# Baseball Research Journal

Volume 48, Number 1

Spring 2019

Published by the Society for American Baseball Research

**BASEBALL RESEARCH JOURNAL, Volume 48, Number 1**

**Editor:** Cecilia M. Tan
**Design and Production:** Lisa Hochstein
**Cover Design:** Lisa Hochstein
**Copyediting assistance:** King Kaufman
**Proofreader:** Norman Macht
**Fact Checker:** Clifford Blau

**Front cover photo:** Library of Congress, G.G. Bain Collection

**Published by:**
Society for American Baseball Research, Inc.
Cronkite School at ASU
555 N. Central Ave. #416
Phoenix, AZ 85004

**Phone:** (602) 496–1460
**Web:** www.sabr.org
**Twitter:** @sabr
**Facebook:** Society for American Baseball Research

# Contents

# Note from the Editor

Every spring, the preparation of the year's first issue of the BRJ gets me ready for the baseball season. The anticipation of the drama and action that will captivate the nation (or at least parts of it) only builds as I read about the game's past, present, and future. And I am continually captivated by watching the events of my lifetime run downstream to become "history."

I recently was a guest on a podcast called "Movie vs Expert." The concept of the podcast is the hosts, Mike and Kyle, watch a Hollywood movie and discuss it with a person who knows the subject. For example, they watched Arnold Schwarzenegger's *Kindergarten Cop* with an actual schoolteacher to thought-provoking and occasionally hilarious effect. The episode I recorded was me versus the movie *Moneyball*. To prep for the show, I re-read Michael Lewis's book for the first time since it was published.

I remember well the avid attention I gave the book the first time around in 2003. I was a baseball blogger at the time, a newly minted member of SABR in the middle of a two-year reading jag in which I devoured around 150 books on baseball. Yes, I went down a rabbit hole. I read most of the "canon" (Roger Angell, Ed Linn, Jules Tygiel, Roger Kahn, et. al.), built myself a reference library (*Total Baseball*, *Baseball Prospectus*, Neft & Cohen), and picked up most of the new baseball books coming out, *Moneyball* included. The book (and movie) suffer the reductive flaw that they don't actually tell the whole story. You can't tell the story of the 2002 A's success with barely a mention that their starting rotation had three of the best pitchers in baseball. But perhaps that's the point. The book (and movie) aren't about the A's so much as they are about a way of thinking—and about a sea change that was taking place in baseball's way of thinking.

It being 2019, when I re-read the book I read it digitally on my phone. The ebook edition has an afterword that I had not previously seen, in which Lewis chronicles major league baseball's intense negative public reaction to the book and to the sabermetric concepts in it. From here in 2019 I'll confess I had almost forgotten things didn't change overnight, because they certainly did change rapidly after that. Boston adopting a sabermetric approach—and even hiring Bill James—and then winning the World Series in 2004 certainly helped silence the critics, though. And here we are not even 20 years later and every major league team has sabermetricians in the front office— whole departments of them sometimes. The revolution is total and complete. The book *Moneyball* itself ended up being part of the story of how things changed.

Of course SABR itself is a large part of that story, too, and the generations of SABRen, old and new, who have been threads in that tapestry. In this issue of the *BRJ* we celebrate the current winners of the Chadwick award. One of them, Allan Roth, can be said to have been the first saber-metrician hired by a major league team, though he came several decades before the coining of that term. Another, Rob Neyer, comes out of my generation of pioneering Internet bloggers! This is what I mean about the events of my life becoming history. And we mavericks, whether named James or Neyer or Beane or any number of the names that have graced SABR publications, have become the institutions. In the words of Dizzy Dean (and Mortimer Snerd): who'da thunk it?

It all gives me hope that backward or outdated ways of thinking in other reaches of life aside from baseball can also be overcome by science and truth. Hopefully within my lifetime.

— Cecilia M. Tan
Publications Director

# Sweet!

## *16-Year-Old Players in Major League History*

### Chuck Hildebrandt

On June 10, 1944, during the ninth inning of a 13–0 blowout, an event occurred that is known to many fans with at least a passing knowledge of baseball history: Joe Nuxhall, at a mere 15 years and 316 days of age, made his way into an actual regular-season major league game, becoming the youngest player to ever do so.

This event did not occur out of left field (as it were). Joe Nuxhall was already well-known before his big-league debut. It was widely reported earlier that year that the Cincinnati Reds had signed the 6'3", 195-pound ninth-grader to a major league contract.[1] He'd thrown two no-hitters and two one-hitters in his "knothole league" the previous year.[2] Joe's father had himself played semipro ball, and had been training his son to be a pitcher since Joe was a little kid.[3] Joe sat on the Reds' bench that Opening Day, and it was anticipated that he would see game action at some point that season.[4,5] When Joe was finally called up to the active roster on June 8—after his junior high school graduation, of course—there was a feature story in which he was quoted, "Would I like to get into a big-league game? What do you think I've been waiting for all these months?"[6,7]

Of course, it's also well known that Joe's debut performance fell far short of the hype. Pitching against the St. Louis Cardinals, after retiring two of the first three hitters he faced, he fell apart in a manner one might expect of a junior high student: wild pitch, walk, single, walk, walk, walk, single. Five runs later, he was yanked from the game.[8] Five days later, he was on his way to the Birmingham Barons farm club, where he essentially replicated his Reds debut performance.

Today it seems absurd to think it was a good idea for a boy—technically still a minor—to be allowed to compete alongside full-grown men. And yet, although Joe was a once-in-history fluke player as a 15-year-old, there have been several times in the history of professional baseball when teams allowed *16*-year-olds (themselves not much closer to physical maturity[9]) to make that same leap onto a major league roster. That's what happened on fifteen separate occasions between 1872 and 1956.[10]

In this article, we will explore three aspects of the phenomenon of the 16-year-old major leaguer:

1. Who were the fifteen boys who make up this exclusive club?

2. How did it come to pass that 16-year-olds were even allowed to play major league ball in the first place?

3. Is it possible that a 16-year-old could ever again play in the major leagues?

## 1. THE FIFTEEN 16-YEAR-OLD MAJOR LEAGUERS

### Jacob Doyle
**Position**: Shortstop, Second Base
**Born**: November 26, 1855
**Debut**: April 20, 1872
**Team**: Nationals of Washington (National Association)
**Age**: 16 years, 146 days

| G | PA | R | H | AVG | OBP | SLG | wRC+ | fWAR |
|---|----|----|----|-----|-----|-----|------|------|
| 9 | 41 | 6 | 11 | .268 | .268 | .293 | 56 | -0.5 |

The first 16-year-old player in major league history stepped onto the field for the first-ever game the National Association version of the Nationals played, and his stint at baseball's then-highest level ended after his ninth game on May 25.[11] Little is known about how Jacob made his way onto the team. The newspapers around the District of Columbia saw fit only to note his appearances in box scores, not his origin story. Given the nascence of organized professional baseball, the presence of a school-aged boy in a top professional game likely seemed unremarkable. Jacob acquitted himself nicely enough: 11 hits, including a double, in 41 at-bats for a .268 batting average. He even managed a base hit off eventual two-time 50-game winner and future Hall of Famer Al Spalding. Nevertheless, Jacob's entire career spanned those nine games for the

Nationals, who themselves disbanded after eleven games in total, all losses. (This being the era of "erratic schedule and procedures," they were not the only team to close shop before a full slate of fixtures could be played.) Jacob Doyle passed away in 1941 at the ripe old age of 85.

## Jim Britt

**Position**: Pitcher
**Born**: February 25, 1856
**Debut**: May 2, 1872
**Team**: Atlantics of Brooklyn (National Association)
**Age**: 16 years, 67 days

| G | GS | W | L | ERA | IP | WHIP | ERA- | bWAR |
|---|----|----|----|-----|-----|------|------|------|
| 37 | 37 | 9 | 28 | 5.06 | 336.0 | 1.73 | 120 | 0.3 |

Unlike his predecessor above, this 16-year-old actually logged a full season as the sole pitcher for the Atlantics, hurling all 336 innings of the team's 37 games and shouldering their entire 9–28 record. Alternately referred to in the *Brooklyn Daily Eagle* as both "Britt"[13] and "Brett"[14]—sometimes in the same story[15]—there's no mention of how this particular 16-year-old happened to land with the Atlantics in the first place. The team must have had high hopes for Jim, though, particularly after some of the thrashings he administered to amateur teams in exhibition play.[16,17,18] However, once the season switch flipped to "regular" mode, the effectiveness of the team, and of Jim, waned. The Atlantics were one of a handful of clubs to use a single pitcher the entire season, and it was noted of the club that "[having] no change pitcher, when Jim failed to be effective[,] their strong point was at an end."[19] Remarkably, Jim hung on with the Atlantics for the 1873 campaign as well, during which he hurled another 480⅔ innings and compiled

*Ben Chapman gives young Tommy Brown some tips in the Dodgers dugout in 1944.*

a 17–36 record. He left the Atlantics after his age 17 season and played several more seasons for lesser Brooklyn-based clubs before moving to the West Coast.[20] Jim Britt passed away at age 67 in 1923.

## Frank Pearce

**Position**: Pitcher
**Born**: March 30, 1860
**Debut**: October 4, 1876
**Team**: Louisville Grays (National League)
**Age**: 16 years, 188 days

| G | GS | W | L | ERA | IP | WHIP | ERA- | fWAR |
|---|----|----|----|-----|-----|------|------|------|
| 1 | 0 | 0 | 0 | 4.50 | 4.0 | 1.50 | 178 | 0.0 |

Frank holds the distinction of being the first 16-year-old "one-and-done" player, but he would not have appeared at all were it not for a grisly injury-*cum*-cruel insult suffered by the Grays' starting pitcher, Jim Devlin, during the team's penultimate game of the season against the Hartford Blues. Devlin had reached first base in the fourth inning on a muffed grounder, and while taking second on a high throw to that bag, "he slid just before reaching it, his foot caught in the large iron ring holding the base-bag down, wrenching and twisting his foot severely." Devlin knocked the base bag several feet away with his slide and was lying on his back in agonizing pain when Blues second baseman Jack Burdock came back with the errantly thrown ball and tagged Devlin, who was called out by umpire Dan Devinney to complete the insult. Devlin was carted off the field on the shoulders of two teammates but, being the only pitcher on the roster, bound up his ankle and pitched the fifth. He then thought the better of it and insisted on coming out, and so Frank, a pitcher with a local amateur team, was conscripted to finish the match. He pitched "creditably" enough, yielding only four runs in the final four innings on five hits despite eight errors committed behind him.[21] Frank promptly disappeared into local amateur ball, playing into the early 1880s before becoming a local collector and traveling salesman.[22] Frank Pearce died in 1926 at the age of 66.

## Leonidas Lee

**Position**: Outfielder, Shortstop
**Born**: December 13, 1860
**Debut**: July 17, 1877
**Team**: St. Louis Brown Stockings (National League)
**Age**: 16 years, 216 days

| G | PA | R | H | AVG | OBP | SLG | wRC+ | fWAR |
|---|----|----|----|-----|-----|-----|------|------|
| 4 | 18 | 0 | 5 | .278 | .278 | .333 | 101 | 0.0 |

Leonidas is among the more interesting 16-year-olds who played at the top level of the game. Ostentatiously christened Leonidas Pyrrhus Funkhouser—his father was a leading businessman in St. Louis and a member of the Sons of the American Revolution[23]—Leonidas had already attended Princeton University before joining the St. Louis ballclub during his summer vacation. As his family was well-established in St. Louis, given the prevailing social taboo against gentlemen engaging in roughneck activities such as "base ball," perhaps Leonidas chose "Lee" as an alias to spare his family name embarrassment. While the circumstances under which he came to join the "Brown Sox" are a mystery, he appeared in four league games and fared nicely with a 5-for-18 performance, including a double, although his fielding left something to be desired (four errors in 11 chances at four different positions). He graduated from Princeton the following June and made his way to Omaha.[24] Now reestablished as a Funkhouser, Leonidas was an up-the-order hitting outfielder and first baseman with that city's Union Pacifics club in 1882, on which his brother Mettelus also appeared, but he would never again reach the major leagues.[25,26,27] Leonidas moved on to Lincoln, Nebraska, where by 1902 he held officer-level positions with several companies simultaneously.[28] Funkhouser/Lee died in 1912 en route from Florida to Bryn Mawr, Pennsylvania, for a summer retreat.[29]

### Piggy Ward

**Position**: Third Base
**Born**: April 16, 1867
**Debut**: June 12, 1883
**Team**: Philadelphia Quakers (National League)
**Age**: 16 years, 57 days

| G | PA | R | H | AVG | OBP | SLG | wRC+ | fWAR |
|---|----|----|----|-----|-----|-----|------|------|
| 1 | 5 | 0 | 0 | .000 | .000 | .000 | -48 | -0.1 |

Piggy was the youngest player in big-league history for more than six decades, arriving just 57 days after his 16th birthday. He was also the first 16-year-old player to emerge from his maiden appearance to enjoy a fairly lengthy career, whereas Doyle, Pearce, and "Lee" were all out of the game before they turned 17, and Britt made it through just one more season. After a hiatus following his sole teenage appearance, Piggy re-entered the majors at age 22, then again at 24. He was a bench player until achieving nearly full-time status with the 1894 Washington Senators, playing mainly second base and slashing a respectable .303/.446/.375, including 80 walks—good for tenth in the league. He then faded into minor league obscurity for the next 12 seasons, retiring for good in 1906 after his age 39 season. In his very first big-league appearance back in 1883, though, Piggy—referred to as a "handball expert"[30]—was tried out at third base, and although he did ring up two assists there, he also went 0-for-5, striking out twice, and then slipped out of pro ball until popping up with the Johnstown and Shamokin clubs in the Pennsylvania minors in 1887 to begin his second act in the game. As did so many in his day, Piggy Ward came to a rough end: he fell off a telephone pole in Altoona, Pennsylvania, in 1909 and died three years later after suffering paresis resulting from his injuries.[31]

### Willie McGill

**Position**: Pitcher
**Born**: November 10, 1873
**Debut**: May 8, 1890
**Team**: Cleveland Infants (Players League)
**Age**: 16 years, 179 days

| G | GS | W | L | ERA | IP | WHIP | ERA- | fWAR |
|----|----|----|---|------|-------|------|------|------|
| 24 | 20 | 11 | 9 | 4.12 | 183.2 | 1.73 | 101 | 1.5 |

Despite that he was out of the bigs by 23, Willie still fashioned the best career of any major leaguer who debuted as a 16-year-old: 14.6 fWAR, split between his pitching and hitting. Invited to try out for Cleveland's Players League club during 1890 spring training, Willie made his debut for the coincidentally nicknamed Infants on May 8 against the Buffalo Bisons.[32] He made an immediate impact due to his appearance ("he is like the little girl's definition of a sugar plum, 'round and rosy and sweet all over'"), stuff ("throws barrel-hoops and corkscrews at the plate...with a swift, straight ball that is as full of starch as though it had just come out of a laundry"), and performance (struck out ten batters while going 1-for-4 with a walk at the plate in a 14–5 victory).[33] Willie delivered an impressively average season for a high-school-age boy. Once the Players League folded after season's end, Willie, who'd been playing without a contract anyway, moved on to King Kelly's Cincinnati "Killers" club of the American Association, then was sold to the St. Louis Browns early that next season.[34] He eventually pitched in the National League with Cincinnati, Chicago, and Philadelphia until his final season in 1895 at age 22. He broke his pitching hand the following year, spoiling any chance for a return to the bigs, although he continued pitching in the minors and in top Chicago amateur leagues for more than a decade afterward.[35,36] Willie

McGill eventually became head baseball coach at Northwestern University before moving to Indianapolis, where he died in 1944 at age 70.[37]

**Tom Hess**
**Position**: Catcher
**Born**: August 15, 1875
**Debut**: June 6, 1892
**Team**: Baltimore Orioles (National League)
**Age**: 16 years, 296 days

| G | PA | R | H | AVG | OBP | SLG | wRC+ | fWAR |
|---|----|---|---|-----|-----|-----|------|------|
| 1 | 2 | 0 | 0 | .000 | .000 | .000 | -77 | 0.0 |

A good deal of mystery surrounds the saga of Tom Hess. Listed on Baseball-Reference as having started his minor league career in 1890 with Albany at the age of 14,[38] Hess was another 16-year-old one-gamer, playing catcher for the Orioles in a 23–1 laugher over the Chicago Colts. Nothing is known about how Hess ended up on the Orioles in the first place—only that he entered the game in the fifth inning for the O's that June day and exited in the seventh after getting busted in the kneecap with a ball. Despite the pummeling the Baltimores laid on the Chicagos, Hess did nothing at the plate, making out both times.[39] Hess was released by the Orioles about a week later and returned to Albany to finish out the season for the Senators there.

However, there is some dispute as to whether Tom Hess was a 16-year-old major leaguer at all, as well as whether the player in question was even Tom Hess in the first place. David Nemec's book, *The Rank and File of 19th Century Major League Baseball*, maintains that the player for the Orioles that game was a man of unknown provenance named Jack Hess, and that Tom Hess was a career minor leaguer who did not pass through Baltimore at all. As evidence, Nemec cites gaps in Tom's minor league record between 1895 and 1899.[40] However, Baseball-Reference shows Tom as having played minor league ball each season from 1890 through 1909, including A-level minor league ball in 1891; while Jack's record is complete from 1890 through 1897, without gaps, including playing B-level minor league ball in 1892. Given this, and the lack of conclusive evidence contradicting Baseball-Reference's record, we've included Tom Hess here. He passed away in 1945, aged 70.

**Joe Stanley**
**Position**: Pitcher
**Born**: April 2, 1881
**Debut**: September 11, 1897
**Team**: Washington Senators (National League)
**Age**: 16 years, 162 days

| G | GS | W | L | ERA | IP | WHIP | ERA- | fWAR |
|---|----|---|---|-----|-----|------|------|------|
| 1 | 0 | 0 | 0 | 0.00 | 0.2 | 0.00 | 0 | 0.0 |

Joe was one of the few 16-year-olds who enjoyed a big-league career spanning several years, with an unusual twist: he debuted for the Senior Circuit Senators as a one-and-done teenage pitcher, then returned to the Junior Circuit Senators as a 21-year-old outfielder. There he remained for six seasons and 215 games, with two mop-up mound appearances. In that teenage debut game in 1897, with his squad being crushed by the Cincinnati Reds, 14–5 after seven innings, Senators manager Tom Brown called on Joe to take one for the team. The 5' 9", 150-pound pitcher was brought in along with 5' 7", 168-pound catcher Tom Leahy to serve as Brown's "mustang pony battery"[41] and finish the first game of a doubleheader. Joe, a local "District lad," was "nervous" and ended up walking three and throwing a wild pitch while yielding another five runs in the final two frames, a number the Senators matched in their half of the ninth before finally falling, 19–10. He also went 0-for-2 at the plate.[42] (It should be noted that this account from the next day's *Washington Times* stands at odds with the record of Joe's one-game performance as reflected in Retrosheet: ⅔ IP; no runs, hits, walks or strikeouts; one wild pitch; 0-for-1 at the plate. For consistency, it is this record reflected above.[43]) From there, Joe next showed up on the Newport News club of the Virginia League in 1900, then in Raleigh and New Orleans during the 1901 season before making his way up to the American League Senators that season. He bounced up and down between the bigs and the bushes before settling into the minors from 1910 through his retirement in 1917. When Joe Stanley died in Detroit in 1967, he had been one of the last living nineteenth century players.[44]

### "Coonie" Blank

**Position**: Catcher
**Born**: October 18, 1892
**Debut**: August 15, 1909
**Team**: St. Louis Cardinals (National League)
**Age**: 16 years, 301 days

| G | PA | R | H | AVG | OBP | SLG | wRC+ | fWAR |
|---|----|---|---|-----|-----|-----|------|------|
| 1 | 2 | 0 | 0 | .000 | .000 | .000 | -94 | 0.0 |

The first 16-year-old player of baseball's modern era, "Coonie" (or more likely "Connie"[45,46]) capped a momentous year of baseball by playing in his one and only big-league game for his hometown Cardinals. Coonie started the year on a St. Louis "trolley league" team that had traveled to Springfield, Missouri, for an exhibition series against the Class C Midgets of the Western Association.[47] The Midgets liked him well enough to try him out as their catcher before quickly releasing him.[48,49] He moved on to the Guthrie and Muskogee clubs in the same league during May before making his way back to Springfield by July, where he stuck into August.[50,51,52] Then, on the 15th of that month, Coonie found himself substituting for starting catcher Jack Bliss in the first game of a late season doubleheader in St. Louis as the Redbirds were winding up a stretch of 14 games in 13 days before hitting the road. He was less than impressive during the game: the Brooklyn paper mentioned that "the Dodgers ran wild on the sacks," against Coonie and that he would "need a lot of seasoning."[53] He wouldn't get it: Coonie was one-and-done as far as the majors were concerned. There's no record of where he went after his sip of coffee, and he was out of pro ball entirely by age 18. Coonie Blank died in his hometown in 1961.

### Roger McKee

**Position**: Pitcher
**Born**: September 16, 1926
**Debut**: August 18, 1943
**Team**: Philadelphia Phillies (National League)
**Age**: 16 years, 336 days

| G | GS | W | L | ERA | IP | WHIP | ERA- | fWAR |
|---|----|---|---|-----|----|------|------|------|
| 2 | 0 | 0 | 0 | 16.20 | 3.1 | 3.30 | 385 | -0.1 |

The first 16-year-old major leaguer of the World War II era, Roger Hornsby McKee is also the first whose rise to the majors was well-chronicled in contemporaneous newspaper reports. The previous year he'd earned several mentions in the nearby Asheville, North Carolina, daily paper as a star pitcher for his hometown

Shelby American Legion Juniors team. Roger was 9–1, averaged 14 strikeouts per game, and batted .500 in 1943.[54] He was signed August 12 by the Phillies as a "17"-year old, his smiling face appearing in papers across the country via AP Wirephoto.[55] Roger made his debut in Philly less than a week later, relieving Jack Kraus in the seventh inning against the Cardinals, who were already down, 5–0. Roger pitched well despite an especially tough assignment: the first four batters he faced were All-Stars Harry "the Hat" Walker (bunt single), Stan Musial (base on balls), Walker Cooper (5–4–3 double play), and Whitey Kurowski (fly out to right to retire the side without a run). Roger finished the game, giving up only one run in three innings. He pitched once more as a 16-year-old, four days later, yielding an ignominious result: three hits, three walks and five runs, all earned, in ⅓ inning. Roger pitched two more games that season after turning seventeen, and one final big-league game as an 18-year-old in late 1944 after a season at Class B Wilmington before shipping out to the Navy in 1945.[56] After the war, Roger sailed into a long minor league career as an outfielder, retiring at age 30 before returning home to Shelby to become a postal carrier. Roger McKee passed away in 2014.[57]

### Carl Scheib

**Position**: Pitcher
**Born**: January 1, 1927
**Debut**: September 6, 1943
**Team**: Philadelphia Athletics (American League)
**Age**: 16 years, 248 days

| G | GS | W | L | ERA | IP | WHIP | ERA- | fWAR |
|---|----|---|---|-----|----|------|------|------|
| 6 | 0 | 0 | 1 | 4.34 | 18.2 | 1.45 | 131 | -0.4 |

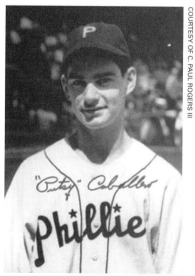

*Ralph "Putsy" Caballero was signed fresh out of high school in 1944 by the Phillies, who were in a push to find talent younger than draft age.*

Carl, the first 16-year-old (and still youngest player) in American League history, took a slightly different path from the 16-year-olds before him. He racked up notices in newspapers around his hometown of Gratz, Pennsylvania, about his stellar pitching and hitting during 1941 and 1942. Though still a 15-year-old in August 1942, he received a tryout with Connie Mack's A's. Carl impressed the old man greatly. "There's only one thing against the boy and that's his age," Mack was quoted as saying, "However, bring him down next year as soon as school closes [and we'll] take care of him. In the meantime, don't let Carl pitch too much."[58] The following year, Carl spent the entire season with the Athletics as a batting practice pitcher, a job for which he'd quit high school.[59] He also pitched for the Athletics in several off-day exhibition games.[60] Eventually, with the Pittsburgh Pirates and "another major league club" reportedly interested in Carl, Mack signed him to a big-league contract and brought him into his first game in relief against the New York Yankees.[61] Carl was greeted roughly by hitter Nick Etten's triple, after which Joe Gordon plated Etten with a groundout. Nevertheless, Carl "did O.K."[62] Unlike most 16-year-old rookies, Carl stuck around the majors for a while, pitching with the A's until age 27, passing through the Cardinals that same year, and winding up his career in the Pacific Coast and Texas Leagues before retiring at age 30. Carl Scheib passed away in San Antonio in 2018 at the age of 91.

## Tommy Brown

**Position**: Shortstop
**Born**: December 6, 1927
**Debut**: August 3, 1944
**Team**: Brooklyn Dodgers (National League)
**Age**: 16 years, 241 days

| G | PA | R | H | AVG | OBP | SLG | wRC+ | fWAR |
|---|----|----|----|------|------|------|------|------|
| 46 | 160 | 17 | 24 | .164 | .208 | .192 | 11 | -2.0 |

Tommy Brown holds two distinctions: he is the youngest 16-year-old player of the twentieth century, and he is the only starting position player on this list. He appeared in more games as a 16-year-old than any other player in major league history. The Dodgers did not bring Tommy to Ebbets Field as a novelty—they brought him there to play. Signed by the club after an open tryout, he was assigned to their Class B Newport News farm club and showed some serious skills there. Tommy was leading the Piedmont League in triples, as well as socking 21 doubles and even a towering home run over a right-center-field fence, practically forcing the then last-place Brooklyns to purchase his contract on July 28.[63,64,65] So popular was Tommy in Newport News that they held a "day" in his honor before he left, and the local paper continued to report on his performance while he was with the Dodgers.[66] But Tommy wasn't a big deal just in Virginia—New York papers wrote feature pieces heralding the arrival of the Dodgers' new boy wonder.[67] Unique among 16-year-olds, Tommy was immediately installed by his team as their starting shortstop. He had a promising start, clouting a double and scoring a run in his debut, and was batting .278 after his first six games. Alas, his youthful inexperience eventually caught up with him: his batting average plummeted below .200 for good by Labor Day, and his 16 errors in only 364 innings marked him as one of the worst defenders in the league. He was strong-armed but wild, earning the nickname Buckshot Brown, because "you know how buckshot scatters."[68] Tommy started 1945 with the Dodgers' top affiliate in St. Paul before finishing the season back in Brooklyn, where he became the only 17-year-old to hit a homer in a big-league game. He found his niche as a backup shortstop with the Dodgers, Phillies, and Chicago Cubs through 1953, eventually settling into the high minors before retiring for good in 1959. As of this writing, Tommy Brown is alive and well and living in Brentwood, Tennessee.[69]

## Putsy Caballero

**Position**: Third Base
**Born**: November 5, 1927
**Debut**: September 14, 1944
**Team**: Philadelphia Phillies (National League)
**Age**: 16 years, 314 days

| G | PA | R | H | AVG | OBP | SLG | wRC+ | fWAR |
|---|----|----|----|------|------|------|------|------|
| 4 | 4 | 0 | 0 | .000 | .000 | .000 | -100 | -0.2 |

Ralph "Putsy" Caballero was a two-sport star in his native New Orleans and was named to the all-American Legion team twice by the time he'd graduated high school in 1944 at age 16. But rather than take a dual basketball/baseball scholarship to Louisiana State University, he decided to travel to Nashville to attend a tryout with the Cubs. His high school baseball coach was also a scout for the New York Giants; however, the Phillies, who had just undertaken efforts to sign high school-age talent, swooped in with an $8,000 bonus offer and stole Putsy out from under Giants manager (and fellow Louisiana native) Mel Ott.[70] Although Ted McGraw, the Phillies scout who signed him, predicted Putsy would be a major leaguer in one year, he actually made his big-league debut just a week later in the eighth inning of an 11–1 blowout at the hands of the Giants.[71] Putsy did mop-up duty at third base, where he handled one chance, a pop fly from (coincidentally) Mel Ott, and went 0-for-1 at the plate, a popout to short. He appeared in three more games as a 16-year-old: twice as pinch runner, and once as a pinch hitter-turned-third baseman in another blowout. Putsy spent parts of seven more seasons with the Phillies, finishing his career at age 27 in 1955 after three more seasons with their AAA teams in Baltimore and Syracuse. He went into his father-in-law's extermination business and then ran his own business until his retirement in 1997. Putsy Caballero passed away in New Orleans in 2016 at the age of 89.[72]

### Alex George

**Position**: Shortstop
**Born**: September 27, 1938
**Debut**: September 16, 1955
**Team**: Kansas City Athletics (American League)
**Age**: 16 years, 354 days

| G | PA | R | H | AVG | OBP | SLG | wRC+ | fWAR |
|---|----|---|---|------|------|------|------|------|
| 5 | 11 | 0 | 1 | .100 | .182 | .100 | -23 | -0.3 |

The first of the two 16-year-old players of the 1950s was a locally famous four-sport superstar at Kansas City's Parkhurst High School who graduated early and was all set to enroll and play basketball and baseball at the University of Kansas when the Athletics came calling. On September 15, they signed him to a contract with an $18,000 bonus, spread over two years, that mysteriously fell outside the Bonus Baby rules of the time, which stated if a first-time amateur received a bonus over $4,000, he had to be placed on the team's big-league roster for two seasons.[73] Even so, while the A's could have—indeed, should have—sent Alex immediately to the minors for seasoning, they instead inserted him into the very next day's game against the Chicago White Sox as a pinch hitter. Sherm Lollar, the catcher, told him every pitch that was coming, and Alex still struck out.[74] It didn't get any better for Alex from there: he appeared at the plate eleven times in five games, struck out in seven of those trips, took one walk and got one hit, a drag bunt single.[75] The following season he was sent to Class D Fitzgerald in the Georgia-Florida League and ended up riding buses for the next eight seasons, rising as high as AA, but never getting another crack at the majors. Alex quit baseball in 1963 at age 24, then went into ad sales for local radio and TV stations in Kansas City. As of this writing, Alex George still lives in Prairie Village, Kansas, a suburb of his hometown.[76]

### Jim Derrington

**Position**: Pitcher
**Born**: November 29, 1939
**Debut**: September 30, 1956
**Team**: Chicago White Sox (American League)
**Age**: 16 years, 306 days

| G | GS | W | L | ERA | IP | WHIP | ERA- | fWAR |
|---|----|---|---|------|-----|------|------|------|
| 1 | 1 | 0 | 1 | 7.50 | 6.0 | 2.50 | 182 | -0.2 |

Jim was a bona fide Bonus Baby, having signed for $78,000.[77] The White Sox had high enough hopes for him that they signed the 16-year-old knowing that, by major league rules, they would have to carry him on their big-league roster for two seasons. They had good reason to be optimistic: Jim, ace pitcher-first baseman for South Gate High School, had been named Los Angeles All-City Player of the Year earlier that summer of 1956, during which he went 10–2, struck out 159 in 88 innings, had a 0.23 ERA, batted .452, and threw at least two no-hitters.[78,79,80] Jim was given the start of the final game of the 1956 season in Kansas City against the Athletics and, for a still-growing

*A four-sport star at Kansas City's Parkhurst High School, Alex George graduated early and was nabbed by the hometown big league club (then the Kansas City A's).*

boy, pitched a man-sized game: 31 batters faced, six innings, six runs (five earned) on nine hits (two homers) and six walks (five on 3–2 pitches), and three strikeouts. He took the 7–6 loss when the Chisox fell just short on their comeback bid. Jim came to bat twice, striking out his first time up but singling to right on his second trip, before he was lifted for pinch hitter Larry Doby in the seventh.[81] Jim remains the youngest pitcher since 1876 to start a major league game. Bonus Baby rules dictated his return to the big club in 1957, during which he appeared in 37 innings across 20 games, including five starts, and finished with a 4.86 ERA. After that, Jim suffered the same fate so many other 16-year-old major leaguers did: he kicked around the minors for a few years before retiring from the game after the 1961 season at the tender age of 21. After baseball, Jim Derrington worked at a variety of jobs and coaching gigs in the LA area, where he still lives as of this writing.[82]

Those are the fifteen 16-year-old major leaguers. In major league terms, nearly all of them performed awfully, as would be expected. So the question now becomes:

## 2. UNDER WHAT CIRCUMSTANCES COULD A 16-YEAR-OLD HAVE BEEN ALLOWED TO PLAY MAJOR LEAGUE BASEBALL IN THE FIRST PLACE?

It should barely rate mention that a 16-year-old boy would be a suboptimal choice for a spot on a major league roster, not only because his physical strength is still more than a decade away from its peak, but also because his baseball skills are still in the early stages of development.[83] After all, it's a safe bet that most players on any given major league roster have already been playing the game for more than 16 years, let alone having been alive for that long. Experience matters.

Nevertheless, there are certain rare circumstances when it might actually make sense for a 16-year-old to be included on a major league roster. Three major circumstances are:

A. **The game of baseball was so new, hardly anybody was an expert at playing it.** This was obviously true in the very early days. The first clubs that played what most resembles today's game of baseball were founded in New York between the late 1830s and mid-1840s. However, key rules—such as nine innings per game, nine men per side, and ninety feet between bases—were not officially codified until 1857 by the Convention of Base Ball Clubs, and the first professional league launched a mere 14 years later. At that time, playing baseball for money was still considered by many to be a disreputable activity, the province of gamblers and corruptible players, casting a pall on its integrity.[86] Even as the game began to "[gain] in popularity, never before equaled by anything of the sort invented," many believed the game should remain an amateur affair, contested strictly for love of competition and not for the crass goal of making money and thus reducing the game "to the level of horse racing and other gambling pursuits."[87,88] This controversy may have had the effect of restricting the flow of some of the better ballplayers to professional leagues during its first few years.

In addition, the earliest baseball leagues for children did not form until the 1880s (and even those that were established did not flourish). Children could play sandlot ball, but with substandard equipment that was invariably adult sized.[89] As such, it would have been exceedingly difficult for children to acquire advanced baseball expertise. Since organized baseball activity was essentially non-existent for children before 1871, a large age cohort of boys from this era could not have achieved enough proficiency to ensure a tightly-aged group of the highest-skilled professional players. Of the cohort we would consider to be of peak professional baseball age, only a small sliver—much smaller than today—would have been available to play, simply because so many had still not played the game to a serious enough degree to do so professionally.

In other words, just about anybody of this era with a rugged enough body who could learn to play the game as an adult with a passable level of skill would have been considered suitable to play professional "base ball." As a result, the early and middle 1870s saw some of the highest compositions of both teenage players[90]—and players over 35[91]—in professional baseball history.

B. **World War II.** This particular war took a drastic toll on professional baseball's player pool. Unlike the first World War, which for the United States spanned only the 1917 and 1918 seasons, the second great war lasted almost four complete seasons. In the immediate shock of Pearl Harbor and the declaration of a two-front war, the major leagues continued with business as usual, as affirmed by President Roosevelt's famous "Green Light" letter.[92,93] Even so, more than 500 major leaguers and over 4,000 minor leaguers "swapped flannels for khakis" during this period.[94]

This obviously created a shortage of professional-quality ballplayers, so the pool of candidates had to be widened outside the boundaries of draft age, which in November 1942 Congress expanded to ages 18 to 37.[95] As a result, 1944 saw ten 16- and 17-year-old players in the majors, by far the most of any season in history.[96] (The 1944–45 seasons also saw the highest composition of players age 38 and older by a wide margin.[97]) Several ballclubs actively sought underage ballplayers—notably the Dodgers (six) and Phillies (five)—to "man" positions for their teams.[98] The Dodgers conducted tryouts across the country, sending letters to 20,000 coaches and others "requesting recommendations of promising athletes." One camp in Lancaster, Pennsylvania, drew 252 teenage hopefuls.[99] Perhaps not surprisingly, these two clubs also occupied the bottom two slots of the 1944 National League standings. Other clubs such as the Giants—led by Mel Ott, a former 17-year-old major leaguer himself—recruited underage players to populate the rosters of their minor league affiliates. This allowed them to call up minor leaguers—themselves bereft of true major league skill, but at least possessing the quality of adulthood—to sip their own cups of coffee courtesy of the wartime talent shortage.[100]

**C. The Bonus Baby Rule.** Implemented by MLB in 1947, the Bonus Baby rule was intended to prevent the wealthiest clubs—e.g., Yankees, Boston Red Sox, Dodgers, Cardinals—from using their vast financial resources to sign all the best amateur talent and then stash them away in their farm systems.[101] The original Bonus Baby rule was weak and eventually rescinded in 1950, but was reinstated in 1952 in stronger form: any "Baby" signed for more than a $4,000 bonus was required to be assigned to the major league roster for a full two years, or else be exposed to the waiver wire.[102]

This led to some teams deciding that signing incredibly young, barely proven talent would be worth the risk of major bonus money and potentially wasting a mandated roster spot on them—at least in principle. In practice, the rule was routinely circumvented by many teams, accompanied by rumors of secret under-the-table payments to signees to avoid the two-year-rostering part of the rule.[103] This may have been true of Alex George in 1955, who relayed in an interview that his bonus was $18,000, paid to him across two years. It is likely that the Athletics found some loophole that allowed them to exceed the $4,000 Bonus Baby Rule limit while also allowing them to ship Alex out to Class D Fitzgerald for his second season.

The rule also led to the signing of Jim Derrington, the only acknowledged 16-year-old Bonus Baby, who did remain with the White Sox for his age 17 season. Typical of how disrespected the rule was, even Jim's bonus was misstated: widely reported as being $50,000, Derrington confirmed in an interview that the true amount was $78,000, simply because "that's the way it was done."[104]

The Bonus Baby rule led to an uptick in both 17- and 18-year-old big-league players as well. In the seven seasons between the war and the second Bonus Baby rule, only two 17-year-olds reached the majors; during the years 1953–57, fifteen littered various big-league rosters.[105] Also, in 1955 there were nine 18-year-old big leaguers, and in 1957 there were eight, the highest totals in a single season since 1912.[106]

The Bonus Baby rule was rescinded in December 1957 for multiple reasons—it penalized "honest" teams, young Babies suffered "arrested development" sitting unused on a big-league bench for two whole seasons, and the rule was so widely flouted anyway.[107,108] Without it, the incentive to place a 16-year-old boy on a big-league roster disappeared for good.

There has not been a 16-year-old major league player in the six-plus decades since, which leads to the question:

### 3. IS IT POSSIBLE THAT A 16-YEAR-OLD COULD EVER PLAY IN THE MAJOR LEAGUES AGAIN?

Technically, yes. Practically, no.

Two sets of rules govern a team's acquisition of first-time amateur talent, pertaining to either the First-Year Player Draft or signing of amateur free agents.

The draft is the only way for players in the United States and Canada to join a team in either Major League Baseball or their affiliated minor leagues—together: Organized Baseball.[109] (The professional leagues independent of Organized Baseball, such as the Frontier League and Atlantic League, provide no direct path to the big leagues and explicitly stipulate a minimum age of 18 years.[110,111]) As of 2019, to be draft-eligible a player must have completed four years of high school or at least one year of junior college. There is no explicit age requirement, which leaves open the possibility that a player could be eligible for the draft as a four-year high school graduate at age 16. A player is also eligible if he graduates from high school in three years (i.e., received a diploma after 11th grade) *and* he will be 17 years old within 45 days after the draft, again leaving open the possibility of being drafted at age 16.[112]

So, technically, a drafted player could enter Organized Baseball at the age of 16 and go directly to the major leagues to play. In real terms, however, draft rules are designed to make this a practical impossibility. During the first 54 years of the amateur draft, the youngest player ever selected was Alfredo Escalera, age 17 years and 114 days, in 2012.[113] Beyond this, only four drafted high schoolers have gone directly to the majors once they were selected: David Clyde in 1973, and Tim Conroy, Brian Milner, and Mike Morgan, all in 1978, and all having already turned 18.[114]

A player living outside the US and Canada (i.e., a foreign player) has a marginally better chance of making the major leagues at age 16, although it is still practically as unlikely. A foreign player may enter Organized Baseball under contract as an amateur free agent if he is age 16 at the time of the signing, but only if he turns 17 prior to September 1 of the first season covered by the contract.[115] Therefore, it is technically possible for a 16-year-old whose birthday is in late August to be signed during the winter and then play almost an entire season in professional ball as a 16-year-old. Jefferson Encarnacion (born August 28, 2001) did this in 2018. However, he, along with the vast majority of 16-year-old professional ballplayers, played in the Dominican Summer League (DSL), a short-season rookie league designed specifically to launch the careers of still-underage foreign-born talent signed as amateur free agents.

As such, very few foreign players make it onto an American diamond as 16-year-old professionals. According to Baseball-Reference, from 2009 through 2018, there were 355 sixteen-year-old professional baseball players. Ninety-three percent of them played exclusively in either the DSL or the Venezuelan Summer League (suspended in 2015). Of those 16-year-olds that did play pro ball in America, fifteen played in the Gulf Coast League, eight in the Arizona League, two in the Pioneer League and one in the Appalachian League—all rookie leagues. Not a single player during this period made it even as high as short-season A at age 16.

Adding all this up, it is clear the system is simply not designed to shortcut 16-year-old players directly onto major league rosters. Indeed, since the founding of the DSL in 1985, the youngest Dominican player to have reached the majors has been Adrian Beltre, who debuted at 19 years and 78 days, and only after he had apprenticed in the minor leagues for 318 games.

To illustrate once more the extreme unlikelihood of a 16-year-old player ever again making a big-league roster, briefly consider the case of one of the best and most-hyped high school players of our time: Bryce Harper, who first broke through America's consciousness on the cover of *Sports Illustrated* in June 2009. That October, he earned his GED after his sophomore year of high school specifically to accelerate his eligibility for the draft by one year. To satisfy draft eligibility requirements, he enrolled in a Nevada junior college for the 2010 season, where he put up astounding numbers (.443/.526/.987 in 272 plate appearances).[116] The Washington Nationals selected Bryce Harper number one overall in the 2010 draft. He was already age 17 years, 224 days. And instead of putting the greatest underage hitter in recent memory directly onto their major league roster, the Nationals sent him to the minors for 164 games of seasoning. This is consistent with contemporary baseball practice. Since 1996, only two drafted players have gone directly to the majors without minor league experience, both college graduates past their 21st birthdays.[117]

The inescapable conclusion is that—given the vast physical and developmental differences between high school age boys and fully grown men, combined with the stringent way in which the acquisition of amateur talent is regulated, and the process by which major league organizations develop that talent—we will not see another 16-year-old play major league baseball ever again. ∎

## APPENDX

### Table 1. Season and Career Records for All 16-Year-Old Major Leaguers

| BATTERS | 16-Year-Old Stats | | | | | | | | | Career Stats | | | | | | | | |
|---|---|---|---|---|---|---|---|---|---|---|---|---|---|---|---|---|---|---|
| Player | Year | G | PA | R | H | AVG | OBP | SLG | wRC+ | fWAR | G | PA | R | H | AVG | OBP | SLG | wRC+ | fWAR |
| Jacob Doyle | 1871 | 9 | 41 | 6 | 11 | .268 | .268 | .293 | 56 | -0.5 | 9 | 41 | 6 | 11 | .268 | .268 | .293 | 56 | -0.5 |
| Leonidas Lee | 1877 | 4 | 18 | 0 | 5 | .278 | .278 | .333 | 101 | 0.0 | 4 | 18 | 0 | 5 | .278 | .278 | .333 | 101 | 0.0 |
| Piggy Ward | 1883 | 1 | 5 | 0 | 0 | .000 | .000 | .000 | -48 | -0.1 | 221 | 959 | 172 | 223 | .286 | .419 | .360 | 115 | 3.5 |
| Tom Hess | 1892 | 1 | 2 | 0 | 0 | .000 | .000 | .000 | -77 | 0.0 | 1 | 2 | 0 | 0 | .000 | .000 | .000 | -77 | 0.0 |
| Joe Stanley | 1897 | (Stanley was a pitcher for his 16-year-old season) | | | | | | | | | 216 | 694 | 77 | 148 | .213 | .275 | .272 | 68 | -2.1 |
| Coonie Blank | 1909 | 1 | 2 | 0 | 0 | .000 | .000 | .000 | -94 | 0.0 | 1 | 2 | 0 | 0 | .000 | .000 | .000 | -94 | 0.0 |
| Tommy Brown | 1944 | 46 | 160 | 17 | 24 | .164 | .208 | .192 | 11 | -2.0 | 494 | 1384 | 151 | 309 | .241 | .292 | .355 | 72 | -2.4 |
| Putsy Caballero | 1944 | 4 | 4 | 0 | 0 | .000 | .000 | .000 | -100 | -0.2 | 322 | 706 | 81 | 150 | .228 | .273 | .274 | 48 | -2.8 |
| Alex George | 1955 | 5 | 11 | 0 | 1 | .100 | .182 | .100 | -23 | -0.3 | 5 | 11 | 0 | 1 | .100 | .182 | .100 | -23 | -0.3 |

| PITCHERS | 16-Year-Old Stats | | | | | | | | | Career Stats | | | | | | | | |
|---|---|---|---|---|---|---|---|---|---|---|---|---|---|---|---|---|---|---|
| Player | Year | G | GS | W | L | ERA | IP | WHIP | ERA- | fWAR | G | GS | W | L | ERA | IP | WHIP | ERA- | fWAR |
| Jim Britt | 1872 | 37 | 37 | 9 | 28 | 5.06 | 336.0 | 1.73 | 120 | 5.3 | 91 | 91 | 26 | 64 | 4.38 | 816.2 | 1.61 | 125 | 7.9 |
| Frank Pearce | 1876 | 1 | 0 | 0 | 0 | 4.50 | 4.0 | 1.50 | 178 | 0.0 | 1 | 0 | 0 | 0 | 4.50 | 4.0 | 1.50 | 178 | 0.0 |
| Willie McGill | 1890 | 24 | 20 | 11 | 9 | 4.12 | 183.2 | 1.73 | 101 | 1.5 | 168 | 150 | 72 | 74 | 4.59 | 1251.0 | 1.66 | 101 | 13.4 |
| Joe Stanley | 1897 | 1 | 0 | 0 | 0 | 0.00 | 0.2 | 0.00 | 0 | 0.0 | 3 | 0 | 0 | 0 | 9.39 | 7.2 | 1.57 | 324 | -0.3 |
| Roger McKee | 1943 | 2 | 0 | 0 | 0 | 16.20 | 3.1 | 3.30 | 385 | -0.1 | 5 | 1 | 1 | 0 | 5.87 | 15.1 | 1.30 | 175 | -0.1 |
| Carl Scheib | 1943 | 6 | 0 | 0 | 1 | 4.34 | 18.2 | 1.45 | 131 | -0.4 | 267 | 107 | 45 | 65 | 4.88 | 1070.2 | 1.52 | 120 | 3.0 |
| Jim Derrington | 1956 | 1 | 1 | 0 | 1 | 7.50 | 6.0 | 2.50 | 182 | -0.2 | 21 | 6 | 0 | 2 | 5.23 | 43.0 | 1.70 | 138 | -0.7 |

## Notes

1. "Lad of Fifteen Picked by Reds To Do Hurling," *Cincinnati Enquirer*, February 19, 1944.
2. "Maybe You Need Different Glasses, Deacon! Things First Look Rosy, Then Gloomy," *Cincinnati Enquirer*, March 5, 1944.
3. Davis J. Walsh, "Reds to Expect Great Things From Hamilton Rookie, Joe Nuxhall," *The Daily Herald* (Circleville, OH), March 29, 1944.
4. Si Burick, "15-Year-Old Joe Nuxhall Tagged A Typical Southpaw; "Plays Hooky" To Sit With Reds On Opening Day," *Dayton* (OH) *Daily News*, April 19, 1944.
5. Oscar Fraley, "Two Items: Definite With Deacon; Baseball To Keep Rolling, View Of McKechnie, Who Also Opines That Redlegs Cannot Be Counted Out—Nuxhall Is Lauded." *Cincinnati Enquirer*, May 26, 1944.
6. Paul B. Mason, "Kid Pitcher Thrilled By Big League Chance," *The Times Recorder* (Zanesville, OH), June 13, 1944.
7. Al Cartwright, "School's Out, Nuxhall Joins Reds," *The Dayton* (OH) *Herald*, June 8, 1944.
8. Except where noted, all career and game statistics are sourced from either Baseball-Reference.com or Retrosheet.org.
9. Centers for Disease Control and Prevention, "2 to 20 years: Boys Stature-for-age and Weight-for-age percentiles," published May 30, 2000 (modified November 21, 2000).
10. Baseball-Reference.com Play Index, "For Single Seasons, From 1871 to 2018, For age 16, sorted by earliest date," accessed February 15, 2019, https://www.baseball-reference.com/tiny/C9qSv (case-sensitive).
11. Although in 1968 the Special Baseball Records Committee ruled that the National Association, which was active from 1871 to 1875, was not to be considered a major league, consistent with the National Association's appearance in major league research sources such as Retrosheet, it is included here.
12. John Thorn, "Why Is the National Association Not a Major League… and Other Records Issues," May 4, 2015, accessed February 19. 2019, https://ourgame.mlblogs.com/why-is-the-national-association-not-a-major-league-and-other-records-issues-7507e1683b66.
13. "Sports and Pastimes. Base Ball," *Brooklyn* (NY) *Daily Eagle*, May 21, 1872.
14. "Sports and Pastimes. Base Ball," *Brooklyn* (NY)) *Daily Eagle*, April 8, 1872.
15. "Sports and Pastimes. Base Ball," *Brooklyn* (NY)) *Daily Eagle*, May 4, 1872.
16. "Sports and Pastimes. Base Ball," *Brooklyn* (NY)) *Daily Eagle*, April 20, 1872.
17. "Sports and Pastimes. Base Ball," *Brooklyn* (NY)) *Daily Eagle*, April 27, 1872.
18. "Sports and Pastimes. Base Ball," *Brooklyn* (NY)) *Daily Eagle*, May 1, 1872.
19. "Sports and Pastimes. Base Ball," *Brooklyn* (NY)) *Daily Eagle*, May 21, 1872.
20. David Nemec, *Major League Baseball Profiles, 1871–1900, Volume 1: The Ballplayers Who Built the Game* (Lincoln, NE: Bison Books), 21.
21. "Base-Ball. Louisvilles vs. Hartfords," *The Courier-Journal* (Louisville, KY), October 5, 1876.
22. Nemec, *Major League Baseball Profiles, 1871–1900, Volume 1: The Ballplayers Who Built the Game*, 67.
23. David Nemec, *Major League Baseball Profiles, 1871–1900, Volume 2: The Hall of Famers and Memorable Personalities Who Shaped the Game* (Lincoln, NE: Bison Books), 321
24. "The Colleges. A Rainy Class Day at Princeton. The Festivities Marred by the Disagreeable Weather. A List of the Graduates—A Description of the New Library at Lehigh University to be Dedicated This Week," *The Times* (Philadelphia), June 19, 1878
25. "The Jumbos Floored. Another Expedition of Muscular Giants Bagged Between Bases, The Stannards of St. Louis Follow the Footprints of the "Reds," And Retire from the Field Minus Their Scalps," *Omaha* (NE) *Daily Bee*, August 28, 1882.
26. "Well Whitewashed. The Union Pacifics Receive Nothing But Goose Eggs, While the Council Bluffs Get One Tally," *Omaha* (NE) *Daily Bee*, September 25, 1882.
27. "Again Downed. The Union Pacifics Suffer Another Defeat at the Hands of the Council Bluffs Nine," *Omaha* (NE) *Daily Bee*, October 23, 1882.
28. "Leonidas P. Funkhouser," *The Courier* (Lincoln, NE), March 15, 1902.
29. [News item without title], *The Haddam* (KS) *Clipper-Leader*, June 21, 1912, 2.

30. "A Great Battle of Bats. Victory Won After Twelve Innings. A Remarkable Game of Base Ball at Recreation Park—The Philadelphia Club Defeats the Cleveland by a Score of 4 to 3—The Athletics Win," *The Times* (Philadelphia), June 13, 1883.

31. "Piggy Ward Dead, Once Played Here," *Hartford* (CT) *Courant*, October 26, 1912.

32. Society for American Baseball Research, *Baseball's First Stars* (Phoenix: SABR), 105.

33. "Haddock Hammered. Cleveland Paying Buffalo Back With Interest. The Internationals Also Beaten—League and Association Scores—Sports of All Sorts," *The Buffalo* (NY) *Express*, May 9, 1890.

34. Nemec, *Major League Baseball Profiles, 1871–1900, Volume 1: The Ballplayers Who Built the Game*, 127.

35. Society for American Baseball Research, *Baseball's First Stars*, 105.

36. Nemec, Major League Baseball Profiles, *1871–1900, Volume 1: The Ballplayers Who Built the Game*, 127.

37. "William (Wee Willie) McGill, Major League Pitcher in 1890s, Dies Here," *The Indianapolis Star*, August 31, 1944.

38. Tom Hess player card, accessed February 15, 2019, https://www.baseball-reference.com/register/player.fcgi?id=hess--001tho.

39. "Pity Poor Anson. His Colts Scamper in Confusion Before the Orioles. Overwhelmed by a Score of 23 to 1. Great Batting and Fine Fielding and Base-Running Against Chicago—President Harrison Sees the Washington Game—Other Contests," *The Sun* (Baltimore), June 7, 1892.

40. David Nemec, *The Rank and File of 19th Century Major League Baseball: Biographies of 1,084 Players, Owners, Managers and Umpires* (Jefferson, NC: McFarland), 107.

41. "Slugging Won the First Game. The Reds at Last Find Their Batting Eyes And Pound McJames To Their Hearts Content. 'Twas Different in the Second Game at Washington—Baseball News," *Cincinnati Enquirer*, September 12, 1897.

42. *Cincinnati Enquirer*, September 12, 1897.

43. Joe Stanley player card, accessed February 15, 2019, https://www.retrosheet.org/boxesetc/S/Pstanj103.htm.

44. Nemec, *The Rank and File of 19th Century Major League Baseball: Biographies of 1,084 Players, Owners, Managers and Umpires*, 77.

45. "Bonehead-Bonehead-Bonehead-Bonehead. Bartlesville Takes Three Straight From Midgets—Worst Game of the Season," *The Springfield* (MO) *Republican*, July 6, 1909.

46. "Monett Beats Sarcoxie. Only Four Local Men Play In Cassville Game," *The Springfield* (MO) *Republican*, August 7, 1909.

47. "Baseball," *The Springfield* (MO) *Republican*, April 4, 1909.

48. "Baseball," *The Springfield* (MO) *Republican*, April 6, 1909.

49. "Baseball," *The Springfield* (MO) *Republican*, April 15, 1909.

50. "Railroaders Walloped Senators. Foot Racing Qualities of Visitors Declared Good," *The Guthrie* (OK) *Daily Leader*, May 14, 1909.

51. "Line Drives," *The Muskogee* (OK) *Times-Democrat*, May 26, 1909.

52. "Bonehead-Bonehead-Bonehead-Bonehead. Bartlesville Takes Three Straight From Midgets—Worst Game of the Season," *The Springfield* (MO) *Republican*, July 6, 1909.

53. "Even Break at St. Louis Ends Superbas' Western Trip. Swamp the Cardinals in the First Game and Lose the Second When Scanlon Blew Up—Record, Five Games Won; Ten Lose and Two Tied—Play at Boston To-Morrow," *The Brooklyn* (NY) *Daily Eagle*, August 16, 1909.

54. "'Mail-Order' Rajah Signed by Phillies," *The Brooklyn* (NY) *Daily Eagle*, August 13, 1943.

55. "Baseball Break," *Des Moines* (IA) *Tribune*, August 12, 1943.

56. "Pitcher McKee Enters Navy," *Mount Carmel* (PA) *Item*, January 3, 1945.

57. Alan Ford, "Local baseball legend McKee passes away," September 4, 2014, accessed February 15, 2019, https://www.shelbystar.com/20140904/local-baseball-legend-mckee-passes-away/309049793.

58. "Sport Shots," *Mount Carmel* (PA) *Item*, September 1, 1942.

59. Jim Sargent, "Carl Scheib," accessed February 15, 2019, https://sabr.org/bioproj/person/93562fe6.

60. "Gratz Hurler Bought by Phila. Athletics," *The Elizabethville* (PA) *Echo*, September 9, 1943.

61. "Sport Shots," *Mount Carmel* (PA) *Item*, September 10, 1943.

62. "Sport Shots," *Mount Carmel* (PA) *Item*, September 9, 1943.

63. C. Paul Rogers III, "Tommy Brown," accessed February 15, 2019, https://sabr.org/bioproj/person/7913ae6c.

64. Vann Dunford, "Codde Right, Dodgers Trim Cards By 9 To 3. Blast Couple of Hurlers for Eleven Bingles," *Daily Press* (Newport News, VA), June 18, 1944.

65. "Brooklyn Dodgers Purchase Tom Brown," *Daily Press* (Newport News, VA), July 29, 1944.

66. Vann Dunford, "Dodgers Lose 'Pitler Day' Tilt To Tars, 16–2. Norfolk Homers Spell Locals' Doom As Visitors Thump Out 17 Safe Hits," *Daily Press* (Newport News, VA), July 31, 1944.

67. "Newcomers," *Daily News* (New York), August 4, 1944.

68. "Schultz Ignores Low, Outside One—Poles 15 Hits," *Brooklyn* (NY) *Eagle*, September 5, 1944.

69. Rogers, "Tommy Brown," https://sabr.org/bioproj/person/7913ae6c.

70. Jim Sweetman, "Putsy Caballero," *The Whiz Kids Take the Pennant—The 1950 Philadelphia Phillies* (Phoenix: SABR), 45.

71. Stan Baumgartner, "Caballero, 16, Signed by Phils," *The Philadelphia Inquirer*, September 10, 1944.

72. Sweetman, "Putsy Caballero," 45.

73. Dan Blom, "Prairie Village's Alex George played major league baseball with the Kansas City Athletics as a 16-year-old," October 30, 2014, accessed February 16, 2019, https://shawneemissionpost.com/2014/10/30/prairie-villages-alex-george-played-major-league-ball-kansas-city-athletics-16-year-old-33366.

74. "Lollar Called Pitches, But A's Rookie Whiffed Anyhow," *Sporting News*, September 26, 1955.

75. Blair Kerkhoff, "Can you imagine a 16-year-old playing in the majors? This Rockhurst 75 grad did, for the KC Athletics," *The Kansas City Star*, June 8, 2018.

76. Blom, "Prairie Village's Alex George."

77. Brent P. Kelley, *Baseball's Bonus Babies: Conversations With 24 High-priced Ballplayers Signed from 1953 to 1957* (Jefferson, NC: McFarland), 84.

78. "Four Valley League Players on All-City," *The Valley News* (Van Nuys, CA), June 10, 1956.

79. "South Gate's Derrington Signs Chisox Bonus Pact," *Los Angeles Times*, September 11, 1956.

80. "Derrington Registers His Second No-Hitter," *Los Angeles Times*, May 30, 1956.

81. Robert Cromie, "Bonus Hurler and Sox Lose to A's, 7 to 6," *Chicago Daily Tribune*, October 1, 1956.

82. Tom Birschbach, "He Started for the White Sox at 16, but Was Through at 22," *Los Angeles Times*, June 29, 1991.

83. Samantha Olson, "How Old Is Usain Bolt? Fastest Man In The World Tests His Age In 100-Meter Sprint," August 14, 2016, accessed February 16, 2019, https://www.medicaldaily.com/usain-bolt-fastest-man-world-394814.

84. John Thorn, "Origins of the New York Game: How did a regional game become the national pastime?," October 31, 2018, accessed March 4, 2019, https://ourgame.mlblogs.com/origins-of-the-new-york-game-bf9b330042d6.

85. John Thorn, "Nine Innings, Nine Players, Ninety Feet, and Other Changes: The Recodification of Base Ball Rules in 1857," August 22, 2012, accessed March 4, 2019, https://ourgame.mlblogs.com/nineinnings-nine-players-ninety-feet-and-other-changes-the-recodification-of-base-ball-rulesin-39684873f818.

86. Aaron Feldman, "Baseball's Transition to Professionalism," accessed February 16, 2019, https://sabr.org/sites/default/files/feldman_2002.pdf.

87. "Base-Ball," *Louisville* (KY) *Journal*, May 1, 1868.

88. "Base Ball Gambling," *The Brooklyn* (NY) *Daily Eagle*, April 10, 1868.

89. "History of Little League," accessed February 16, 2019, https://www.littleleague.org/who-we-are/history/.

90. "For Single Seasons, From 1871 to 2018, From Age 16 to 19, sorted by greatest number of players matching criteria in a single season," accessed February 16, 2019, https://www.baseball-reference.com/tiny/oNjtV (case-sensitive).

91. "For Single Seasons, From 1871 to 2018, From Age 35 to 99, sorted by greatest number of players matching criteria in a single season," accessed February 16, 2019, https://www.baseball-reference.com/tiny/BqfEi (case-sensitive).

92. "Major Leagues Plan 'Business as Usual,'" *The State Journal* (Lansing, MI), January 14, 1942.

93. Shirley Povich, "'Green Light' from No. 1 Umpire Rallies Game Through Nation," *Sporting News*, January 22, 1942, 1.

94. Gary Bedingfield, "Baseball in World War II," accessed February 16, 2019, http://www.baseballinwartime.com/baseball_in_wwii/baseball_in_wwii.htm

95. "Draft age is lowered to 18," accessed February 16, 2019, https://www.history.com/this-day-in-history/draft-age-is-lowered-to-18.

96. "For Single Seasons, From 1871 to 2018, From Age 16 to 17, sorted by greatest number of players matching criteria in a single season," accessed February 16, 2019, https://www.baseball-reference.com/tiny/2pwJ9 (case-sensitive).

97. "For Single Seasons, From 1871 to 2018, From Age 38 to 98, sorted by greatest number of players matching criteria in a single season," accessed February 16, 2019, https://www.baseball-reference.com/tiny/xwihn (case-sensitive).

98. "For Single Seasons, From 1942 to 1946, From Age 16 to 17, sorted by most recent date," accessed February 16, 2019, https://www.baseball-reference.com/tiny/7R65w (case-sensitive).

99. Don Basenfelder, "Rickey Scouts Scour U.S. for Teen-Age Prospects," *The Sporting News*, August 5, 1943, 7.

100. Ken Smith, "Mel Ott to Test 20 Youngsters," *The Sporting News*, February 10, 1944, 12.

101. Steve Treder, "Cash in the Cradle: The Bonus Babies," November 1, 2004, accessed February 16, 2019, https://www.fangraphs.com/tht/cash-in-the-cradle-the-bonus-babies/.

102. Robert F. Burk, *Much More Than a Game: Players, Owners, and American Baseball since 1921* (Chapel Hill, NC: The University of North Carolina Press), 127.

103. Treder, "Cash in the Cradle: The Bonus Babies," https://www.fangraphs.com/tht/cash-in-the-cradle-the-bonus-babies/.

104. Kelley, *Baseball's Bonus Babies: Conversations With 24 High-priced Ballplayers Signed from 1953 to 1957*, 84.

105. "For Single Seasons, From 1871 to 2018, For age 17, sorted by greatest number of players matching criteria in a single season," accessed February 16, 2019, https://www.baseball-reference.com/tiny/5y1s8 (case-sensitive).

106. "For Single Seasons, From 1871 to 2018, For age 18, sorted by greatest number of players matching criteria in a single season," accessed February 16, 2019, https://www.baseball-reference.com/tiny/GMFGZ (case-sensitive).

107. Edgar Munzel, "Bankrolls Now Only Limit on Bonus Bids," *The Sporting News*, December 18, 1957, 11.

108. Ray Gillespie, "Busch to Lead Fight to Put End to Bonus Rule," *The Sporting News*, October 9, 1957, 1.

109. For the purposes of the draft, The United States also includes its territories, e.g., Puerto Rico.

110. "Player Eligibility," accessed February 16, 2019, https://www.frontierleague.com/league/playereligibility/.

111. "Open Tryouts For Many Atlantic League Teams," accessed February 16, 2019, http://atlanticleague.com/about/newswire/index.html?article_id=411.

112. "MLR 3(a)" *The Official Professional Baseball Rules Book* (New York: Office of the Commissioner of Baseball), © 2018, 32.

113. Globalize LLC, "Royals Draft The Youngest Player In Baseball History," June 7, 2012, accessed February 16, 2019, http://www.i70baseball.com/2012/06/07/royals-draft-the-youngest-player-in-baseball-history/.

114. "Straight to the Major Leagues", accessed February 16, 2019, http://www.baseball-almanac.com/feats/feats9.shtml. (NOTE: Although Brian Milner is listed at this source as having gone directly to the majors in 1978 from Texas Christian University, contemporary reports of the time confirm that he was indeed drafted out of Southwest High School in Fort Worth Texas. Example: "Pro Draft," *The Tampa Times*, June 8, 1978, page 10.)

115. "MLR 3(a)," *The Official Professional Baseball Rules Book*, 32.

116. Bryce Harper player card, accessed February 16, 2019, http://www.thebaseballcube.com/players/profile.asp?ID=156293 (case-sensitive).

117. "Straight to the Major Leagues," http://www.baseball-almanac.com/feats/feats9.shtml.

# Playing with the Boys

*Gender, Race, and Baseball in Post-War America*

## A.J. Richard

The highest grossing baseball movie of all time, *A League of Their Own*, features a 15-second scene where an African-American woman picks up an errant ball and throws it back with such snap that it raises eyebrows.[1] The film tells the story of what is now known as the All-American Girls Professional Baseball League (AAGBPL), a real-life professional women's baseball league in the Midwest 1943–54. The AAGPBL is remembered for creating a golden era in women's baseball when women were paid well to play a game that otherwise barred their participation, but this brief scene is an allusion to the fact that black women were barred from the league.

During this unprecedented period for women in baseball, African American women had two strikes against them: they were women and they were black. Even with the success of the AAGPBL, female players of color were largely invisible. Three African American women, however, broke gender and racial barriers by playing in the Negro Leagues. By playing professional baseball with men, Mamie "Peanut" Johnson, Toni Stone, and Connie Morgan directly challenged the belief that women were the "weaker sex."[2]

## WOMEN'S ROLE

The demand for workers during World War II when millions of American men served overseas led to un-precedented work opportunities for women outside of the home, although these jobs remained largely sex-segregated.[3] Once the war ended and men returned from overseas, women were expected to return to domestic duties and give up their jobs.[4] But many did not. Although after the war they were relegated to low-wage jobs considered appropriate for women, as scholar Ruth Milkman writes: "Yet a permanent shift had occurred for women as a social group, and despite the postwar resurgence of the ideology of domesticity, by the early 1950s the number of gainfully employed women exceeded the highest wartime level."[5] It was in this era that Johnson, Stone, and Morgan found their way into a previously all-male occupation.

## NO BLACKS ALLOWED

The official Rules of Conduct of the AAGPBL strictly enforced standards of femininity and beauty for the players.[6] While "No Blacks Allowed" was an unofficial rule, it was no less strictly enforced. Unlike Major League Baseball, the AAGPBL never integrated. The league promoted a middle class American ideal of beauty and femininity that excluded African American women. According to Carol J. Pierman, professor of women's studies at the University of Alabama at Tuscaloosa, the All-American "girl next door" was white, not black.[7]

Mamie Johnson tried the AAGBPL before the Negro Leagues, but "[t]hey didn't let us try out."[8] After seeing an advertisement for women baseball players in the newspaper, the teenage Johnson and her friend Rita traveled to Alexandria, Virginia, for the tryout. Johnson described standing there with her baseball glove. She and Rita were the only people of color. Johnson said they looked at her and Rita but said nothing. "They wouldn't give us the opportunity to try out."

The refusal of the white AAGPBL to integrate women's professional baseball led to black women

*Mamie "Peanut" Johnson was a starting pitcher in the Negro Leagues, playing alongside male teammates on the Indianapolis Clowns.*

INDIANAPOLIS CLOWNS

playing baseball with black men, which may seem surprising in the context of postwar policing of male and female roles in America. As described by Pierman, dual segregation created a paradox for black women ball players in postwar America.[9] Black women could neither play baseball with white women nor with men of any race. But the upheavals of postwar America would create an unexpected opportunity within the Negro Leagues.

**DECLINE OF THE NEGRO LEAGUES**

Since the early twentieth century, Negro Leagues teams had served as centers of cultural life for African-American communities.[10] For instance, the Newark Eagles hosted NAACP fundraisers, black charity events, and ceremonies to honor black achievement.[11] Team owners understood the central role of Negro Leagues teams in African-American communities, and knew the teams provided a source of pride and something to cheer about at a time when race relations in America caused intense suffering. But several factors would play into the downfall of the leagues.

In 1945, Jackie Robinson broke the color barrier in Major League Baseball by signing with the Brooklyn Dodgers organization, debuting in the big leagues in 1947.[12] By 1953, increasing numbers of black players were signing MLB and minor league contracts.[13] By the 1950s, most American homes had radios, and televisions had become common in American households and in eating and drinking establishments.[14] Baseball fans could now follow the games from the comfort of home.[15] At the same time a great postwar migration brought an influx of black workers to urban areas, resulting in population shifts. Many MLB stadiums were located in neighborhoods that shifted from majority white to majority black, making it easier for black fans to attend MLB games at the same time those games were featuring more and more black players.[16] As fans followed their heroes like Robinson on TV, radio, and by attending MLB games in person, attendance at Negro Leagues games plummeted. As more Negro Leagues stars moved to the major leagues, many of their fans switched their allegiance and money to MLB teams. Birmingham Black Barons owner Tom Hayes said, "The golden era has passed. Teams that are to survive must retrench and proceed with caution."[17]

The raid on the Negro Leagues for the best players presented a unique financial problem for team owners. The Brooklyn Dodgers president Branch Rickey, who signed Jackie Robinson, felt no compunction to honor the contracts players had signed with Negro Leagues teams. The loss of their stars resulted in crit-ical financial losses for the team owners even after Newark Eagles owner Effa Manley leveraged to get some reimbursement for star player Larry Doby, which established an important precedent.[18] Amira Rose Davis, Assistant Professor of History and Women's, Gender and Sexuality Studies at Pennsylvania State University, wrote, "Negro League owners were hemorrhaging players, fans, and revenue and desperately looking for a way to stop the bleeding."[19]

By the early 1950s, only six teams were left in the Negro American League.[20] In the *Los Angeles Sentinel*, Negro American League President Dr. J.B. Martin cautioned, "The color line has not been erased nearly as much in baseball as you might be led to believe. There is still great resistance to colored players in organized baseball."[21] The decrease in gate receipts led Negro League team owners to try a variety of public relations ventures to keep the league afloat.[22] In the *Sentinel* article, Dr. Martin wrote, "The NAL does not even bar a person because of sex if that person can play baseball."[23] The door was open for black women to play with the boys.

**SYD POLLOCK AND THE INDIANAPOLIS CLOWNS**

Syd Pollock, the owner of the Indianapolis Clowns, told *The Frederick Times-Post*, "You have to give the fans something different each year and that's our objective. We keep adding new and colorful players from time to time."[24] The Clowns were a highly theatric team known as, "the Harlem Globetrotters of baseball." *The Frederick News-Post* article described an upcoming game between the Clowns and Birmingham Black Barons: "Unmatched comedy, stellar big-league baseball, plus all sorts of added attractions are on tap."[25] Clowns games featured comic acts which were sometimes criticized as perpetuating harmful racial stereotypes. The Clowns were also a competitive team and won Negro American League pennants in 1950, 1951, 1952, and 1954, a year they fielded two women players. With declining gate receipts and continued loss of star players to the majors, Pollock was willing to try women players as a strategy to keep the team afloat. He even hired women as umpires for some Clowns games.[26] According to Neil Lanctot, professor of modern American history at the University of Delaware, the theatrics paid off because the Indianapolis Clowns were the most profitable Negro American League team in the 1950s.[27]

**WOMEN PLAYING A MAN'S GAME**

Pollock's scouts discovered Toni Stone playing for the New Orleans Creoles, a Negro minor league team.[28] She was born Marcenia Lyle Stone in St. Paul, Minnesota.[29]

She was a gifted athlete and became known as "Tomboy" or "Toni" at an early age.[30] Like many women, Stone played softball because it was more accessible for women than baseball. However, she expressed a preference for baseball, which antagonized her parents who emphasized the importance of education. In the Stone family home, African-American educator Mary McLeod Bethune was admired, not Satchel Paige.[31]

Stone had already generated pre-game publicity for the Creoles: "A girl second-sacker…should be something to see here Sunday."[32] The *Atlanta Daily World* elaborated that Stone was "more than a novelty but slightly a miracle."[33] The *Council Bluffs Nonpareil* stated, in July 1950, "Something new and different in the way of a baseball attraction will be offered Council Bluffs baseball fans at American Legion park Tuesday night. Playing second base for the New Orleans Creoles will be Tony [sic] Stone-Miss Tony Stone that is."[34] The article elaborated, "Yes, a girl ball player on a men's team. And there entirely on her merits, they say." The newspaper highlighted Stone's play against the town team in two additional articles the same week.[35]

For two years Stone turned down Pollock's offer of a contract with the Clowns because "I felt I wasn't ready, but when he said $12,000 for the season, I ran to get my fountain pen."[36] Stone seized an unprecedented opportunity to play professional baseball in the Negro Leagues. The team's star player, Hank Aaron, had just signed with MLB's Milwaukee Braves. After signing Stone, Pollock proclaimed, "The latest masculine enterprise to fall before the advance of wearers of skirts and panties is the baseball diamond."[37] Many, including sportswriter Sam Lacy, were skeptical of the authenticity of Stone's reported salary: "At least that's what your bosses say and that's what they tell you to say when you're asked the question."[38]

According to Davis, Stone's image was commonly featured on scorecards, fliers, and other promotional materials.[39] Stone said Pollock wanted her to play in a skirt or shorts, in contrast to her all-male teammates. She refused, effectively distinguishing herself from the white women playing in the AAGPBL who were required to wear skirts.[40] However, wearing a men's baggy uniform did not insulate Stone from comments about her body. *Our World* remarked Stone wore an "oversized shirt…to accommodate her size 36 bust."[41]

The press was well aware the signing of Stone was a public relations strategy. As *Our World* reported, "They are counting on her to bring back the huge crowds that have been lost to the major league."[42] *Ebony* magazine reported, "While most sports fans

were sure the Clowns signed Toni merely as an extra box office attraction (the team features baseball comedy and 'Spike-Jones-like' music on barnstorming tours), the young lady has surprised everybody by turning in a businesslike job at both second base and at the plate."[43] A caption accompanying the article read, "Toni is never afraid to hit the dirt. Gardening and bicycling are her hobbies." This had also been a common feminization tactic used by the AAGPBL in their publicity.

According to SABR researcher Stew Thornley, it can be difficult to determine fact from fiction when researching Negro Leagues players. Records were not systematically kept. Thornley wrote, "With Toni Stone, however, the misinformation was in part by design as the league, in attempting to enhance her status as a drawing card, shaved years off her age and added thousands to the salary she was actually being paid."[44] An *Ebony* article from 1953 listed her age as 24 even though she turned 32 that year.[45] She was commonly referred to as "Miss Stone" even though she was married.

Signing Stone did increase gate receipts in 1953, and *The Frederick Times-Post* referred to the signing of Stone as "the female innovation of '53," which, "was little short of melodramatic." According to the paper, the Clowns "are more popular than ever before, having set new attendance records in the NAL circuit in '53, and the demand for dates this year has them booked months in advance, and over a wider area than in any previous season."[46]

As attendance rose at Clowns games, the team was deluged with mail and messages from players, coaches, and promoters offering the talent of potential female players.[47] According to Davis, Pollock was not interested in an all-women's team, black women's league, or too many women on one team because it would take away from the novelty.[48] Pollock was interested in fielding a few personally vetted women to sell more tickets. At the end of the 1953 season, a scout saw Mamie Johnson playing on an all-men's team in the DC area. According to *The Michigan Chronicle*, "After the Clowns completed their season last year, Miss Johnson accompanied the team on a month's barnstorming tour."[49]

Eighteen-year-old Connie Morgan wrote a letter to the Clowns requesting a tryout.[50] Morgan was successful and impressed the management with her "good arm" and appearance. Morgan had lighter skin, a curvy figure, and curled hair which came closer to fitting the ideal of beauty and femininity than Stone's muscular build and darker skin.[51] According to Davis, Morgan's physical appearance meant she was more marketable than Stone.[52] At an exhibition game against Jackie Robinson's All Stars, photos were taken of Morgan with Jackie Robinson and featured a photo of Morgan "getting pointers from Gil Hodges of the Brooklyn Dodgers."[53] Davis noted Pollock did not invite Stone to take part in the photo shoot. A picture of Jackie Robinson and Morgan graced the official scorecard of the Clowns for the 1954 season.[54]

According to Lanctot, Stone grew disgruntled with the Clowns and wanted more playing time. However, the team manager referred to Stone as "box office bait," and she typically played only the first few innings of games.[55] It became clear Pollock was going to sign Johnson and Morgan for the upcoming 1954 season.[56] Stone voiced her discontent to Pollock, who sold her contract to the Kansas City Monarchs.[57]

In 1954, Pollock signed both Morgan and Johnson to contracts with the Clowns. "This season Connie Morgan of Philadelphia, is gracing the Clowns' defensive position at second base. In addition, a second girl star has been signed in the person of Mamie (Peanut) Johnson of Washington D.C. whose specialty is pitching, and who has earned her way to a regular starting berth among the Clowns' pitching staff."[58] Another paper reported, "Always good for something novel each season, owner Syd Pollock of the Indianapolis Clowns, three-time champions of the Negro American League, announced this week the sale of Miss Toni Stone to the Kansas City Monarchs for an undisclosed sum."[59] A flier featuring Stone, Johnson, and Morgan with the title "Feminine Stars" was used during games between the Monarchs and Clowns.[60] Davis asserted the inclusion of Morgan and Johnson in *The Laff Book*—a Clowns' publication which featured jokes and cartoons—served to frame the women as sideshow acts, not athletes.[61]

The *Chronicle* reported Connie Morgan "was scouted personally by the Clowns' new manager, Oscar Charleston, who claims she is one of the most sensational girl players he has ever seen."[62] Before signing with the Clowns, Morgan played on a North Philadelphia women's softball team called the "Honeydrippers."[63] The team name "Honeydrippers" has sexual connotations. Cheryl D. Hicks, associate professor of history at the University of North Carolina, described how black women in America have been hypersexualized: "Black women, whom whites characterized as innately promiscuous because of their African ancestry and the legacy of American enslavement were seen as less amendable to rehabilitation."[64] Black women were viewed as "dark temptresses" and had to negotiate grotesque stereotypes while pursuing their interests.[65]

*Marcenia Lyle Stone picked up the nickname "Tomboy" or "Toni" as a youngster. She would be a gate draw first for the New Orleans Creoles and then for the Indianapolis Clowns.*

Like Stone, Mamie Johnson's childhood was spent playing baseball with the boys. Johnson stated her uncle taught her to play baseball: "I was very, very young when I started playing ball down South. That was all we had to do at that particular time. We made our own baseballs out of stone, twine, and masking tape. I learned to play with the fellows and it was enjoyable to me."[66] Many black women played baseball on sandlots and for amateur teams, especially in rural areas like the South Carolina countryside where Johnson grew up.[67]

Johnson played on sandlot, Police Athletic League (PAL), Catholic Youth Organization (CYO), and semi-professional black teams with men. She experienced strong resistance to playing with the boys through PAL until they saw she was a strong player and relented. Johnson told Cottingham she started playing "big Pro in 1953 and played 1954 and 1955 with the Clowns — but semi pro it started back in 1949."[68] Johnson earned the nickname "Peanut" when pitching to Hank Bayles of the Kansas City Monarchs. Johnson stood 5 feet, 3 inches tall.[69] Baylis declared, "Why, that little girl's no bigger than a peanut. I ain't afraid of her." She struck him out.

Like Stone, Johnson was married when she played for the Clowns, and she had a young son. When asked what her husband thought of her playing baseball she responded, "It didn't make any difference because I was going to play anyway."[70]

## ATTENDANCE AND REACTION

According to newspaper accounts, the presence of Stone on the Clowns did increase attendance. On June 19, 1953, *The Call* reported the Clowns "are breaking attendance records through the nation this season, climaxed by their 18,205 paid at Kansas City."[71] Lanctot wrote that a Clowns game in Birmingham in May 1953 drew the largest crowd there since 1949.[72] A game between the Clowns and Monarchs in Detroit attracted over 20,000 attendees in June 1953.[73]

Like Stone before her, Morgan's presence generated pre-game publicity, as found in *The Call* in 1954. The Kansas City-based newspaper featured descriptions of her fielding while reporting on the upcoming opening of the season: "The Clowns officially open the home season for the Kansas City Monarchs at Blues Stadium this Sunday afternoon, May 30." The paper advised, "to avoid tie-ups at the gates because of the anticipated crowds for these games, advance tickets have already been placed on sale at both the Kansas City and St. Louis stadium box offices."[74]

According to Tracy Everbach, journalism professor at the University of North Texas, Stone, Johnson, and Morgan were given credit by black newspapers for fighting gender and racial discrimination.[75] In *The Call*, Stone was referred to as, "the female Jackie Robinson" who would "break down the prejudice against women players in the N.A.L."[76] Stone's heroism was further hailed in the same article: "From Longview, Tex., and Chattanooga, Tenn., come stories of Miss Stone visiting hospitals and schools, spreading cheer and goodwill with her interviews." On August 27, 1954, *The Call* went further in praising Stone and Morgan: "These two ladies prove that we no longer can refer to them as the weaker sex."[77]

Everbach notes, though, that the women received little mention in white newspapers such as the *Kansas City Star*, *Kansas City Times*, or *The Sporting News*.[78] *The Call* credited record turnout at a 1953 game in Kansas City to Stone, while the white owned-and-operated *Kansas City Times* didn't mention Stone as a factor when reporting on the crowd of 18,205 at the same game.[79] On the rare occasion when the *Kansas City Star* did mention Stone, she was not referred to by name: "The Clowns will feature a girl at second base."[80] According to Everbach, this was part of a larger circumstance.[81] *The Sporting News* was the oldest sporting publication in the United States and was called "The Bible of Baseball," but this national publication rarely

*Connie Morgan (right) pictured here with manager with Oscar Charleston and "King Tut" (holding giant glove).*

mentioned the women players and when they covered the Negro Leagues, the information appeared on the back pages. In 1954, when there were three women playing in the Negro Leagues, including Stone in Kansas City, *The Kansas City Star* and *Times* ignored the three women players completely.[82] That year the Clowns won the Negro American League Championship with two women on the roster. To many Americans, the three women of color playing professional baseball with and against men were invisible.

Not all black newspaper sportswriters were impressed with Stone, Johnson, and Morgan. The *Chicago Defender*'s Doc Young described the reaction when a woman tried out for an organized baseball club: "Men rose up in all their male mightiness and quickly returned her to her place in the home. And among those who applauded was the woman's unathletic husband, who obviously had been forced to wear the apron in the family while she went out shagging flies and hitting batting practice home runs." Young wrote, "The opinion here is that girls should be run out of men's baseball on a softly-padded rail both for their own good and for the good of the game." Young conceded that women "have proven themselves capable as defense workers, cab drivers, garage mechanics, factory hands, and drill press operators, they just aren't 'cut out' for the game of baseball."[83]

Wendell Smith wrote about Toni Stone on June 20, 1953, in the *Pittsburgh Courier*, "She is the hunk of femininity employed by the Indianapolis Clowns."

Smith wrote that Pollock "owned, operated, and exploited" Stone. He added, "She is a lady making a living in a profession designed strictly for men. It is a profession in which only the hale, hearty and strong are likely to succeed, certainly not one to which gentility and refinement are the prerequisites for success."[84] Young belittled Stone for her batting average, although he did write, "I'll have to admit it's not bad for a dame." He imagined a long dialogue between Stone and her husband which included references to Stone powdering between innings, admiring the curves of the pitcher she faced, her husband apologizing for not having dinner ready, spending money on a silver mink baseball glove, planning a shopping spree, and getting angry at her husband for putting starch in her sliding pads. Smith bemoaned, "Negro baseball has collapsed to the extent it must tie itself to a woman's apron strings in order to survive."

Luix Virgil Overbea wrote in the *Baltimore Afro American*, "Although the ladies appear to be a sure fire hit at the box office, I am not going to be one of their enthusiasts. This does not mean I'm against the fair sex on the diamond, but it does mean I am for them only if they play baseball."[85] He continued, "They'll have to show me. My recommendation is that they try and make some of these pro women teams. I don't want to see women in baseball togs on the basis of curiosity." It is curious Overbea suggested they play in the AAGPBL since it was well known the league allowed only white women to play. The columns by Young, Smith, and Overbea cited here demonstrate patterns of gender discrimination and enforcement of traditional gender roles that existed in the black community.

The same black press that voiced hostility, skepticism, and sexism also found it necessary to promote the women via affirming stories. Often, their femininity was contrasted with their athleticism to maximize the "spectacle." In *The Call*, Stone was a "rough-and-tumble player" who played as hard as the men."[86] A photo in *The Call* article showed Stone in an athletic pose with her legs wide apart, mouth open, and arm extended. The article described Stone as being a "tough sister," and "murder-minded in her effort to aid her team." The black media sometimes contrasted Stone's athletic performance with feminine descriptions such as, "She belts home runs as easily as most girls catch stitches in their knitting, and the sports boys are goggle-eyed." In the same article, Stone was described as "a cute second baseman."

## WOMEN IN A MAN'S GAME

The women of the Negro Leagues traveled extensively. Toni Stone grew to appreciate the rich African-American culture in the South, saying, "I wanted to travel. I wanted to go places. Now, that was my education."[87] Stone's upbringing included an emphasis on education. She carried on that value when she visited black colleges, black churches, and libraries. She met the prominent educator Mary McLeod Bethune, whom her family idolized. These atypical experiences caused Stone to believe, "I know who I am, and I know how to carry myself accordingly."[88]

Unlike Stone, Johnson was not interested in checking out libraries and learning about African-American history on road trips. Johnson told Cottingham she played in "every state there is, Canada and wherever. I don't think that there is a state I haven't played in."[89] SABR researcher Jean Hastings-Ardell pointed out Stone was from a Northern urban background in St. Paul, Minnesota, and her family emphasized the importance of education. On the other hand, Johnson spent much of her childhood in the rural South, where her family supported and influenced her interest in sports.[90]

According to Hicks, black women were hypersexualized and their morals questioned due to their race.[91] Davis wrote that the women had to deal with gender discrimination and assumptions about sexuality and whenever possible they stayed at the homes of local black families.[92] Stone was often not allowed to stay at the same hotel as her teammates because the hotel managers assumed a lone woman traveling with a group of men was a prostitute, and hotel managers would direct her to local brothels to find accomodations.[93] Reporters often asked Stone about her sleeping arrangements and whether her teammates took advantage of her sexually. Davis wrote, "Both management and players on the team were unable or chose not to defend her presence, so Stone frequently lodged in brothels."[94] Stone said of one of the prostitutes who welcomed her, "She was a 'wrong woman', but a beautiful human being. She taught me many things… the walks of life. I had no crime with her."[95] Davis stated the prostitutes gave Stone money, food, rides, and would even launder her uniform.[96] They made her a special protective bra to wear when playing baseball.[97] These women urged Stone to "represent" black women, cheered her at games, and kept newspaper articles about her. Through these women, Stone experienced a network of women supportive of each other. Stone was a woman breaking traditional gender norms and earned a living independently by doing what had been deemed men's work. It was something other marginalized black women could appreciate.

According to Davis, the reaction of women baseball fans to the women baseball players could be enthusiastic and appreciative.[98] Former Kansas City Monarch Buck O'Neil said, "Women really came out to watch."[99] Toni Stone was greeted by women fans who wanted to kiss and hug her. Stone said, "I think I brought more women to the game," because she was approached by women and girls wanting her autograph.[100] Morgan was greeted with hugs and kisses by a hometown crowd in 1954.[101]

Johnson reported that on road trips, "We sleep on the bus most of the time because we travel like in the day, because we played mostly night games. When we did get up to nice towns that had nice hotels we stayed in them, but it was still a segregated thing."[102] Cottingham asked Johnson if the women (Johnson and Morgan) stayed together. Johnson responded, "Oh yes, I mean we stayed in the hotels then there was provision made for the women we would stay like in people's homes and they were very nice people. The fellows would stay mostly in the dingy hotels or whatever, but we stayed in people's homes where it was very nice."[103] Johnson explained how they negotiated the locker rooms and facilities as the only women on a men's baseball team: "Well, what we did we would either change before the guys or after the guys but we share the same facilities but a whole lot of time there weren't any facilities for changing we had to change on the bus."[104]

According to Davis, the historical record is sparse regarding the attitudes of male teammates and opposing players as to the inclusion of women in the league.[105] The men may have recognized that the presence of the women in the league boosted ticket sales, so they were essentially a meal ticket for the men. Hastings-Ardell believed the women may have been reluctant, like any team member, to publicly reproach the behavior of teammates, and a woman who reported incidents of harassment, hazing, and discrimination ran the risk of gaining a poor reputation.[106] According to Davis, the women did encounter verbal harassment, physical harassment, jokes, catcalls, isolation, and sexual comments.[107] Darlene Clark Hine described a "culture of dissemblance," where women adopt the attitude that these were incidents of "hazing" or they were "earning respect" by being "tough" and being able to "take it."[108] Stone said, "Once you make it clear there ain't going to be no monkey business…they give you your respect."[109] Likewise, Johnson was clear she was "here to play

ball and nothing else." Johnson did admit sometimes throwing at batters on purpose. "Sometimes, honey, you just get mad."[110]

Stone, Morgan, and Johnson faced fastballs, jeers, sabotage, sexism and Jim Crow. Like Jackie Robinson, they preferred to let their athletic talent speak for them. Unlike Jackie Robinson, their struggles, successes, and defeats have not become icons of American history. They were women playing a man's game and largely ignored by the white press.

## "TOMBOYISM" AND FEMININITY

Women baseball players faced admonishment for being "tomboys." For some, it was a negative label and marked them as "others" and was used to mock and deprecate. For others, a "tomboy" was a strong girl.[111] The term "tomboy" is used to mark athletic girls as different from other girls. A girl who climbed trees, played sports with boys, and loved the outdoors might be embraced by her family or reprimanded. It differed among families and communities.[112]

Pierman pointed out the paradox women athletes face by competing in a sport which is considered a masculine endeavor, and women athletes run the risk of being branded "deviant."[113] In addition, she identified baseball as especially challenging terrain for women athletes because it has been branded both a "man's game" and America's "national pastime." Therefore, it became necessary to feminize such women in the media. In the *Afro American*, Ruth Rolen wrote of Morgan, "The trim second baseman in her becoming blue and red uniform will be ready to 'play ball.'"[114] The article featured side-by-side photos of Morgan in her baseball uniform and being fitted for a dress.

Stone, Johnson, and Morgan persistently struggled to prove they were good enough to play with the men. Their struggle has been complicated by the fact that they were signed to boost sagging ticket sales. Forty years after playing in the Negro Leagues, Johnson said, "People say Toni and Connie and I were gimmicks. Well, we weren't gimmicks, we were good enough to be there."[115] Ray Doswell, curator of the Negro Leagues Baseball Museum, concurred. "It probably was a gimmick when it started. But those three held their own. They were extremely talented."[116]

## 1955 AND AFTER

After two years in the Negro Leagues, Stone left professional baseball because she had become disenchanted with the business of baseball and being objectified and exoticized.[117] Stone said she felt like a "goldfish" when she played for the Clowns.[118] Everywhere she went there were agents, scouts, fans, and reporters. Morgan stopped playing after the 1954 season and returned to business school.[119] *The Call* reported, "All her opponents were male, but that didn't bother the Philadelphia girl."[120] The same article stated, "Her real ambition is to become a top-flight worker in a business office." Johnson held on for one more year before returning home to her young son and husband at the end of the 1955 season.[121]

By playing baseball with men, these women exercised "female agency and choice which has actually challenged aspects of male supremacy."[122] At a crossroads in American history, when gender roles were strictly enforced yet women were pushing the envelope by continuing to work after the war ended, Stone, Johnson, and Morgan expanded the public sphere for black women.[123] This gain was temporary and celebrated exclusively in the black media. White female baseball players in the AAGBPL were accepted as "good" women by adhering to feminine standards and playing in a league of all women, as opposed to with and against men.[124]

The narratives of Stone, Morgan, and Johnson rewrite the historical narrative by expanding the public sphere of black women within the context of the novelty of coed baseball.[125] Stone and Johnson were consistently referred to as "Miss" despite the fact they were both married. The press and the American public had difficulty reconciling the fact these women were participating in what had been branded a man's sport instead of being at home taking care of husbands and children as the gender roles of the time dictated. It was part of a larger shift in American society regarding ideas about black women.[126]

The reaction of black sportswriters demonstrated that sports were still viewed largely as exclusively male terrain within the black community. Journalists who wanted to see the Negro Leagues succeed financially depicted the women as "nice girls" and drew attention to their femininity to promote their inclusion in the league. Davis wrote, "Black women athletes were not supposed to forgo their traditional responsibilities as wives and mothers who had decent careers as teachers, social workers, or nurses."[127] The presence of black women athletes caused black male journalists to fear the "manliness" of the game had been devalued and black men had been "emasculated." Malcolm Poindexter of the *Philadelphia Tribune* painted the picture of women baseball players emasculating men by manipulating them with their female charms when he claimed, "We saw Toni Stone's head in Buster Haywood's lap," and, "Womanly wiles are okay everywhere but trying to get in the starting lineup."[128]

According to Susan K. Cahn, professor of history at the University of Buffalo, baseball was a central proving ground for masculinity in America.[129] In 1957, the *Science Digest* featured a study conducted by the American Psychiatric Association. The study determined just 14 of 102 gay men had played baseball as children.[130] The implication was the national pastime made "normal" men out of boys. Cahn wrote, "If sport

*Toni Stone speaking to some young fans.*

represented masculinity and sexual desire for women, female athletes might also be mannish types who sexually disdained men and desired women."[131] "Good" or "nice" women didn't upset traditional gender norms. The perceived status of black women as being of innately questionable character made black women playing baseball even more susceptible to the label of "wrong" or "bad" women.

The women had to be careful not to appear too masculine while playing a sport deemed a man's sport for fear of being labeled homosexual. If they complained too much about sexual harassment, it could also give rise to suspicions of them being sexually deviant and not "nice girls". In the same vein, if they did not obey proper decorum or appeared too interested in their male teammates they could be labeled as "bad girls". An *Ebony* article featured Stone wearing a dress with the caption, "Stone is an attractive young lady who could be somebody's secretary."[132] The use of the term "lady" necessitates the existence of a "wrong" or "evil" woman who does not conform to feminine standards. In the same article, Stone asserted, "I am out here to play the game. I can take knocks as well as anyone else. Don't worry I can take care of myself." *Ebony* reassured its black audience that Stone was not upsetting gender roles with a photo of Stone washing windows, "washing windows while her husband enjoys the sun," and, "Toni Stone is an excellent housewife and cook."[133]

It was important to depict Stone and the other women players in domestic roles because, after nearly two decades of depression and war, the emphasis was on reestablishing traditional feminine roles in the realms of family and domesticity. Pierman wrote that women baseball players from the postwar period typically would not speak about the subject of lesbianism even decades later "Indoctrinated into a culture of sport that denied a lesbian presence, they are also women of a time of war—and then Cold War—when to be deviant was to be without rights, possibly to be hunted down, investigated, and publicly shamed."[134] Accordingly to Cahn, the "homosexual menace" was a postwar fear as a result of wartime changes in gender roles and sexuality.[135] Women in sports were among the most suspect groups because they publicly did not fit into traditional feminine roles. During the postwar period, the government and military were taking action against gays and lesbians through purges, intense investigations, and legal prosecutions. The police were raiding gay bars and other areas of gay social activity. Cahn wrote this was due to the "perceived need to reestablish gender and sexual order in the wake of wartime disruptions."[136] The hostility and fear

contributed to a "homosexual panic." Black women like Stone, Morgan, and Johnson came under even greater scrutiny because racial stereotypes branded black woman as "naturally" sexually delinquent.[137]

Despite the barriers, harassment, and exploitation, all three women did benefit from the opportunity to play baseball with men. They enjoyed the rare experience of being paid to play a game they loved. Professional baseball was a career option for few women and even fewer black women. The travel they experienced deeply impacted them as related by Johnson, "It was a tremendous thing to wake up and look out the window and be five hundred miles from where you were before."[138] Travel throughout the United States and Canada gave these women an opportunity to experience different regions, people, and cultures. Few women of the era had such opportunities to travel. According to Davis, Morgan finished business school and worked for the AFL-CIO in Philadelphia, Johnson became a nurse, and Stone became a personal care assistant.[139] Both Stone and Johnson coached Little League and youth baseball. Stone continued to play baseball on men's teams and lesbian teams.[140]

With the reemergence of interest in the Negro Leagues in the 1970s, the three women remained a footnote in history.[141] However, in the 1990s Stone was featured in over twenty articles and Morgan and Johnson were rediscovered. Davis reported they became "romanticized symbols of multiculturalism."[142] A series of recognitions, awards, and books followed. However, Davis added, "The narratives that were used to recall the history of Stone, Morgan, and Johnson were similar to the ones that sanitized Rosa Parks."[143] These stories largely ignored the roots of institutionalized racism. Instead these stories focused on the values of self-determination and persistence. The women were transformed into sports icons in a patriarchy which refused to honestly assess racism.[144]

According to Davis, the narratives of these women etched the memory of them into American history because they transcended race and gender to accomplish their goals.[145] However, by acknowledging them merely as trailblazers, the complex realities they faced are marginalized. As reflected in the different views of their experiences, each woman had to determine for herself how to negotiate these barriers and constraints as well as manage the way they were depicted as much as they could. As Davis pointed out, to a large extent, they had little control over how they were depicted.[146]

In the postwar period, women baseball players were publicly changing the perception of baseball as an exclusively male domain. This is part of the larger history of women's struggles to define their role in society. For women baseball players, baseball enabled them to expand the boundaries of women's activities, and to assert that strength, skill, aggressiveness, and competitiveness could be characteristics genuinely possessed by women. ■

## Notes

1. Gabe Zaldivar, "Power Ranking The 11 Highest Grossing Baseball Movies Of All Time, *Forbes*, retrieved February 8, 2019, https://www.forbes.com/sites/gabezaldivar/2016/03/31/power-ranking-the-11-highest-grossing-baseball-movies-of-all-time/#25985bd67138

2. Tracy Everbach, "Breaking Baseball Barriers: The 1953–1954 Negro League and Expansion of Women's Public Roles." *American Journalism* 22(1) 92005) 14.

3. Ruth Milkman. "The Sexual Division of Labor During World War II," in *Women's America: Refocusing on the Past*, ed. Linda K. Kerber, Jane Sherron DeHart, Cornelia Hughes Dayton, and Judy Tzu Chu (New York & Oxford University Press, 2016). 536-546.

4. Milkman, "The Sexual," 537–40.

5. Milkman, "The Sexual," 541.

6. All-American Girls Professional Baseball League: Rules of Conduct. Northern Indiana Historical Society. Retrieved from https://www.aagpbl.org/history/rules-of-conduct.

7. Carol J. Pierman. "Baseball, Conduct, and True Womanhood." *Women's Studies Quarterly*, Vol 33, No. ½: 73.

8. Mamie Johnson, interview by the National Visionary Leadership Project, 2009, retrieved from http://www.visionaryproject.org/johnsonmamie/.

9. Pierman, "Baseball," 69–74.

10. James Overmyer, *Queen of the Negro Leagues: Effa Manley and the Newark Eagles* (Lanham, MD & London: The Scarecrow Press, 1998) 5, 52–53.

11. Overmyer, *Queen*, 52–53.

12. Neil Lanctot, *Negro League Baseball: The Rise and Ruin of a Black Institution* (Philadelphia: University of Pennsylvania Press, 2004). 281–92.

13. Lanctot, *Negro League*, 360.

14. Lanctor, *Negro League*, 330.

15. Lanctot, *Negro League*, 360.

16. "Negro Ball Clubs Hope to Make Comeback This Season," *Ebony*, May 1949.

17. Lanctot, *Negro League*, 342.

18. Overmyer, *Queen*, 217–23.

19. Amira Rose Davis, "No League of Their Own: Baseball Black Women, and the Politics of Representation." *Radical History Review*. Issue 125 (2016): 72–78.

20. Lanctot, *Negro League*, 281–90.

21. Dr. J.B. Martin. "Negro League President Comments." *Los Angeles Sentinel*, June 11, 1953.

22. Lanctot, *Negro League*, 380.

23. Martin, "Negro League President."

24. "Clowns to Play Saturday," *The Frederick Times-Post*. July 15, 1954.

25. "Clowns to Play," 1954.

26. Everbach, "Breaking Baseball," 15.

27. Lanctot, *Negro League*, 380.

28. Martha Ackmann. *Curveball: The Remarkable Story of Toni Stone* (Chicago: Lawrence Hill Books, 2010) 119.

29. Ackmann, *Curveball*, 3.

30. Davis, "No League," 76.

31. Ackmann, *Curveball*, 21.

32. Marion E. Jackson, "Sports of the World," *Atlanta Daily World*, May 11, 1950.

33. Jackson, "Sports of," 1950.

34. "Girl Handles Fielding Chances," *Council Bluffs Nonpareil*, July 25, 1950; "Girl Player to Return Monday," *Council Bluffs Nonpareil*, July 23, 1950.

35. "Negro Girl Second Baseman Will Oppose Rainbows Tuesday Night," *Council Bluffs Nonpareil*, July 1950.

36. "Woman Player Says She Can 'Take Care of Self' in Game," *Ebony*, 1953. 48.

37. *Los Angeles Sentinel*, February 26, 1953.

38. Sam Lacy, "A to Z," *Baltimore Afro-American*, July 25, 1953.

39. Davis, "No League," 78.

40. Davis, "No League," 80.

41. "The Gal on Second Base," *Our World*, 1953, 8–11.

42. "The Gal," *Our World*, 1953.

43. "Lady Ball Player on Male Team," *Ebony*, 1953.

44. Stew Thornley, "Toni Stone," Society for American Baseball Research, retrieved December 3, 2018 https://sabr.org/bioproj/person/2f33485c

45. "Lady Ball Player," 1953.

46. "Clowns to Play," 1954.

47. Davis, "No League," 81.

48. Davis, "No League," 81.

49. "Clowns Sell Toni Stone. Sign New Female Star," *Michigan Chronicle*, 1954.

50. Davis, "No League," 81.

51. Davis, "No League," 82.

52. Davis, "No League," 82.

53. "Clowns' Girl Second Baseman Thrills Birmingham Fans With Speedy Plays," *The Call*, May 28, 1954.

54. Davis, "No League," 82.

55. Lanctot, *Negro League*, 381–83.

56. "Clowns Sell Stone to KC Nine," *Pittsburgh Courier*, March 13, 1954.

57. Ackman, *Curveball*, 164.

58. "Clowns' Girl Second," *The Call*, 1954.

59. "Clowns Sell Toni Stone: Sign New Female Star," *Michigan Chronicle*, 1954.

60. "Feminine Stars," *Philadelphia Courier*, 1954.

61. Davis, "No League," 78.

62. "Clowns Sell Toni," *Michigan Chronicle*, 1954.

63. "Honeydrippers' Torrid Pace Scares off Opposition in North Softball Division," *Philadelphia Tribune*, August 26, 1952.

64. Cheryl D. Hicks. "Mable Hampton in Harlem: Regulating Black Women's Sexuality in the 1920s," in *Women's America: Refocusing on the Past*, ed. Linda K. Kerber, Jane Sherron DeHart, Cornelia Hughes Dayton, and Judy Tzu-Chu (New York & Oxford: Oxford University Press, 2016), 437.

65. Hicks, "Mable Hampton," 439.

66. Mamie Johnson, interview by Reba Goldman Cottingham, 1998, Negro League Oral History Collection, Archives and Special Collections, Langsdale Library, University of Baltimore.

67. Davis, "No League," 77.

68. Johnson, interview, 1998.

69. Alan Schwarz, "Breaking Gender Barriers in Negro Leagues," *The New York Times*, June 12, 2010.

70. Jean Hastings Ardell, "Mamie 'Peanut' Johnson: The Last Female Voice of the Negro Leagues," *NINE: A Journal of Baseball History and Culture*, Vol. 10 No. 1, 2000, 181–92.

71. "Clowns Setting New Attendance Records," *The Call*, June 19, 1953, 10–12.

72. Lanctot, *Negro League*, 381.

73. Lanctot, *Negro League*, 381

74. "Clowns Girl," 1954.

75. Everbach, "Breaking Baseball," 27.

76. "Clowns to Battle Monarchs in Sunday Twin Bill," *The Call*, August 27, 1954.

77. "Clowns to Battle," 1954.

78. Everbach, "Breaking Baseball," 21.

79. "Crowd of 18,205 Watches Monarchs Trim Clowns," *The Kansas City Times*, May 25, 1953, 14.

80. "Richardson to Hurl for Monarchs," *The Kansas City Star*, Mary 24, 1953, 3B.

81. Everbach, "Breaking Baseball," 23.
82. Everbach, "Breaking Baseball," 23–24.
83. Doc Young, "Should Girls Play Ball: No, Says Doc," *Chicago Defender*, August 28, 1954.
84. Wendell Smith, "The Lady's Playing a Man's Game," *Pittsburgh Courier*, 1953.
85. Luis Virgil Overbea, "Beating the Gun: Players in Baseball Not Excited Over Women," *Baltimore Afro-American*, July 25, 1953.
86. "Clowns to Battle," 1953, 10.
87. "Syd Pollock, Clowns' Owner to Watch Monarchs Home Opener May 24," *The Call*, May 22, 1953.
88. Susan K. Cahn. *Coming on Strong: Gender and Sexuality in Twentieth Century Women's Sports* (New York, Free Press) 233.
89. Johnson, interview, 1998.
90. Hastings Ardell, "Mamie," 186.
91. Hicks, "Mable Hampton," 436–39.
92. Davis, "No League," 85.
93. Ackmann, *Curveball*, 157.
94. Davis, "No League," 85.
95. Ackmann, *Curveball*, 157.
96. Davis, "No League," 85.
97. Davis, "No League," 85.
98. Davis, "No League," 85.
99. Buck O'Neill, *I Was Right on Time: My Journey from the Negro Leagues to the Majors* (New York: Simon & Schuster, 2010) 195.
100. Davis, "No League," 85.
101. "Clowns Girl Player Returns to School," *The Call*, October 29, 1954.
102. Johnson, interview, 1998.
103. Johnson, interview, 1998.
104. Johnson, interview, 1998.
105. Davis, "No League," 84.
106. Hastings Ardell, "Mamie," 185.
107. Davis, "No League," 85.
108. Darlene Clark Hine, "Rape and the Inner Lives of Black Women in the Middle West," *Signs: Journal of Women in Culture and Society* (1989): 912–20.
109. Davis, "No League," 85.
110. Hastings Ardell, "Mamie," 185.
111. Cahn, *Coming on Strong*, 230–31.
112. Cahn, *Coming on Strong*, 230–31.
113. Pierman, "Baseball," 70.
114. Ruth Rolen, "Connie Morgan to Join Clowns," *Afro-American*, March 27, 1954.
115. Candus Thomson, "Making pitch for women; Baseball: After breaking the gender barrier 40 years ago as a Negro Leagues pitcher, Mamie Johnson returns to the baseball world," *The Baltimore Sun*, June 22, 1999.
116. Thomson, "Making pitch."
117. Davis, "No League," 88.
118. "Lady Ball Player," 1953.
119. "Clowns Girl Player Returns," *The Call*, 1954.
120. "Clowns Girl Player Returns," *The Call*, 1954.
121. Johnson, interview, 1998.
122. Adrienne Rich, "Compulsory Heterosexuality and Lesbian Existence," in *Blood, Bread, and Poetry: Selected Prose, 1979–1985* (New York: W.W. Norton, 1986) 72.
123. Joanne Meyerowitz, *Not June Cleaver: Women and Gender in Postwar America 1945–1960* (Philadelphia: Temple University Press, 1994) 84–98.
124. Davis, "No League," 75.
125. Davis, "No League," 75.
126. Cahn, *Coming on Strong*, 11.
127. Davis, "No League," 75.
128. Malcolm Poindexter, "Sports View," *Philadelphia Tribune*, May 11, 1954.
129. Cahn, *Coming on Strong*, 180.
130. *Science Digest*, September 1957, 37.
131. Cahn, *Coming on Strong*, 180.
132. "Lady Ball Player," 1953.
133. "Lady Ball Player, 1953.
134. Pierman, "Baseball," 77.
135. Cahn, *Coming on Strong*, 178.
136. Cahn, *Coming on Strong*, 177.
137. Hicks, "Mable Hampton," 437.
138. Davis, "No League," 88.
139. Davis, "No League," 88.
140. Davis, "No League," 88.
141. Davis, "No League," 88.
142. Davis, "No League," 88.
143. Davis, "No League," 88.
144. Davis, "No League," 88.
145. Davis, "No League," 88.
146. Davis, "No League," 88.

# All The Duckys in a Row

*In Search of the Real Ducky Holmes*

Joan Wendl Thomas

When quintessential baseball buff Douglas Heeren first approached me about a player named Ducky Holmes, I failed to grasp the depth of the subject. Pointing out my misidentification of Ducky in a team photo in my book about baseball in Northwest Iowa, Heeren simply wanted to set the record straight.[1] A young man from rural Akron, Iowa, Heeren had some familiarity with one major-league baseball player known as Ducky Holmes. In 1941, Heeren's uncle, Robert Tucker, was a first baseman and pitcher for the Dayton Ducks, a Middle Atlantic League team managed by one Howard "Ducky" Holmes. The Ducky Holmes in my book is James William Holmes, who played for and managed the Sioux City Packers in 1908. The photo caption is correct about that, but it incorrectly adds that he "caught for the St. Louis Cardinals in 1906."

It was Howard, not James, who was a catcher for St. Louis that year. Although Howard Holmes had an extensive career in baseball, his time as a big-league player consisted of a mere nine games for the Cardinals. But the conflation of Duckys does not end there. Enthusiastically handing me articles and records he had judiciously gathered from reliable Internet sources, Heeren proved that at least three different baseball players by the name of Ducky Holmes played in the major leagues during the same era.

Appalled by my own error, I thanked the young man, promising to somehow make restitution. Thus I embarked on a perplexing, mesmerizing quest to detail and separate the three Duckys. Little did I know that my research would yield not just three, but five professional baseball players named Ducky Holmes. Numbers four and five never advanced beyond the minor leagues, but their very existence plunged my study down a multitude of wrong-way paths. Of course, as a historian, that only deepened my stubborn need to "set the record straight."

The following short biographies should assist anyone seeking the true identity of any one of these Duckys. Here are all five Duckys in a row:

## JAMES WILLIAM "DUCKY" HOLMES 1869–1932

Born in Des Moines, Iowa, James William Holmes, frequently referred to as William, is the first—or some would say "the real"—Ducky Holmes in baseball. Born over a decade before the others, his stretch as a professional baseball player surpasses those of his namesakes by far. A good all-around athlete who batted left and threw right, he proved capable at any position but was typically designated as an outfielder. Significantly, the annals of baseball history portray him as an archetypal bad boy of the sport. Stories of his quick-tempered nature abound. One could easily envision a Hollywood movie featuring him as the title character. There would be no need for hyperbole, as his escapades prove the adage that truth is stranger than fiction.

The son of Arch and Eliza Holmes, William grew up on a farm near Truro, Iowa, about 40 miles south of Des Moines. At one point during his youth, he worked in the hay camps and barns of the small town of Rolfe. He also caught for that town's baseball club during the season that was reportedly "Rolfe's greatest baseball year."[2] William began his professional playing career in Beatrice, Nebraska, sometime between 1890 and 1892, and he was sold to the Western Association's St. Joseph club in 1893.[3] In the same league the following year, he played for Des Moines, then Quincy in early 1895. His first major-league job was with the Louisville Colonels in 1895. From there, he spent nearly a decade bouncing to six more clubs, three more in the National League, then three in the American League. As a player, he posted respectable, sometimes above-average, statistics. His best year was with Baltimore in 1899, when he ended the season with a batting average of .320. By the time a knee injury suffered in 1905 with the White Sox effectively ended his big-league career, he had built a reputation for spawning quarrels and controversy.

While playing left field for Baltimore against the New York Giants at the Polo Grounds on July 25, 1898, James William "Ducky" Holmes, a former Giant, responded to fans' jeers by referring to Giants owner

Andrew Freedman as a "Sheeney." Freedman, who was Jewish, took exception to the ethnic slur. When the umpire refused to eject Holmes from the game at Freedman's request, he ordered Giants manager Bill Joyce to keep his players on the bench. The umpire then forfeited the game to Baltimore. This sparked an ongoing feud in what SABR's Bill Lamb describes as a "bruising 17-month battle among National League magnates that culminated in nothing less than the restructure of major-league baseball."[4]

Playing for Detroit in 1902, Ducky traded barbs with his former teammate John McGraw in a game at Baltimore. After getting a hit and heading for third on an infield play, he jumped high and slid into McGraw, resolutely stationed at third, striking him on the knee with both feet. Getting up, McGraw punched Ducky, who landed one on Mugsy's jaw. The Orioles' player-manager, destined to manage the Giants for 30 seasons, sometimes called "Little Napoleon," and eventually enshrined in the Hall of Fame, left the field that day "never to return again as a regular player."[5]

Following his stint with Chicago, Holmes purchased the Lincoln, Nebraska, team in 1906, the year it joined the Western League. He served as player-manager for the Class A club, named the Ducklings after him. After finishing second with a 75–74 record in 1906, Ducky's team started '07 as the Lincoln Tree Planters. Notably, the Planters' lead pitcher was Eddie Cicotte, who later gained notoriety in the Chicago Black Sox scandal. At season's end, Ducky sold the Lincoln Club to Guy W. Green, then purchased the Sioux City Packers in the same league. Several years later, Green contended that at the time of the sale, Holmes manipulated the Lincoln players in an effort to "land them in Sioux City."[6] He claimed that one of the men Ducky tried to influence was center fielder Bill Davidson, who moved up to the Chicago Cubs in 1909.

Ducky's Packers captured the Western League pennant in 1908. And even if the charge that Ducky tried to recruit Lincoln players was true, it does not appear to have been successful. The next season, Sioux City finished second in the eight-team league, just a hair behind the Des Moines Boosters. Despite his questionable reputation, William "Ducky" Holmes had proven his aptitude for management. That likely persuaded Toledo Mud Hens ownership to sign him as player-manager in 1910.

However, his time with that American Association club was short-lived. When he returned from a road trip, the club's president reportedly called him to task for unspecified offenses. It was also rumored that Ducky wanted his own club and "had bought an interest in the Des Moines club of the Western League."[7] Rather than face firing, he announced his resignation on June 6. News soon surfaced that revealed he had more than baseball on his mind at the time.

The marriage of William "Ducky" Holmes to Merte Rogers, a Sioux City public school teacher, was announced on June 11. The Waterloo Evening Courier reported that the wedding had taken place several weeks earlier while "the Toledo team was playing in the Twin Cities."[8] That of course, would be during the road trip in question. The news item reporting the marriage also included the fact that Ducky had divorced the previous winter. Significantly, in a suit in Rapid City, South Dakota, his ex-wife had charged him with desertion. Yet none of the adverse publicity prevented him from being chosen as manager of the Mobile Sea Gulls of the Southern Association for 1911. But his position there proved contentious from the start.

Late in April of that season, word came of the quarrelsome Mobile manager's suspension by the league president. Ducky was charged with insulting Umpire Collidower by referring to him as a "common vegetable."[9] The suspension didn't last long, but neither did Mobile's new manager. On June 12, Holmes was fired after he engaged in a fistfight with Mobile director Harry Hartwell. One newspaper account claimed that "trouble had been brewing for some time."[10] Following his suspension over the umpire incident, Holmes had been fined $500 for language on the field and for an alleged attempt to get recompense in the sale of pitcher Frank Allen to Brooklyn.[11] (Allen would go to the Dodgers in 1912.) Additionally, there were charges that Ducky incited the Mobile players to mutiny, made side contracts, and attempted to keep players from the field in order to cause forfeiture of games.[12] The same news story that made these charges reported that Holmes blamed his firing on Southern prejudice against a Northerner.

Taking his dispute with Mobile to the National Commission, Holmes presented his contract as evidence that he was the club's business manager. He claimed that he should have been paid his salary for the unexpired portion of the contract.[13] The end result of his claim, or if he was ever forced to pay the fine, are unknown. There is some evidence that he finished the 1911 season with the Victoria Bees, who finished last in the six-team Northwestern League. The following season found him back managing clubs in the Midwest, starting with a short stay with the Class D Nebraska City Forresters, then back to Sioux City in 1912 and part of 1913. One undated newspaper account of his resigning from the Packers on June 6, 1913, reveals that he had a ranch in Montana. That was reportedly his next destination.[14] This fits with records of his time with the Union Association's Butte Miners in 1914. But he soon returned to Nebraska, managing Lincoln in 1916–17.

In 1918, managing Sioux City again, the restless Ducky Holmes prepared to travel to France to represent the YMCA in war welfare work, but the Armistice that ended World War I canceled his journey.[15] Then, in January 1919, his purported interest in the Des Moines club again surfaced. He attempted to purchase that Western League franchise from Des Moines Mayor Tom Fairweather, former president of the Sioux City club. Ducky offered to buy the Class A Boosters outright, with the intention of moving the team to Lincoln, whose club did not have a minor-league franchise at the time. When that offer was turned down, Holmes proposed to lease the Des Moines ballpark and to keep the Boosters in that city. Both offers were refused.[16]

A curious side note to this story is that in January 1918, a devastating fire had destroyed the former Western League Lincoln ballpark's grandstand and the clubhouse, which served as caretaker Edward McConnell's residence. McConnell was away at the time, but his wife and five-year-old daughter were at home and suffered serious burns. Fortunately, the ballclub carried $3,000 insurance on the grandstand. The *Lincoln Daily State Journal* reported that just before the fire started, Mrs. McConnell heard the sound of an automobile and voices. The story goes on to say: "It is not the belief of Ducky Holmes that anyone would intentionally set fire to the ball park."[17] This sheds some suspicion on Holmes himself, having managed Lincoln the previous season. It is conceivable that he might have had a financial interest in the concern at the time.

Unable to acquire a Western League franchise in 1919, Ducky finally settled for an amateur team in Brownville, Nebraska, in 1920. That year he managed and played third base for the Apple Pickers, and he may have owned the club. The townsfolk were elated that not only would a prominent baseball figure control its team, but that a municipal election yielded a go-ahead for Sunday baseball.[18] (Some Midwestern towns banned the practice at the time.) Still living in Brownville early in 1921, Ducky umpired in a number of Class B Three-I League games and also served as "one of Charles Comiskey's scouts."[19] In July, his contrary nature surfaced in his umpiring, as evidenced by an altercation that resulted in fines being levied on the Moline Plowboys' manager and a player, and Holmes taking a short leave of absence, which he would soon make permanent. "Ducky Holmes is no longer on Al

*James William Holmes, baseball's "original" Ducky Holmes.*

CHICAGO HISTORY MUSEUM

Tearney's officiating corps," the *Moline Dispatch* reported. "After the breakdown here last Monday it is said Ducky beat it for home in Lincoln, Nebraska. Enuf is enuf, is the way Holmes put it."[20]

In 1922, Ducky started the season managing the Fort Smith Twins of the Western Association in Arkansas. Transient as ever, he ended up in Nebraska, helming the Beatrice Blues in July. True to form, late in August, he got into a brouhaha with an umpire and was escorted from the field by the local police. He was promptly fired and "ordered out of the lot for assaulting umpire 'Dutch' Meyers."[21] By then, he was no longer married to Merte. She married Elmer Eugene Theno in Lincoln on January 7, 1922.

As time passed, Ducky continued working in baseball as an umpire and scout. In an undated letter from John J. McMahon, an insurance representative from Des Moines, addressed to Billy Coad, owner of the semipro Le Mars (Iowa) Orioles, the writer recommends Mr. "Ducky" Holmes, "a former Western League umpire," to serve as umpire "in that part of the country."[22] McMahon adds that Holmes "comes reasonable and can also give you reference Chas. Dexter, a former Major League…" The mention of Dexter confirms that the Ducky being backed is James William. Charlie Dexter was a teammate of his when he played for the National League Louisville Colonels in the 1890s. As Coad's Le Mars club was founded in 1926, the correspondence was typed then or later. During that year, Ducky was living in Sioux City, which is near Le Mars. Soon, stories arose that he was bargaining to purchase Lincoln's Class A Western League Links.[23]

Apparently, Ducky's plan to buy the Links failed: During the summer of 1927, a Le Mars paper announced that he had been hired to manage a new

Sioux City Stockyards team.[24] The city didn't have a minor-league club at the time. In the same publication, a story appeared about his appointment as coach of the team in Merrill, a small town between Le Mars and Sioux City. Some of the players being sought by Ducky for Sioux City were then with the Merrill and Le Mars clubs.

Finally, after suffering from ill health for several years, James William "Ducky" Holmes died at the age of 63 in his hometown of Truro on August 5, 1932. He was survived by two brothers and two sisters. But he had outlived his ex-wife, Merte. Lincoln newspapers confirm that Merte, Mrs. E. E. Theno, retired from an 11-year teaching position in Lincoln in 1927. She died on October 29, 1929, while on a trip to Pasadena, California. There is no mention of children or of her first husband in her obituary.[25] Local news items reveal that people in Lincoln had fond remembrances of both her and Ducky.

In 1911, the *Lincoln Star*, in a story about Ducky's career up until then, states, "Holmes has made friends and enemies galore…. He is afflicted with a temper that easily breaks bounds, but is gifted with an equal ability to forget grudges…he is the best of friends, and a man who always gives all he has to his employers."[26] In a 1926 Lincoln newspaper story about his interest in buying the town's Western League team, he is described as a "resourceful, heady baseball general." A *Rolfe Arrow* story of August 18, 1932, describes him as one of baseball's best known players, who had a remarkable career in the game. These words intimate a legacy befitting the first, or "real," Ducky Holmes.

### HOWARD ELBERT "DUCKY" HOLMES 1883–1945
Howard Elbert Holmes, the most colorful of all the Duckys in baseball, was born in Dayton, Ohio. His full career in the sport included catching for one major-league club and a number of minor league teams, umpiring in the minors and both major leagues, founding and managing several minor-league clubs, and serving in an executive position for at least one. References to his nose as an "elongated proboscis" and "big schnozzola," as Douglas Heeren observed, suggests that it resembled a duck's bill.[28] That may explain how he acquired the moniker Ducky. Although not as notorious for his temperament as James William "Ducky" Holmes, Howard did gain a reputation for being a "fiery manager."[29]

At the age of 19, Howard "Ducky" Holmes launched his professional playing career as a catcher in 1902 with the Saginaw/Jackson White Sox in the short-lived Class D Michigan State League. He then caught for

Savannah in the Sally League for several years before being signed by the Cardinals in 1906. Following his brief stay in St. Louis, he moved on to Indianapolis, then to Canton in 1907. Some records indicate that he played for the Sioux City Packers in 1908, but that is highly doubtful.

Studies of numerous reports of the Packers' games of 1908, including lineups, never reveal a catcher named Holmes. Player-manager Ducky Holmes is frequently named, and that is, without doubt, James William Holmes. Moreover, there are never two players with the surname Holmes listed. Notably, several April 1908 news items report that the American Association Louisville club's new catcher would be Ducky Holmes from Dayton.[30] On June 25, another story revealed that "Catcher Holmes, of Birmingham, has been reinstated, and will be used regularly."[31] The term "reinstated" does leave some question. Then, late in July, Birmingham announced that catcher Holmes was released to Montreal in the Eastern League.[32] So it appears that Howard started the season in Louisville, then went to Birmingham and finally to Montreal. This is the sort of detective work that would have prevented my error of placing him in Sioux City in 1908. That settled, on with the story of Howard "Ducky" Holmes.

After Montreal, Howard played for three Central League clubs over the next four years—Zanesville, South Bend, and Grand Rapids—before taking on his first managing position. In 1913, the Southern Michigan League's Saginaw club changed its name from the Trailers to the Ducks, after its new player-manager, Howard "Ducky" Holmes. He led the Ducks to pennants that year and the next. His star hurler in 1914 was none other than 20-year-old Jesse Haines. The future Hall of Famer won 17 games. Following one more season in Saginaw, Ducky went on to manage the Class D Frankfort Taylors of the Ohio State League. That season, 1916, proved to be his last as a player and Frankfort's last with a minor-league club. Howard spent most of the next decade umpiring.

After starting out in the Three-I League in 1917, Ducky signed with the American Association.[33] In March 1921, the *Nebraska State Journal* reported that he was included on the staff of Western League umpires for that season. Later that year, an incident occurred that might have involved James William "Ducky" Holmes, but was likely Howard instead.

During an Oklahoma City-Tulsa game in Tulsa on August 10, 1921, disgruntled fans hurled pop bottles and cushions at umpires William Guthrie and "Ducky" Holmes. "One bottle bounced off Guthrie's stomach," reported the *Pella Chronicle*.[34] Outside the park after the game, the two arbiters retaliated by assaulting Sgt. Tom Haines, a war veteran in uniform, who apparently had taken no part in their attack. The local police arrested Guthrie and Holmes, who were fined $50 and $10, respectively. American Legion posts all over the country demanded that they be fired from the Western League and barred from organized baseball. The matter was taken up with the league and with baseball's new commissioner, Kenesaw Mountain Landis.

The quandary here is the identity of the umpire named Ducky Holmes. Not one of the related news articles gives a first name, which was often the case with James William "Ducky" Holmes. However, as William was never actually recognized as a league umpire, and Howard was an official Western League ump, that would indicate it was the latter. The pugnacious nature of the Ducky in question proves nothing, as neither Ducky was averse to fisticuffs. Moreover, there was always the possibility of misidentification by the media. Regardless, if Judge Landis ruled on the matter, it did not affect either of their careers. Neither was banned from professional baseball, and Howard went on to umpire in the major leagues. He got a trial in the National League late in 1921 but was held "to the Western" in 1922.[35]

Following his brief stint with the National League, Howard umpired for the American League in 1923 and '24. An episode in St. Louis in June 1924 may have resulted in the end of his career as a baseball arbiter. He infuriated fans by ejecting Browns manager George Sisler, catcher Pat Collins, and coach Jimmy Austin. Following the game, he was confronted by an irate fan, who struck him in the eye. Holmes blamed the attack on a conspiracy by gamblers.[36] Paul Farina, the disgruntled Browns fan, eventually pleaded guilty to the offense and paid a $25 fine. Explaining his actions, Farina said, "I was excited and did it in the heat of passion."[37] One story claimed that Browns owner Phil Ball made it his business to get Ducky removed from the umpire roster.[38] In fact, that was his last season in the majors. He soon turned his attention back to managing.

After purchasing his hometown's minor-league club in 1932, Howard, who also served as manager, changed the Dayton team name from Aviators to Ducks. By the following season, he'd gained permission to move the club from the Central League to the Mid-Atlantic League. He oversaw the start of lefty Johnny Vander Meer's professional career, as the future four-time All-Star pitched for the Ducks in 1933. Firmly stationed in Dayton by 1935, when the club was associated with the Brooklyn Dodgers, Howard lived up to his reputation as a fiery manager. He was suspended for three months for striking an umpire. Demonstrating his "colorful" label, he continued to manage the Ducks by signaling from his perch on "an electric tower in back of the ball park."[39] Another incident that year involving Howard "Ducky" Holmes is the stuff of baseball legend.

Just prior to a playoff game between Dayton and Huntington on September 13, 1935, a fan presented Ducky with a real duck as a gift. When none of the Dayton players had reached base by the seventh inning, he took the bird to first base and stationed it there. Relating this story, SABR's Ira L. Smith claims that Holmes had said, half to himself, that he'd make sure a duck got to first base before the inning was over. He adds, "Very soon thereafter that duck gained the distinction of being the first member of its species to be 'thumbed' off the baseball field by an umpire."[40]

Howard continued managing the Dayton Ducks through 1942, with brief interruptions in 1939 and again in 1940. Early in August of that year, it was announced that he'd been appointed acting manager of the Michigan State League's Grand Rapids team, also a Brooklyn farm club. He replaced Burleigh Grimes, who'd been suspended following a dispute with an umpire.[41] So it seems the theme of umpire disputes followed Ducky throughout his career.

At one point in 1942, Howard was presented with a huge floral horseshoe by his Zanesville admirers.[42] That year was the last season for the Middle Atlantic League, and also for the Ducks. During his tenure in Dayton, he not only managed, but served as president, general manager, and treasurer of the club. After his team folded, he worked in a grocery store for some time. In 1944, an article related that if he could "get away from his war job," he would attend a meeting of the Ohio State League.[43] This indicates that he was still involved in baseball, and was also doing more than working at a store. After suffering two strokes, he died at home at the age of 62 on September 18, 1945. He was survived by his wife, Lillian, who passed away in 1960. Originally buried at Woodland Cemetery in Dayton, Howard's remains were moved to Calvary Cemetery in Kettering, Ohio, in 1946. His tombstone reads HOLMES — H E "Ducky."

### JAMES SCOTT "DUCKY" HOLMES 1881–1960

Little is known about James "Ducky" Holmes, and news items often confuse him with the other Ducky Holmeses in baseball. What is certain is that he was born in Lawrenceburg, Kentucky, on August 2, 1881. He was a right-handed pitcher. His career description on his 1912 Imperial Tobacco card makes the claim that his first "professional engagement was with the Albany Club in the New York League in 1908."[44] Yet all other evidence has him starting with Huntsville of the independent Tennessee-Alabama League in 1904.

He spent time with Augusta of the Sally League in 1905, and his first major-league assignment was with the 1906 Philadelphia Athletics, with whom he appeared in three games. He then went back to Augusta for 1907. There, he tallied his best season, with a 26–16 won-loss record in 1906. His last major-league assignment was in 1908 with Brooklyn, where he appeared in 13 games. He definitely spent the next four seasons with Rochester, then was with Buffalo for parts of 1912 and '13, and Newark for the rest of the latter year. A January 1914 *New York Times* story reported that "the veteran pitcher" Ducky Holmes had signed with Baltimore of the new Federal League, but he played for Memphis of the Southern Association that year, his last as a professional player.[45]

James Scott Holmes's name as shown under his photo on his Imperial Tobacco card is simply Holmes. The back side description reads only "Ducky" Holmes. Often, news stories call him Jim rather than James. Few details about his life after 1914 are available, but obituaries reveal that he moved to Jacksonville, Florida, in 1928. He worked in the retail grocery business there before he retired around 1950. Then, following an illness of several months, he died in a Jacksonville hospital on March 10, 1960.[46]

Several news items that appeared after his death contribute to the misidentification caused by too many baseball players named Ducky Holmes. The *Brownsville Herald*, in a story reflecting on the Augusta club of 1906, refers to him as "the original Ducky Holmes."[47] As James William "Ducky" Holmes was in the game, and called Ducky, almost a decade earlier, it would not seem likely that Jim could qualify as the original. Also, a Florida newspaper story in 1959, while Jim was still very much alive, names him as one of the umpires to officiate at the first game at the original Yankee Stadium. It correctly calls the umpire Ducky Holmes but goes on to say how he once played for Augusta in the Sally League.[48] However, it was Howard "Ducky" Holmes who umpired in that first game at Yankee Stadium on April 18, 1923. But Howard never played for Augusta.

The pitcher Ducky Holmes whose major league assignments included Philadelphia and Brooklyn is buried at Riverside Memorial Park in Jacksonville. His tombstone reads "James Scott Holmes."

## ROBERT H. HOLMES OR ROBERT S. HOLMES 1884–?

What little information is available reveals that right-handed relief pitcher Robert H. Holmes, possibly Robert S. Holmes, also called "Bob," was born in Texas in 1883 or 1884. His professional baseball career consisted of four seasons, and he never rose to the major-league level. There is evidence that he too was called "Ducky."

In 1908 he appeared in 21 games for the Altoona Mountaineers of the Tri-State League, and then in 26 games in 1909 for Waco of the Texas League. He pitched in 20 games for the Newark Indians of the Class A Eastern League in 1910, and in 37 more the next year. He never had a winning season. The clue to his "Ducky" handle arises from a *New York Times* report of a 1911 Newark game.

The box score story detailing Newark's game with Jersey City says that the Indians' Holmes "was in good form for seven innings."[49] It adds that "Ducky" blew up in the eighth. One could conjecture that the sportswriter had him confused with the other Newark pitcher, Jim Holmes. However, Jim didn't play for that club until 1913, two years after Bob. Bob's Imperial Tobacco card dubs him "Pitcher 'Bob' Holmes."[50]

Unable to track down solid information about this mysterious Ducky, I did locate an R. S. "Ducky" Holmes living in Amarillo, Texas, in the 1930s and '40s. This might be stretching it a bit, but the "R" could stand for Robert. Moreover, his Texas birthplace enhances this hunch to some degree. Speculations about his possible identity as the former pitcher include several pieces in Amarillo newspapers.

A 1938 *Amarillo Globe* story about girls softball reads, "Ducky Holmes is interested in forming a girls' city league and having a tournament."[51] The name R.S. "Ducky" Holmes appears several times in the 1940s, the most helpful in 1945. A story about a Capt. R.S. Holmes Jr. describes his parents as "Mr. and Mrs. R.S. (Ducky) Holmes," who "now live in Amarillo." It goes on, "Mr. Holmes for years was a Rock Island Dispatcher."[52] Several stories show that the family lived in Dalhart, Texas, while Ducky Junior was growing up. But nothing turns up with the Dalhart clue. However, in a 1927 story about the Texas A&M Aggies, Ducky Holmes is mentioned as "the Aggies fifth flinger (who) has quit going out for baseball."[53] Considering the date, that Ducky is quite likely Ducky Junior. One more piece of the puzzle, perhaps an irregular piece, is a photo found in a magazine published by the New Haven Railroad for its employees in October 1946. On page 262, in a photo featuring Brakeman "Biddy" Comm and Conductor 'Ducky' Holmes, Conductor

Ducky's face looks remarkably like an age-enhanced sketch of Newark's Holmes on the baseball card.[54] And, R. S. "Ducky" Holmes did work for a railroad. But again, that alone does not really prove anything.

Many times there are significant leads in obituaries, but so far none have surfaced for Bob, Robert or R. S. "Ducky" Holmes that prove useful. One hope is that someone reading this will come forward and help fill in the blanks. That would certainly augment baseball history, and honor the memory of pitcher Bob "Ducky" Holmes.

### CHARLES M. HOLMES, AKA DUCKY HOLMES 1907–82

While preparing to wrap up my research, a futile effort, I happened onto yet another minor-league pitcher named Ducky Holmes. Although he was of a later generation than the others, I could not ignore his existence.

In 1927, the Springfield (Missouri) Midgets defeated Fort Smith, 9–5, and "'Ducky Holmes,' youthful Springfield hurler, was the winning slabman."[55] According to Baseball-Reference, a Charles A. Holmes pitched for the Western Association Midgets in 1927, and then for Quincy in 1928. A 1929 news item reported that Ducky Holmes had been released from the Quincy Indians.[56] Another story revealed that Charley "Ducky" Holmes was pitching for the Moline Plowboys by June of that year.[57] It also had him living in Cedar Rapids, Iowa, at the time. Baseball Reference lists C. M. Holmes with the Plowboys in 1930. A June 1930 article in a Burlington, Iowa, newspaper detailing a game between the Burlington Bees and the Moline Plowboys calls him "Ducky Holmes, the bespectacled Moline veteran."[58] As evidenced by a story in a Cedar Rapids newspaper, he was still being considered for the Moline pitching staff early in 1931. The writer reports, "Ducky Holmes and Sally Lambert, veteran right handers, still are the property of the club.... Holmes was one of the most valuable flingers on the staff last year."[59] There is one 1934 story that has a Ducky Holmes pitching for the semipro Manchester Hawks.[60] In all probability, he was the same Ducky who played for the Plowboys.

Thus, we have good evidence that the right-handed pitcher Charles Holmes who played for the Springfield Midgets, the Quincy Indians, the Moline Plowboys, and most likely the Manchester Hawks are one and the same. His middle initial was "M.," and, significantly, he wore eyeglasses. And, he was called Ducky since at least 1927, when he played for Springfield.

Fortunately, we have significantly more biographical information about this Ducky than we have about Robert Holmes. Census records reveal that Charles Moore Holmes was born July 31, 1907, to Robert and Sarah Holmes. This is undoubtedly the Plowboys' Ducky Holmes. He married Elinore B. Berry on September 28, 1935, in Rock Island, Illinois. A 1941 Cedar Rapids City Directory shows him as a foreman at the Quaker Cereal Company there. He died on January 10, 1982, at the age of 74, and was buried at Cedar Memorial Park Cemetery in Cedar Rapids. His wife, Elinore, died in 1993 and was buried beside her husband.

### CONCLUSION

Throughout my probe into the quandary of the multiple Ducky Holmeses, I've pondered the meaning of the nickname "Ducky." In earlier centuries, it had been a slang term for a female breast.[61] Naturally, that can be ruled out. During the time frame covered in this story, it was often used as a term of endearment pertaining to a male. While doing news archives searches, I've found other men named Ducky who were not connected with baseball. One was accused of murder. Another was a prizefighter. Granted, two of the Duckys detailed here were combative, but neither was homicidal or fought for a living. However, it seems all these guys were around during the first half of the 20th century. So, the tag Ducky for a man, especially an athlete, may have been popular then.

Some might suggest that the frequent use of that handle was influenced by Hall of Fame left fielder Joe "Ducky" Medwick. But he came along a bit too late for that. Besides, Medwick did not cherish his nickname, as it was said he got it because he waddled like a duck. One could come up with all sorts of theories, both realistic and farfetched. For instance, Douglas Heeren half-seriously suggested pursuing the origin of the cartoon character Howard the Duck. I actually considered that there might be some connection between him and Howard "Ducky" Holmes. Another even more preposterous notion arose while I searched eBay for images. Inputting "Ducky Holmes" yielded a number of collectibles of Daffy Duck as Sherlock Holmes.

The simple explanation might just be that after James William "Ducky" Holmes gained some prominence in baseball, other players bearing his last name, and/or bearing some resemblance to a duck, got the tag. I have no doubt that there were, or maybe still are, more baseball players out there called Ducky Holmes. But frankly, I would prefer not to hear about them. Case closed. ∎

## Notes

1. Joan Wendl Thomas, *Baseball In Northwest Iowa* (Charleston, South Carolina: Arcadia Publishing, 2017).
2. "Noted Baseball Player Makes Final Home Run," *Rolfe Arrow*, August 18, 1932.
3. Some news items, including obituaries, erroneously report the year as 1900. Others vary between 1890 and 1892.
4. Bill Lamb, "July 25, 1898: The Ducky Holmes Game," in *Inventing Baseball: The 100 Greatest Games of the 19th Century*, ed. Bill Felber (Phoenix: SABR, 2013).
5. "Ducky Holmes Put Out John McGraw," *St. Louis Republic*, July 22, 1907.
6. "Sporting Events," *Lincoln Evening News*, June 26, 1911.
7. "'Ducky' Holmes Out at Toledo," *Waterloo Evening Courier*, June 6, 1910.
8. "'Ducky' Holmes Holding New Job," *Waterloo Evening Courier*, June 11, 1910.
9. "Ducky Holmes Suspended," *Le Mars Semi-Weekly Sentinel*, April 28, 1911.
10. "Release Baseball Manager," *Galveston Daily News*, June 26, 1911.
11. "Ducky Holmes Suspended," *San Antonio Express*, July 14, 1911.
12. "Sporting Events," *Lincoln Evening News*, June 26, 1911.
13. "Holmes Will Test His Case," *Daily Herald* (Biloxi, MS), December 30, 1911.
14. Dean Wheeler, "Ducky Says He Is Done—Veteran Holmes Will Retire to His Ranch in Montana," unidentified news clipping from 1913.
15. "Ducky Going Over," *Fort Wayne News and Sentinel*, October 5, 1918.
16. "Holmes Fails to Buy Club," *Des Moines News*, January 27, 1919.
17. "Two Burned In Fire at Ball Park," *Lincoln Daily State Journal*, January 24, 1918.
18. "Brownville for Sunday Games," *Lincoln Daily Star*, April 9, 1920.
19. "Says the Moline Dispatch," *Rockford Illinois Daily Register*, July 16, 1921.
20. *Moline Dispatch*, July 13, 1921.
21. "Nebraska Minor League Baseball, Nebraska State League, Beatrice Blues," *Nebraska Minor League Baseball History*, http://www.nebaseballhistory.com/beatrice1922.html.
22. Letter on Federal Surety Company letterhead addressed to W. P. Coad, Manager, Le Mars Baseball Club, contributed by Bill Coad, grandson of W. P. "Billy" Coad.
23. "Ducky Holmes Dickers for Lincoln Franchise," unknown newspaper, October 21, 1926.
24. "New Club at Stock Yards," *Le Mars Sentinel*, July 19, 1927.
25. "Mrs. E. E. Theno, Former Lincoln Teacher, Is Dead," *Lincoln Daily Star*, October 31, 1929.
26. "Sporting Review," *Lincoln Star*, July 21, 1911.
27. "Ducky Holmes Dickers for Lincoln Franchise."
28. Howard Spencer, "The Sportacle," *Sunday Times Signal* (Zanesville, OH), September 23, 1945.
29. "Ducky Holmes Dies," *Zanesville Signal*, September 20, 1945.
30. "A. A. Is Post Graduate School for Central Leaguers," *Indianapolis Sun Sports*, April 27, 1908.
31. "Changes in Two Clubs," *Atlanta Georgian*, June 25, 1908.
32. *Atlanta Georgian and News*, July 31, 1908.
33. "Three-Eye Ump Lands Place," (Davenport) *Daily Times*, July 12, 1917.
34. "American Legion News," *Pella Chronicle*, August 18, 1921.
35. "Newest Umpire in Major Show Is Experienced," *Arizona Republican*, March 3, 1923.
36. "Umpire Hit in St. Louis," *The New York Times*, June 26, 1924.
37. "Hits Umpire, Is Fined $25," *The New York Times*, July 29, 1924.
38. "Why His Career as Umpire Ended," *Sunday Times Signal*, September 23, 1945.
39. "Pilots Although Absent," *Burlington Daily Hawkeye Gazette*, June 15, 1935.
40. Ira L. Smith, "Birds, bees, beasts and baseball," *Baseball Research Journal* 1, 1972, https://sabr.org/research/birds-bees-beasts-and-baseball.
41. "Holmes in Grime's Post," *The New York Times*, August 7, 1940.
42. "Ducky Holmes, Former Dayton Baseball Team Manager, Dies," *Zanesville Signal*, September 19, 1945.
43. Howard Spencer, "Ohio State League Meeting Scheduled for Tuesday," *Sunday Times-Signal*, December 3, 1944.
44. 1912 Imperial Tobacco c46 No. 60, Ducky Holmes, Rochester.
45. "Newark Players for Federal League," *The New York Times*, January 31, 1914.
46. "James Scott Holmes," *The Sporting News*, March 23, 1960.
47. Harry Grayson, "Rucker Hurt Arm Pitching Out of Town," *Brownsville Herald*, July 21, 1943.
48. Red Smith, "Views of Sport," *The News* (Sarasota, Florida), April 10, 1959.
49. "Eastern League," *The New York Times*, July 7, 1911.
50. 1912 Imperial Tobacco No. 79, Holmes, Newark.
51. "In Case You Are Interested Department," *Amarillo Globe*, July 20, 1938.
52. "'Hump' Veteran Back in States," *Amarillo Globe*, June 1, 1945.
53. "Aggies Making Strong Battle for Gonfalon," *Bryan Daily Eagle*, May 2, 1927.
54. "The 'Canal Line' Crew," I Know a Railroad, October 7, 2006, http://iknowarailroad.net/photoalbum/page262.htm.
55. "Barage of Hits Wins for Joplin," *Joplin News Herald*, September 3, 1927.
56. Gilbert Twiss, "Twisters," *Decatur Review*, June 5, 1929.
57. "Plow Boys Go to Keokuk," *Moline Dispatch*, June 24, 1929.
58. "Moline Takes 2–1 Victory in Hurling Duel," *Burlington Gazette*, June 13, 1930.
59. "Parker Has Strong Squad of Veterans at Moline This Season," *Cedar Rapids Evening Gazette and Republican*, April 9, 1931.
60. "Dyersville Spills Manchester to Gain on Valley Leaders," *Telegraph Herald and Times-Journal* (Dubuque, IA), August 17, 1934.
61. William Brohaugh, *English Through the Ages* (Cincinnati: Writers Digest Books, 1997).

# An Ever-Changing Story

*Exposition and Analysis of Shoeless Joe Jackson's*
*Public Statements on the Black Sox Scandal*

### Bill Lamb

When it came to his involvement in the corruption of the 1919 World Series, Shoeless Joe Jackson rarely told the same story twice. When the fix first came to light in late September 1920, Jackson, along with teammates Eddie Cicotte and Lefty Williams, abjectly admitted that he had agreed to join the conspiracy to throw the series in return for a gamblers' payoff. And that he had accepted $5,000 of a promised $20,000 bribe before the start of Game Five. But once in the hands of experienced legal counsel, Jackson's story changed. From then on, Jackson was the injured innocent, unaware that teammates had tried to rig the series outcome until after the fact, and entirely blameless in the affair. Even here, however, Jackson had trouble keeping the details of his story straight. His appearance on the witness stand in support of a civil lawsuit that he filed against the White Sox ended in disaster. Jackson was cited for contempt by the trial judge and subsequently charged with perjury by the Milwaukee County District Attorney. That charge ultimately went unprosecuted, and Jackson was still protesting his innocence at the time of his death in December 1951.

The text below examines the evolution of Joe Jackson's public statements on the Black Sox scandal. A forensic examination of those statements follows. We precede that exposition with a brief, Jackson-centric recap of the 1919 World Series and its aftermath.

### THE 1919 WORLD SERIES AND EARLY INQUIRIES ABOUT CROOKED PLAY

The talent-laden Chicago White Sox were the Series betting favorites until a late surge of Cincinnati money gave the Reds a slight edge. Still, the Sox remained the choice of most sportswriters and other baseball insiders. But Chicago got off poorly in Game One when a sudden fourth-inning meltdown by pitching ace Cicotte triggered a lopsided 9–1 defeat. Then, a curious one-inning control lapse by 23-game winner Williams proved the difference in a 4–2 Game Two loss. A three-hit, 3–0 shutout thrown by undersized Dickey Kerr temporarily righted the Sox in Game Three, but

Chicago bats thereupon went silent. The American League's best hitting team went an astonishing 26 consecutive innings without scoring.[1] Shutout defeats in Games Four and Five left the vaunted Sox on the brink of elimination just midway through the extended best-five-of-nine series.

Although hardly without accomplices in underachievement, a fair amount of the blame for the Sox predicament rested with clean-up hitter Joe Jackson. Through the first five games, Shoeless Joe had batted a soft .316 (6-for-19), with two runs scored and zero RBIs. Down 4–0 after four innings in Game Six, Chicago bats suddenly revived. A Jackson single in the sixth plated the first run, and the Sox went on to post a 10-inning, 5–4 victory. Thereafter, Eddie Cicotte put the Sox back in contention with a route-going 4–1 triumph which featured two more RBIs by Jackson. In Game Eight, however, a nightmarish outing by Lefty Williams—he did not survive the first inning—quickly put the Sox in a deep hole. With Chicago trailing, 5–0, Jackson hit a solo home run in the bottom of the third. But Cincinnati kept up the attack against Sox relievers, and held a seemingly insurmountable eighth-inning 10–1 lead when a last-ditch Chicago rally cut the margin to 10–5. Two of those Sox runs were tallied by a Jackson double that upped his series RBI total to six. In their final at-bat, Chicago attempted another rally. But with two on and two out, a Jackson grounder to second brought the 1919 World Series to a close.

A day after the Series ended, a widely-syndicated column by Chicago sportswriter Hugh Fullerton insinuated, without explicitly saying, that the Series had not been played on the up-and-up. But otherwise, the Cincinnati triumph, while unexpected by most, was well-received. Those seeking culprits for the Sox downfall did not focus on Joe Jackson. Superficially at least, his series stats (.375 batting average, with a club-high six RBIs and the championship's only homer) were considered outstanding. Blame for the Sox defeat was more readily pinned on Lefty Williams (0–3, with a 6.61 ERA), shortstop Swede Risberg (.080 BA in 25 at-bats, with four errors in the field), right fielder

Nemo Leibold (.056 BA in 18 at-bats), and manager Kid Gleason.

Unbeknownst to the public, the Series outcome was not accepted at face value by two of the game's most powerful actors: Chicago White Sox club owner Charles Comiskey and American League president Ban Johnson. Shortly after the Series conclusion, each began his own discreet inquiry into the Series bona fides. And neither much liked what such probes uncovered. Information furnished to Comiskey investigators by St. Louis sources lent substance to the report—first received by Comiskey just after the Series began—that Sox players had agreed to dump the Series in return for a payoff from gamblers. In late December, these fix assertions were repeated by in-the-know gamblers Harry Redmon and Joe Pesch during a face-to-face meeting with White Sox brass. Notwithstanding that, Comiskey subsequently extended handsome new contract offers to players implicated in the fix by his informants: Joe Jackson, Swede Risberg, Lefty Williams, and outfielder Happy Felsch.[2] Ban Johnson, meanwhile, had uncovered independent evidence that Sox players had been corrupted, purportedly bribed by a St. Louis businessman-gambler named Carl Zork. For the time being, however, Johnson chose not to make such revelations public.

While scandal simmered quietly out of public view, American League rooters focused on a tight three-way 1920 pennant chase involving the White Sox, New York Yankees, and Cleveland Indians. But early that September, fan attention was mildly diverted by the announcement that a Cook County (Chicago) grand jury had been impaneled to probe allegations that a recent Cubs-Phillies game had been fixed. The grand jurors would also investigate the locally popular but illegal practice of baseball game pool selling. Soon thereafter, prominent Chicago citizen Fred Loomis and sports reporters like Joe Vila of the *New York Sun* were publicly calling for the grand jury probe to be expanded to include inquiry into the integrity of the 1919 World Series.[3] Behind the scenes, AL president Johnson was urging the same course upon a longtime acquaintance, Judge Charles A. McDonald, the presiding judge of the Chicago criminal courts and the overseer of the grand jury. Judge McDonald was agreeable, and within weeks the 1919 World Series became the dominant subject of the grand jury's work.

## EXPOSURE AND ADMISSION

In an extraordinary breach of normal secrecy requirements, the grand jury proceedings were publicly revealed on a daily basis, with many newspapers printing near-verbatim accounts of witness testimony. Thus by September 25, it was widely reported that eight White Sox players, including Eddie Cicotte, Joe Jackson, and Lefty Williams, had been targeted for indictment by the grand jury on conspiracy and fraud-related charges grounded in their play in the 1919 World Series.[4] Two days later, the burgeoning scandal exploded. In an interview first published in Philadelphia and then circulated nationwide, self-admitted fix insider Billy Maharg alleged that Game One, Game Two, and Game Eight of the Series had been dumped by the Sox at gamblers' behest.[5]

The following morning, Eddie Cicotte was summoned to the law office of Alfred S. Austrian, counsel for the Chicago White Sox corporation. Under interrogation, a stressed-out Cicotte quickly broke down, revealing those aspects of the World Series fix that he was privy to. He also identified the other fix participants, including Joe Jackson.[6] Cicotte was then whisked before the grand jury where he elaborated on his admissions about the Series conspiracy under questioning by Assistant State's Attorney Hartley Replogle.[7]

The first public statement attributed to Joe Jackson about the fix allegations disclaimed any personal knowledge of the matter. "I am willing to go before anyone at any time, any place to testify to what I know. I know little except rumors," said Joe early that morning. "I know I have never been approached with any gambling propositions. If anyone ever does approach me, I'll knock their block off."[8]

Jackson soon got his wish to testify. After being confronted privately with Cicotte's admissions in the Austrian law office, Jackson telephoned the chambers of Judge McDonald. At first, Jackson maintained his innocence to an openly skeptical McDonald. During a second call placed shortly thereafter, Jackson asked the judge for the chance to appear before the grand jury and make a clean breast of his involvement in the World Series fix.

Neither the content of Jackson's telephone conversations with Judge McDonald nor the particulars of their subsequent conversation in chambers was contemporaneously memorialized. But testifying four years later during Jackson's civil suit against the White Sox, McDonald stated that Jackson related various fix details to him, and identified his co-conspirators as Eddie Cicotte, Chick Gandil, Swede Risberg, Lefty Williams, Happy Felsch, Buck Weaver, and Fred McMullin.[9] In particular, McDonald "distinctly" recalled that Jackson told him that during the Series "he had made no misplays that could be noticed by the ordinary person, but that he did not play his best."[10]

*Assistant State's Attorney Hartley Replogle and Joe Jackson at the Cook County Courthouse on September 28, 1920.*

On the afternoon of September 28, 1920, Jackson testified under oath before the grand jury. At the core of the Jackson testimony rests a contradiction. On the incriminating side of the ledger, Jackson provided a fairly detailed account of the fix from his perspective, including his acceptance of $5,000 before the start of Game Five. Notwithstanding that, Jackson insisted that he had done nothing in the field to earn his payoff, citing his World Series stats as proof that he had given his best efforts at all times during the action.

Jackson's testimony about the corruption of the Series was precise and specific. He had not attended the mid-September players-only fix meeting at the Ansonia Hotel in New York. Nor had he been present for a follow-up meeting with gamblers in Chicago's Warner Hotel, although Lefty Williams had told him about it afterwards.[11] Rather, Jackson had been propositioned privately by teammate Chick Gandil. At first, Jackson rebuffed him. But in time, Joe agreed to join the plot to throw the Series in return for a $20,000 payoff, to be "split up some way" after each Series game.[12,13] When he went unpaid after the Sox lost Game One, Jackson asked Gandil, "What's the trouble?" but Gandil assured him that "everything is all right," as Gandil had the money. Then, Jackson testified, "We went ahead and threw the second game," only to be unpaid again. Jackson now asked Gandil, "What are you going to do?" and Gandil replied, "Everything is all right" once more.[14] When no money was forthcoming after Game Three, Jackson told Gandil that "somebody is getting a nice little jazz, everything is crossed." But Gandil responded that the fault lay with fix backers Abe Attell and Bill Burns. The two gamblers had crossed him.[15]

On the evening before the White Sox were to return to Cincinnati for Game Five, Lefty Williams entered Jackson's room at the Lexington Hotel and threw $5,000 onto the bed. At that, Jackson asked, "What the hell had come off here?" Williams replied that Gandil "said we got the screw through Abe Attell. He got the money but refused to turn it over to [Gandil]." But Jackson suspected that Gandil actually had the payoff money and had "kept the majority of it for himself."[16] When Jackson later complained to Gandil, Chick told [17] him that he could either "take that [$5,000] or leave it alone." That evening, when Jackson told his wife that he "got $5,000 for helping throw [Series] games," Katie Jackson told Joe that "she thought it was an awful thing to do."[18] Jackson put the $5,000—"some hundreds, mostly fifties" in denomination—in his pocket and took the money with him to Cincinnati.[19]

Regarding the other conspirators, Jackson testified that Cicotte had told him that he had received $10,000 up front, and scolded Joe as "a God damn fool" for not getting paid the same way."[20] Risberg and Williams told Jackson that they received $5,000 each, but Jackson did not believe them. He suspected that Gandil, Risberg, McMullin, Cicotte, and Williams had cut up the Series bribe money "to suit themselves."[21] Jackson understood from "the boys" that Happy Felsch had also received $5,000, but had no knowledge of any payoff money paid to Buck Weaver.[22] All Jackson knew about Buck was that Gandil had told him that Weaver "was in on the deal."[23]

Despite having agreed to the fix and then accepting a payoff, Jackson nevertheless insisted that he had done nothing on the field to earn the money. Throughout the series, he "had batted to win, fielded to win, and run the bases to win."[24] Joe admitted that while he saw some questionable plays by teammates, particularly Cicotte and Williams, Jackson himself had not done anything to throw Series games. He had "tried to win all the time."[25] After the Series was over, Jackson did not discuss the fix with his co-conspirators, and left Chicago for his home in Savannah the following evening.[26] But Jackson was ashamed of himself for accepting the $5,000, and had offered to reveal everything that he knew about the fix to White Sox management later that fall. But club brass had not brought him in.[27] Jackson was also suspicious of late-1920 season performances by Cicotte and Williams, but declared himself anxious to win the pennant and then capture the World Series.[28] This led to a poignant exchange near the end of the Jackson testimony. ASA Replogle: "You didn't want to do that last year, did you?" Jackson: "Well, down in my heart I did. Yes."[29]

Shortly thereafter, the grand jury proceedings recessed for the day.

Upon leaving the courthouse, Jackson was besieged by waiting reporters. Back in his hotel room later that evening, Jackson expounded upon various fix details. For example, following telephone calls that he had placed to an unsympathetic Judge McDonald, Jackson had gone to the jurist's chambers. Once there, "I said I got $5,000 and they promised me $20,000. All I got was the $5,000 that Lefty Williams handed me in a dirty envelope. I never got the other $15,000. I told that to Judge McDonald. He said he didn't care what I got.…I don't think the judge likes me. I never got the $15,000 that was coming to me," said Joe.[30] Jackson further explained that his grand jury revelations were prompted by the attitude of Gandil, Risberg, and McMullin. When he had threatened to expose the Series fix unless paid in full, Jackson was brushed off. "They said to me, 'You poor simp, go ahead and squawk.…Every honest ballplayer in the world will say you're a liar. You're out of luck. Some of the boys were promised a lot more than you and got less.' That's why I went down and told Judge McDonald and told the grand jury what I know about the frame up," Jackson told the press.[31]

Jackson concluded his extemporaneous monologue with this revelation: "And I'm going to give you a tip. A lot of these sporting writers that have been roasting me have been talking about the third game of the World's Series being square. Let me tell you something. The eight of us did our best to kick it and little Dick Kerr won the game by his pitching. Because he won it, those gamblers double crossed us because we double crossed them."[32]

The following day, Lefty Williams confessed his involvement in the Series fix, first in the Austrian law office, thereafter before the grand jury. In the process, Williams named Jackson as one of the eight Sox players who had been in on the deal.[33] Williams also identified several of the gamblers who had agreed to finance the fix. The next day, the *Chicago Evening American* published a confession of fix participation given by Sox center fielder Happy Felsch to reporter Harry Reutlinger. Felsch now regretted his acceptance of a $5,000 bribe, but offered no excuses for his involvement. "I'm as guilty as the rest of them. We are all in it alike," said an unhappy Happy. "Cicotte's story is true in every detail," Felsch continued. "I don't blame him for telling.…I was ready to confess myself yesterday, but didn't have the courage to be the first to tell."[34]

Meanwhile, the other White Sox players who had been cited as grand jury targets publicly protested their innocence, with Buck Weaver in particular vowing to retain the best lawyer available to fight any criminal charges that might be brought against him.[35] Buck would not have to wait long for such charges. On October 29, 1920, the Cook County Grand Jury returned formal indictments which accused eight White Sox players and five gamblers of multiple counts of conspiracy to obtain money by false pretenses and/or a confidence game.[36]

## A NEW-FOUND CLAIM OF INNOCENCE

It appears that Cook County prosecutors presumed that those White Sox players who had confessed their fix involvement to the grand jury would turn State's evidence and testify against the other accused. But pretrial negotiations with Daniel Cassidy, the Detroit lawyer (and personal friend) who represented Eddie Cicotte, foundered, while Joe Jackson and Lefty Williams were reportedly seeking legal counsel to fight the charges. Out in California meanwhile, Fred McMullin asserted that Happy Felsch had told him that his newspaper confession was a "phony."[37] Days later, Joe Jackson signaled a coming change in his story, publicly declaring, "I never confessed to throwing a ball game and I never will."[38] This evidently proved too much for Judge McDonald, who promptly informed the press that "Jackson's testimony was made under oath to the grand jury. If he denies that testimony when he is brought to trial, he will be guilty of perjury and prosecuted under that charge."[39]

In early November, developments in the baseball scandal were briefly overshadowed by an event of far greater national significance: the political elections of 1920. But election results would also have profound effects upon the course of the Black Sox case. Swept into office on the nationwide Republican Party tide was a new Cook County State's Attorney, recently retired Chicago judge Robert E. Crowe. And joining Crowe in office would be an entirely new cadre of staff attorneys, none of whom was familiar with the Black Sox case. As a team of prosecutors headed by newly-installed Second ASA George E. Gorman scrambled to catch up, the Black Sox defense made its first tactical move—a court application which included sworn repudiation of their grand jury admissions by Joe Jackson and Lefty Williams.

Drafted by criminal counsel Thomas D. Nash (defendants Weaver, Felsch, Risberg, and McMullin) and Benedict J. Short (Jackson and Williams), a defense motion for a bill of particulars was supported by affidavits signed by Buck Weaver, Jackson, and Williams.[40] The bill of particulars averred that (1) while acquainted with gambler codefendants Bill Burns and Hal Chase, they had "no business transactions or personal relations" with the two ex-major leaguers; (2) that they had never met the other gambler codefendants (although Williams had once been introduced to strangers named Sullivan and Brown)[41]; and (3) that they were "entirely innocent" of the charges made against them."[42] When it came time for trial in July 1921, however, neither Weaver, Jackson, nor Williams testified before the jury.[43] Nor did any of the other accused players.[44] But out of the jury's presence, Eddie Cicotte, Jackson, and Williams did take the stand midtrial in support of a defense motion to preclude prosecution use of their grand jury testimony. Significant for our purposes, the Black Sox defense did not challenge the bona fides of the grand jury transcripts, nor claim that any of their content was inaccurate or unreliable. Indeed, the authenticity and correctness of the transcripts was conceded. Rather, the defense sought suppression on the grounds that the Cicotte, Jackson, and Williams grand jury testimony had been induced by broken off-the-record promises of nonprosecution made by authorities, and were thus inadmissible in evidence.[45] At the hearing's close, trial judge Hugo M. Friend found the denials that any such promises had been made elicited from former ASA Replogle and Judge McDonald persuasive, and ruled the Cicotte/Jackson/Williams transcripts available for prosecution use. In redacted form, the grand jury admissions of the trio were subsequently read to the criminal trial jury at length via colloquy between Special Prosecutor Edward A. Prindiville and grand jury stenographers Walter Smith and Elbert Allen—all to no avail as it turned out.[46]

Silence proved a sound defense strategy, as the jury acquitted the accused of all charges after deliberations taking less than three hours.[47] Public reaction to the trial's outcome for those acquitted was subdued, but the Black Sox case was far from over. Within hours of the verdict, Commissioner Kenesaw Mountain Landis permanently banished the accused players from Organized Baseball, their acquittal in court notwithstanding. Thereafter, a number of the former defendants, including Joe Jackson, instituted civil lawsuits against the Chicago White Sox.[48]

The particulars of a new Jackson account of the World Series fix emerged during the deposition phase of his lawsuit. And the story now told by Jackson was dramatically different from the sworn testimony that he had provided the grand jury in late September 1920. Appearing before court commissioner Girard M. Cohen on April 23, 1923, Jackson swore that "I knew absolutely nothing about the throwing of the World Series until two or three days after it was over."[49] Jackson further averred that "I played my best during the Series, threw everything that I had into the effort to bring victory to my team. I think the facts and figures [of my performance] will bear me out."[50]

Regarding his acceptance of fix-connected cash, Jackson revised the timing of that event. He now asserted that "two or three days after the Series was over, Lefty Williams…came to my room with two envelopes in his hand. Williams was in an intoxicated condition. He told me that each envelope contained $5,000 in cash. He threw one of the envelopes at my feet and told me that certain players had used my name in negotiating with the gamblers and that the players had informed the gamblers that I was to help throw the games against my own team."[51] Jackson maintained that he was "dumbfounded" by Williams's revelations and immediately informed him that "they had a lot of nerve to use my name under the circumstances."[52] Lefty then departed the room. "The very next day," Jackson continued, "I went to Charles Comiskey's office with the envelope to interview the club president concerning the transaction with Williams," but was denied admittance by White Sox team secretary Harry Grabiner, who told Jackson "to beat it." When he came to Savannah the following February to sign Jackson to a new contract, Grabiner already knew about the $5,000 given Jackson by Williams, and told him that White Sox brass had "the absolute goods on Cicotte, Williams and Gandil concerning their dishonest and crooked play during the 1919 Series."[53] Jackson then signed the new three-year contact proffered by Grabiner, the terms of which would subsequently become the gravamen of the civil lawsuit filed by Jackson against the club.

## MILWAUKEE PERJURY CITATIONS

Of the Black Sox-related civil lawsuits filed in Milwaukee, the only one that ever went to trial was that of Joe Jackson. The specifics of that litigation are not germane to this article. Suffice it to say that Jackson sought recovery of the unpaid portion of the three-season deal that he had signed with the White Sox in February 1920.[54] At first blush, the setting seemed a congenial one for the plaintiff. His attorney, local firebrand Raymond J. Cannon, was an aggressive and wildly successful civil litigator, having reportedly won over 100 cases in a row.[55] The Jackson case, moreover, would be tried before Wisconsin Circuit Court Judge John J. Gregory, a competent and amiable veteran jurist, progressive in his social views (except in divorce matters) and widely perceived as plaintiff-friendly. Gregory was also an avid baseball fan. But before the trial was out, the proceedings would turn into a nightmare for Joe Jackson.

Things began well for the plaintiff, with Jackson's direct examination by attorney Cannon drawing favorable press reviews.[56] The tide abruptly turned, however, when Jackson underwent cross-examination by George B. Hudnall, lead attorney for the White Sox defense. Hudnall was armed with the transcript of Jackson's September 28, 1920, grand jury testimony.[57] He pressed the plaintiff on the inconsistencies between his current account of scandal events and what he had previously told the Cook County grand jury. Remarkably, Jackson did not attempt to harmonize the two or explain away their differences. Instead, he asserted that he had never said the words reposed in black and white on the grand jury transcript pages.

As Cannon sat by helplessly, Hudnall then led Jackson on a painstaking tour of the testimony that Jackson now maintained he had never given. Page space limitations preclude a thorough rendering of the Hudnall-Jackson colloquies, but the following are representative: When referred to his grand jury testimony that the World Series fixers had "promised me $20,000 and paid me $5,000 (at JGJ4-9 to 10)," Jackson told Hudnall, "I didn't make that answer."[58] When asked about what Chick Gandil had said to him about the fix payment shortchange (at JGJ6-10 to 13), Jackson's response was the same. He denied giving the testimony attributed to him in the grand jury transcript.[59] Thereafter, Hudnall: "Were you asked and did you give this answer? Question: What did you say to Williams when he threw down the $5,000? Answer: I asked him what the hell had come off here (quoting JGJ6-25 to JGJ7-5)." Jackson: "No, sir. I don't know anything about that." Hudnall: "And you did not so testify before the grand jury?" Jackson: "No, sir. I didn't."[60] Similarly, when referred to his grand jury testimony about the "jazz" given the players by fixer Abe Attell, Jackson denied the authenticity of the response reported at JGJ9-10 to 13. Hudnall: "You didn't make any such answer before the grand jury?' Jackson: "No, sir."[61]

Elsewhere, Jackson again denied that he had given the answers contained in the grand jury transcript about his acceptance of the money delivered by Williams before Game Five. Insisted Jackson, "I didn't make the answer like you are reading from there. No, sir."[62] Regarding his grand jury testimony about the $10,000 bribe paid Eddie Cicotte, Jackson replied, "I say that I did not make the answer that you read

*Joe Jackson stunned the courtroom in 1924 by claiming that he had never made any of the statements attributed to him in the records of the 1920 grand jury.*

there."[63] Nor had Jackson testified about fix payments to Swede Risberg and Fred McMullin during his grand jury appearance. Hudnall, incredulously: "Those questions were not asked and you did not make those answers?" Jackson: "No, sir."[64] Also repudiated by Jackson were transcript excerpts pertaining to pre-Series conversations with Gandil, fix payments to Happy Felsch, Katie Jackson's reaction to Joe's involvement in the fix, and, by this writer's count, 119 other particulars of Jackson's sworn grand jury testimony.[65,66,67]

Throughout the Jackson cross-examination, Judge Gregory sat impassively. But inside, the normally genial jurist was seething. Several days later, Gregory made his displeasure with Jackson known. As soon as the jury had retired to deliberate its verdict, the plaintiff was unexpectedly summoned to the well of the court. There, Gregory informed Jackson that "you stand here self-convicted of the crime of perjury. You came to the wrong state, to the wrong city, to the wrong court." Gregory then ordered bailiffs to take Jackson into custody, setting his bail at $5,000.[68] Jackson was released shortly thereafter and back in court the following morning, but Judge Gregory was still rankled by the irreconcilability of the sworn testimony that Jackson had provided the grand jury and his testimony under oath at the civil trial, reiterating his view that Jackson "stands self-convicted and self-accused of perjury. Either his testimony here or his testimony before the Chicago grand jury was false. I think the false testimony was given here."[69]

The jury's verdict did little to improve Gregory's mood. It returned a $16,711.04 judgment in Jackson's favor. Astonished and indignant, Gregory lit into the jurors for ruling in favor of a "perjurer" and promptly vacated their verdict, specifying fraud and perjured testimony as the basis for the court's action.[70] When later explained to the press by foreman John E. Sanderson, however, the jury's verdict had a defensible rationale. According to Sanderson, the panel had disregarded Jackson's claims of innocence, but had awarded him his unpaid salary for the 1921 and 1922 seasons (plus the final days of the 1920 campaign) on the principle of condonation. As the jury viewed the proofs, the post-Series investigation of Comiskey's detectives had left the Chisox boss aware of Jackson's Series perfidy well before he tendered Jackson a new three-season contract in February 1920. By so doing, Comiskey had condoned (or forgiven) Jackson's World Series misconduct. That being so, Comiskey could not avoid making good on that contract simply because the public had discovered what White Sox brass had known about Jackson all along.[71]

Although perjury during civil litigation rarely receives law enforcement attention, Milwaukee County District Attorney George A. Shaughnessy announced his office's intention of investigating the Jackson testimony. "We will go over it carefully to see if there is anything that seems to warrant prosecution for perjury. If we find anything, we will make complaint, a warrant will be issued, and Jackson re-arrested," he said.[72,73] By April, the district attorney was satisfied that Jackson, and Happy Felsch, as well, had testified falsely and obtained warrants for their arrest.[74] On May 18, 1925, Jackson failed to appear for pretrial proceedings on a perjury complaint and a bench warrant was issued for his arrest by Judge George F. Page.[75] But as long as Jackson stayed out of Wisconsin, there was little chance of his being apprehended. As far as can be discovered, proceedings on the perjury complaint outstanding against Jackson went no further.[76]

## RENEWED CLAIMS OF INNOCENCE

Happily for Jackson, few outside Milwaukee paid heed to his civil lawsuit. By then, the world had moved on, with baseball, fueled by the unprecedented exploits of pitcher-turned-everyday-slugger Babe Ruth, embarked upon a golden age. To most fans, the Black Sox scandal and the likes of Shoeless Joe Jackson were ancient history.

Contrary to popular belief, the Black Sox did not remain silent after their banishment from the game.[77]

Jackson was among the most talkative, resolute in his claims of innocence but either erratic or inventive in his recall of scandal details. In 1941, Jackson told *Washington Post* sportswriter Shirley Povich that "I'm as innocent as you are. I had no part in that fix in 1919."[78] He then cited his World Series stats as proof of clean Series play. Jackson also complained about the "shoddy tricks" used by prosecutors against him, maintaining that the claim that he had confessed guilt was bogus. "There was no confession by me. That was trumped up by the court lawyers. They couldn't produce it in court. They said it was stolen from the vaults. Does that sound right?"[79] Povich was far too young to have covered the Black Sox trial in 1921, and reported Jackson's assertions without reservation. Presumably, Povich was unfamiliar with the fact that only the original transcriptions of the Cicotte/Jackson/Williams grand jury testimony had been stolen. The theft was discovered well before trial, with the transcripts thereafter recreated by means of the grand jury stenographers' handwritten notes. At trial, the Jackson grand jury confession was read at length to the jury.

Jackson reiterated his claims of innocence the following year to sportswriter Carter (Scoops) Latimer, an old friend.[80] "I'm innocent of any wrongdoing," Joe asserted, adding that "the Supreme Being is the only one to whom I've got to answer."[81] As before, Jackson cited his Series statistics as proof of his innocence. He also debunked the notorious post-grand jury appearance "Say It Ain't So, Joe" anecdote as a fabrication concocted by a "sob sister" sportswriter.[82] Left unmentioned were the incriminating details about the Series fix that Jackson made to the press that same afternoon.[83]

The best-known of the Jackson apologias was published in the October 1949 issue of *Sport* magazine.[84] Presented as a first-person Shoeless Joe narrative (as told to sportswriter Furman Bisher), the piece was treated as the last word on the Black Sox scandal—as Jackson would die only two years later—by Bisher and other Jackson sympathizers too young to have any personal memory of the affair. But Jackson's reminiscences were marred by faulty recollection, confabulation of events, and the occasional outright falsehood. Indeed, the very first sentence of the piece—"When I walked out of Judge Dever's courtroom in Chicago in 1921…I had been acquitted by a twelve-man jury in a civil courtroom of all charges and I was an innocent man in the records"[85]—was historically inaccurate. The jurist who presided over the trial was Judge Friend, not Dever, and Jackson and the others were found not guilty (different from innocent) by a criminal court jury, not a civil court one.[86]

The story then proceeds to the stunning allegation that Jackson was so troubled by World Series fix rumors swirling about that he went to club owner Comiskey's hotel room in Cincinnati the night before Game One and pleaded to be removed from the line-up, lest his reputation be besmirched by playing in a rigged championship match.[87] And this, Jackson said, was all witnessed by syndicated sports columnist Hugh Fullerton "who offered to testify for me at my trial later." In fact, neither Fullerton nor any other witness was summoned to the stand by the Jackson defense.[88] Three years later, however, Fullerton did testify as a White Sox defense witness in the Jackson civil suit. More important, Fullerton's testimony contains no mention of Jackson trying to beg off playing in the 1919 Series. Nor does the alleged event appear anywhere in Fullerton's writings on the scandal, inexplicable given that star player Jackson begging Comiskey to keep him out of the World Series would have been a sensational story that any sportswriter would have rushed into newsprint—had it ever happened.

The article takes another shot at the "Say It Ain't So, Joe" anecdote, this time describing it as a fabrication invented by *Chicago Daily News* reporter Charley Owens. According to Jackson, the only person that he spoke to outside the courthouse after his grand jury appearance was a deputy sheriff whom Jackson gave a car lift home.[89] But if this was true, where did the *Chicago Daily Journal*, *Chicago Tribune* and other news outlets get the specific fix details (Jackson's complaint about being shortchanged on his bribe payout; his resentment of the brush-off given him by Gandil, Risberg, and McMullin; the thwarted Black Sox attempt to throw Game Three, etc.) attributed to Jackson? Like other followers of the fast-breaking scandal, the gathered pressmen were then unaware of such fix minutiae. Jackson's revision of scandal events also made the far-fetched claim that prosecutors "kept delaying the trial until I personally went to the State Supreme Court judge, after which he ordered the case to be tried."[90] As the record documents, the issue was actually joined by a prosecution motion for a continuance of the proceedings presented to Circuit Court Judge William E. Dever who denied the application. Jackson, represented by able and experienced criminal defense lawyer Benedict Short, was no more than a silent bystander in the matter.[91]

Jackson even got small things wrong—his final White Sox contract, for example. It was a three-season deal, not five.[92] He also got the story about the reputed origin of Comiskey's feud with Ban Johnson backward. It was Johnson who had sent the smelly fish to Comiskey, not vice versa.[93] There were others, as well. But misstatements large and errors small made no difference to Jackson admirers. And Shoeless Joe was still protesting his innocence when felled by the last of a series of heart attacks in December 1951.

## FORENSIC ANALYSIS

Joe Jackson was a great ball player and, by all accounts, a nice man. But when it came to the Black Sox scandal, Jackson inarguably perjured himself. The only issue, as observed by Judge Gregory in 1924, is whether Jackson lied under oath to the Cook County grand jury when he admitted entering the conspiracy to fix the outcome of the 1919 World Series, or whether it was Jackson's duly sworn assertions of innocence in the matter thereafter that were false. The paragraphs below are devoted to forensic analysis of the question. Ultimately, the credible evidence—and reason, too—admits but one conclusion: Joe Jackson, while hardly an instigator or a proponent of the fix, was a knowing participant in the plot to rig the 1919 World Series; his protests of innocence, although prolonged, ring hollow.

Our analytical starting point is the grand jury testimony given under oath by Joe Jackson on the afternoon of September 28, 1920. As previously noted, Jackson's account of the World Series fix was specific regarding events that he was involved in, full of peculiar detail, and highly incriminating, his claim of actually trying his best on the field notwithstanding.[94] Jackson biographer Donald Gropman and other Jackson defenders confronting the issue usually try to explain away Shoeless Joe's grand jury testimony by describing it as no more than regurgitation of information supplied to him by his interrogators.[95] And regrettably, false confessions are a phenomenon that the criminal justice system has to deal with on a far-too-frequent basis. The Jackson grand jury testimony, however, betrays none of the indicia of a false confession. Here is why.

The essential component of the false confession is knowledge of the details of the underlying offense by those questioning a suspect—for if the questioner does not know what happened, how can he implant such information in the mind of someone else? When Joe Jackson was first confronted about his fix involvement in the Austrian law office, his inquisitors had only limited information about the matter. Club boss Comiskey, present but silent during the questioning, had presumably imparted the intelligence uncovered by his operatives to Austrian. But Comiskey's minions had spent most of their time on the West Coast, trolling for dirt on Chick Gandil, Swede Risberg, and Fred McMullin. They also spent time investigating reports on Buck Weaver and Happy Felsch. But no fix-related information had been uncovered on the other Black Sox.[96] Rather, the only specific intel that Comiskey had about the fix that implicated Eddie Cicotte, Joe Jackson, and Lefty Williams was the hearsay supplied to him by disgruntled St. Louis gamblers Harry Redmon and Joe Pesch. And that intel lacked detail. Sox attorney Austrian knew even less, while ASA Replogle's grand jury probe had produced only scandal headlines. It had yet to uncover hard evidence against the targeted Sox players.[97]

Nor had Eddie Cicotte been over-enlightening. Summoned to the Austrian office ahead of Jackson, a distraught Cicotte readily admitted his own complicity in the plot to fix the Series outcome. And he specifically named Joe Jackson as one of "the men who were in on the deal."[98] But otherwise, Cicotte had not been particularly forthcoming. And he supplied Austrian, and later Replogle, with none of the fix-specific detail—about being propositioned privately by Chick Gandil; about the hold up of fix payoffs blamed on Abe Attell; about the $5,000 delivered to his hotel room by Lefty Williams prior to Game Five; about the denomination of the payoff currency, etc.—that Jackson would reveal to the grand jury later the same day. In short, Jackson's detail-specific grand jury testimony could not have been implanted in his mind by Austrian or Replogle, because neither they nor Comiskey were aware of such details at the time.[99] Only Jackson knew them.

For Jackson's grand jury testimony about his fix involvement to be some sort of implanted fabrication, one must also conclude that every other Black Sox who named Jackson as a fix participant—Eddie Cicotte, Lefty Williams, inferentially Happy Felsch, even Chick Gandil[100]—maliciously accused an innocent man. No reason why his teammates would implicate Jackson falsely has ever been advanced because there is none. Nor is there any readily apparent reason for Judge McDonald to have testified falsely about Jackson's admission of fix complicity in chambers prior to his grand jury appearance when McDonald appeared as a witness in the Jackson civil trial.

Finally, there are the Jackson quotations published in the *Chicago Daily Journal*, *Chicago Tribune* and elsewhere the day after Joe's grand jury appearance. Once again, Jackson revealed fix details to the press

unknown to Austrian, Replogle, and Comiskey. Indeed, some details—that attempts to dump Game Three had been frustrated by Dickey Kerr's shutout pitching; that his confession was motivated by the brush-off about fix payment received from Gandil, Risberg, and McMullin—even went unmentioned during Jackson's grand jury testimony. This next-day reportage, ignored by Jackson supporters and mostly neglected by scandal chroniclers, has never been discredited and further demolishes the notion that Jackson's grand jury confession of fix guilt was contrived by some third party and then parroted to the panel by Joe as the scandal broke.

Interestingly, Jackson himself never asserted that the details of his grand jury testimony were fictions invented for him by others. Rather, Jackson insisted that he had never spoken the words memorialized on the grand jury transcript pages. This, of course, contradicted the concession of grand jury transcript accuracy made by the Black Sox defense during the criminal trial in Chicago. It was also belied by the testimony of grand jury stenographer Elbert Allen and panel foreman Henry Brigham, both of whom authenticated the transcript and its content during the Jackson civil trial in Milwaukee.[101] In the end, Jackson's dogged witness stand repudiation of his grand jury testimony was mind-boggling, so utterly preposterous that even plaintiff's counsel Cannon effectively abandoned Jackson's innocence claim in summation. Instead, Cannon focused his closing argument for judgment on the legal principle of condonation, maintaining that his client should be awarded his unpaid 1921–1922 contract salary because Comiskey had known that Jackson was a participant in the 1919 World Series fix, but had chosen to sign him to a new three-season contract despite that.

Balanced against the force of Jackson's grand jury admissions of complicity in the fix is...pretty much nothing. Jackson and present-day supporters invariably cite his Fall Classic stats—the Series-leading batting average at .375, the club-high six RBIs—as proof of honest play. But statistics are always malleable, subject to partisan manipulation. More rigorous examination of how the 1919 World Series unfolded, for example, just as plausibly yields a damning assessment of Joe's performance. During the first five games, the outer limit of the fix duration in most minds, clean-up batter Jackson notably under-produced, failing to drive in a single White Sox run. Most of Jackson's gaudy Series stats were compiled only after the fix had been abandoned and the Black Sox had begun trying to win.

Jackson's revised account of his Series conduct, unveiled in the affidavit prepared by his criminal trial attorney and later embellished during his ensuing civil suit against the White Sox, also does the Jackson cause little good. Aside from its obviously self-serving nature, Jackson's new story was plagued by implausible and/or inconsistent particulars. For instance, Jackson was not so traumatized by rampant fix rumors that he had gone to club boss Comiskey's hotel room prior to Game One and begged to be let out of the lineup (as he later told Furman Bisher). Rather, Jackson swore during his civil deposition testimony that he knew nothing of the fix until days after the Series was over, and was "dumbfounded" when Lefty Williams finally clued him in. Of necessity, the revision of fix-related events also required movement of Williams's delivery of the $5,000 payoff to Jackson from before the start of Game Five. It was now relocated to three days after the Series was completed. Not only did this contradict his own sworn grand jury testimony (and that of Williams, as well), it made no sense, as why would Jackson be hanging around a Chicago hotel room three days after the World Series was over? Clearly, there were no post-Series celebrations in town that he needed to attend. Far more likely was Jackson's grand jury testimony that he and his wife had left Chicago for their home in Savannah the evening after the Series concluded. Jackson's insistence that he had later tried to turn over the bribe money to Comiskey also rang false. At the civil trial in Milwaukee, it was established that the $5,000 was deposited in the Jackson account at the Chatham Bank & Trust Company in Savannah.[102]

That Joe Jackson was a likable fellow and persistent in his claims of innocence does not change the historical record. On the evidence, the call is not a close one, as a mere reading of this essay's factual narrative should make plain. As he admitted under oath after first being confronted, Jackson was a knowing, if perhaps unenthusiastic, participant in the plot to fix the 1919 World Series. And damningly, Jackson was just as persistent in his demands to be paid his promised fix payoff money as the Series progressed as he would later be in his disavowals of fix involvement. In the final analysis, Shoeless Joe Jackson, banished from playing the game that he loved while still in the prime of his career, is a sad figure. But hardly an innocent one. ■

## Notes

1. The White Sox led the league in team batting average with .287 and were second in OPS and OPS+.
2. Comiskey later maintained that the evidence of player corruption uncovered by his investigators was inconclusive, and that the new contracts offered Jackson, Risberg, Williams, and Felsch had been predicated upon the legal advice of Alfred Austrian, counsel for the White Sox corporation. A far more critical view of Comiskey's conduct is provided in current Black Sox scholarship's seminal work. See Gene Carney, *Burying the Black Sox: How Baseball's Coverup of the 1919 World Series Fix Almost Succeeded* (Dulles, Virginia: Potomac Books, 2006).
3. Decades later, it was revealed that Loomis's call for a probe of the 1919 series had been ghostwritten by *Chicago Tribune* sportswriter James Crusinberry. See "A Newman's Biggest Story," *Sports Illustrated*, September 17, 1956, 69–70. Crusinberry himself would later be a significant witness in early grand jury proceedings.
4. See e.g., *Boston Globe*, *Chicago Tribune*, and *The New York Times*, September 20, 1920.
5. *Philadelphia North American*, September 27, 1920.
6. As per notes of the Cicotte admissions taken down by Austrian and now preserved at the Chicago History Museum, Black Sox File, Box 1/Folder 2.
7. Unlike that of Joe Jackson and Lefty Williams, the grand jury testimony of Eddie Cicotte has not survived intact. But substantial portions of the Cicotte grand jury testimony were embedded in the transcript of his sworn January 14, 1924, deposition for the Jackson civil case and thereafter read into the civil trial record.
8. *Chicago Evening Post*, September 28, 1920.
9. Jackson repeated what he told McDonald in chambers, and more, when he subsequently testified before the grand jury. For space reasons, most particulars of the Jackson-McDonald conversation are omitted herein. But the complete testimony of Judge McDonald is preserved in the still-extant but difficult-to-access transcript of the Jackson v. Chicago White Sox civil case, pages 528–54.
10. McDonald civil trial testimony, page 552. See also *Chicago Tribune*, February 5, 1924. Decades later, Happy Felsch reportedly stated, "Playing rotten, it ain't that hard to do once you get the hang of it. It ain't that hard to hit a pop-up while you take what looks like a good cut at the ball." Eliot Asinof, *Bleeding Between the Lines* (New York: Holt, Rinehart & Winston, 1979), 117.
11. Jackson grand jury testimony [hereafter JGJ]5-21 to JGJ6-8. The long-lost transcript of the Jackson grand jury testimony first resurfaced in 1988, and is now viewable on various websites. See e.g., www.blackbetsy.com.
12. JGJ6-13 to 16.
13. JGJ6-17 to 24.
14. JGJ9-4 to 19.
15. JGJ4-19 to 23.
16. JGJ6-25 to JGJ7-9.
17. JGJ7-10 to 12.
18. JGJ4-20 to JGJ5-3.
19. JGJ12-5 to 12.
20. JGJ16-25 to JGJ17-12.
21. JGJ 17-23 to JGJ19-6.
22. JGJ16-9 to 14.
23. JGJ20-3 to 7.
24. JGJ11-11 to 24.
25. JGJ12-20 toJGJ13-24 and JGJ 14-3. Like Cicotte, Jackson was victimized by specious accounts of his testimony circulated by the Associated Press. Among other things, newspapers that subscribed to the AP wire printed that "Jackson said throughout the series he either struck out or hit easy balls when hits would have meant runs." See e.g., *Los Angeles Times*, September 29, 1920. In fact, Jackson had said nothing of the sort.
26. JGJ15-13 to 14.
27. JGJ14-18 to 19; JGJ12-13 to 16.
28. JGJ22-11 to JGJ23-3; JGJ23-16 to JGJ24-5.
29. JGJ24-6 to 7.

30. Initially published in the *Chicago Daily Journal* and *Chicago Tribune*, September 29, 1920, and then re-printed nationwide via the AP wire. See e.g., *Cincinnati Post* and *New Orleans State*, September 29, 1930, and *Philadelphia Inquirer*, September 30, 1920. Unlike the more famous "Say it ain't so, Joe" anecdote, the authenticity of these Jackson remarks has never been credibly challenged.

31. *Chicago Daily Journal*, *Chicago Tribune*, September 29, 1920, and other newspapers nationwide.

32. Ibid.

33. During his grand jury appearance, Williams testified that eight White Sox players had agreed to the series fix, naming for the record "Cicotte, Gandil, Weaver, Felsch, Risberg, McMullin, Jackson, and myself." See transcript of grand jury testimony of Claude Williams, September 29, 1920, page 30–20 to 24.

34. *Chicago Evening American*, September 30, 1920.

35. As reported in the *Boston Globe*, *Chicago Evening Post*, and *The New York Times*, September 29, 1920.

36. The original indictments returned in People of Illinois v. Edward V. Cicotte, et al, can be reviewed via the website www.cookcountyclerkofcourt.com. Joe Jackson was among the Sox players charged, while indicted fix backers included professional athletes-turned-gamblers Abe Attell and Bill Burns, and banished star Hal Chase. Separate indictments were returned against a number of Chicago-area baseball pool operators. In March 1921, the original Black Sox indictments were administratively dismissed by SA Crowe, replaced by superseding indictments that re-charged all of the previously accused while expanding the roster of non-player defendants by five, including St. Louis gambler Carl Zork.

37. *Los Angeles Times*, November 13, 1920.

38. As reported in the *Boston Globe* and *Los Angeles Times*, November 24, 1920.

39. As quoted in the *Boston Globe* and *Chicago Tribune*, November 24, 1920. Although the venue would prove different from that envisioned by McDonald, his observation that Jackson risked exposing himself to a perjury charge proved prophetic.

40. A "bill of particulars" is a pretrial pleading that seeks more specific information about the charges from the prosecution.

41. Notorious Boston bookmaker Joseph "Sport" Sullivan and the shadowy Rachael Brown (probably Nat Evans, a capable lieutenant and business junior partner of reputed, but unindicted, fix financier Arnold Rothstein) were among the gamblers indicted in the Black Sox case.

42. An excerpt from the bill of particulars appears in Black Sox Scandal Research Committee Newsletter, Vol. 6, No. 2 (December 2013), 10.

43. Outside the jury's presence, Cicotte, Jackson, and Williams testified in support of a defense motion to suppress their grand jury testimony. That testimony, however, was restricted to events attending their grand jury appearances, with no prosecution questioning about the actual fix of the World Series permitted by Judge Hugo Friend. At the hearing's end, the motion was denied and redacted versions of the Cicotte/Jackson/Williams grand jury transcripts were later read to the jury at length. But to no avail, as the defendants were acquitted notwithstanding their grand jury admissions of guilt.

44. The only defendant who testified in his own defense at trial was gambler David Zelcer.

45. Partial transcripts of the motion proceedings survive in the Black Sox archive maintained at the Chicago History Museum (Box 1/Folder 4). The proceedings were also memorialized in reportage by the *Chicago Herald Examiner*, *Chicago Tribune*, and *Savannah Daily News*, July 26, 1921, and elsewhere. If defense claims were true, admission of the grand jury transcripts in evidence would have violated the constitutional due process rights of the accused.

46. Redaction means the removal of extraneous or inadmissible portions of the evidence. In the case of the Cicotte/Jackson/Williams grand jury transcripts this entailed the deletion of the names of the other defendants (Gandil, Felsch, Weaver, etc.) from the text, the anonym Mr. Blank being inserted wherever such a name appeared.

47. In the writer's view, the prosecution presented a compelling case at trial against defendants Cicotte, Jackson, and Williams, and a strong one against codefendants Chick Gandil, Swede Risberg, and David Zelcer (if not versus the remaining accused). For one hypothesis about the verdict, see William Lamb, "Jury Nullification and the Not Guilty Verdicts in the Black Sox Case," *Baseball Research Journal*, Vol. 44 (Fall 2015), 47–56.

48. The first of these lawsuits was instituted by Buck Weaver in October 1921, and sought unpaid salary for the 1921 season per the three-year contract that he had signed previously. Originally filed in Chicago Municipal Court, the Weaver suit was quickly transferred to the United States District Court for the Northern District of Illinois on diversity of citizenship grounds, the White Sox being incorporated in Wisconsin. In April 1922, Happy Felsch, Joe Jackson, and Swede Risberg filed state court suits against the White Sox in Milwaukee. Same posited various injury claims.

49. The press was barred from the Jackson deposition, and only ill-informed snippets appeared in newsprint until verbatim excerpts of the deposition were published by syndicated sports columnist Frank G. Menke. See e.g., the *Lincoln* (Nebraska) *Star*, April 23, 1923. Menke had previously authored a fawning portrait of Raymond J. Cannon, Jackson's brash young civil attorney, and would prove a reliable Jackson apologist throughout the proceedings.

50. Per Menke in the *Lincoln Star*, April 23, 1923.

51. Menke, *Lincoln Star*.

52. Menke, *Lincoln Star*.

53. Menke, *Lincoln Star*.

54. For a detailed accounting of the civil litigation attached to the scandal, see William F. Lamb, *Black Sox in the Courtroom: The Grand Jury, Criminal Trial and Civil Litigation* (Jefferson, North Carolina: McFarland & Company, Inc., 2013), 149–98.

55. According to Menke, "From Baseball to $100,000 a Year," *Atlanta Constitution*, July 17, 1921, and elsewhere. Cannon, a decent ballplayer himself and once a semipro teammate of Jackson co-plaintiff Happy Felsch, was also actively engaged in trying to revive a major league players union.

56. See e.g., "Find Shoeless Joe Excellent Witness," (Lincoln) *Nebraska State Journal*, January 31, 1924. Closer to home, local reportage was also initially favorable to the plaintiff. See the *Milwaukee Sentinel*, January 30, 1924: "Jackson made an excellent witness. He looked well on the stand. His answers came quickly and cleanly."

57. One of the many fabrications that mar enjoyment of Eliot Asinof's popular treatment of the Black Sox scandal is the assertion that the Jackson grand jury testimony had long been lost, and that Jackson was ambushed when the transcript "suddenly reappeared [from] Hudnall's briefcase." *Eight Men Out* (New York: Henry Holt & Company, 1963), 289–90. The claim is absurd. The transcript of Jackson's grand jury testimony (and that of Eddie Cicotte and Lefty Williams, too) had been used extensively during the earlier Black Sox criminal trial and was tantamount to a matter of public record. Nor was the Jackson side surprised by Hudnall's possession of it, plaintiff's attorney Cannon having made a motion to preclude the transcript's use at the civil trial. That motion was denied by Judge Gregory.

58. Jackson v. Chicago White Sox civil trial transcript [hereinafter JTT], page 151.

59. JTT, page 156.

60. JTT, pages 159–60.

61. JTT, page 162.

62. JTT, page 220.

63. JTT, pages 197-198

64. JTT, page 200.

65. JTT, page 188.

66. JTT, pages 154-155.

67. JTT, page 160.

68. As reported in the *Milwaukee Journal* and *Milwaukee Sentinel*, February 15, 1924. The day before, Judge Gregory had found plaintiff's rebuttal witness Happy Felsch in contempt for repudiating what was incontestably his signature on his 1920 White Sox contract. Felsch was

thereupon taken into custody, but released later that evening when two local attorneys posted his $2,000 bail.

69. JTT, pages 1686–87. See also, the *Milwaukee Evening Sentinel*, February 15, 1924. The perjury-related crime of false swearing can be deemed a sort of self-accusing, self-convicting offense. In one of its forms, false swearing does not require the demonstration that a particular statement given under oath was false. Conviction can rest upon proof that the accused uttered inconsistent statements on the same subject matter while testifying under oath at two different judicial proceedings. It does not matter which of the two inconsistent statements is false, just that one of them has to be (e.g., giving two different birth dates).

70. JTT, pages 1694–96. See also, the *Milwaukee Journal* and *Milwaukee Evening Sentinel*, February 15, 1924.

71. As reported in the *Milwaukee Journal* and *Milwaukee Evening Sentinel*, February 15, 1924.

72. Over more than 30 years as a state/county prosecutor, the writer recalls only three perjury prosecutions, each of which involved false witness testimony during a very serious criminal case. Prosecutors generally take little interest in alleged perjury during civil litigation, leaving the affected parties and/or the court to pursue their own remedies.

73. As per the *Milwaukee Journal*, February 16, 1924, and *Chicago Tribune*, February 17, 1924. The perjury arrest of Jackson ordered by Judge Gregory was a contempt of court-type sanction. Criminal proceedings against Jackson could only be instituted by a law enforcement agency, like the Milwaukee County District Attorney's Office.

74. As reported in the *Chicago Tribune*, April 10, 1924.

75. As reported in the *Milwaukee Sentinel* and *Sheboygan* (Wisconsin) *Press*, May 18, 1925. That same date, Felsch appeared before Judge Gregory and pled guilty to a reduced charge of false swearing. He was sentenced to a one-year term of probation.

76. Decades later, it was reported that the charge had been dismissed. See the *Milwaukee Journal*, March 13, 1986. In 2010, letters to the Milwaukee County District Attorney's Office from the writer about the disposition of the Jackson perjury complaint went unanswered.

77. A complete accounting of statements uttered by the Black Sox is provided in Jacob Pomrenke, "After the Fall: The Post-Black Sox Scandal Interviews," *Black Sox Scandal Research Committee Newsletter*, Vol. 8, No. 1 (June 2016), 6–9.

78. Shirley Povich, "Say It Ain't So, Joe," *Washington Post*, April 11, 1941.

79. Povich, *Washington Post*.

80. Back in 1908, Latimer, then a cub reporter for the *Greenville* (South Carolina) *News*, had hung the Shoeless Joe moniker on Jackson after Joe had discarded tight-fitting new spikes for a few innings during a minor league game.

81. Carter (Scoops) Latimer, "Joe Jackson, Contented Carolinian at 54, Forgets Bitter Dose in His Cup and Glories in His 12 Hits in '19 Series," *The Sporting News*, September 24, 1942.

82. Latimer, *The Sporting News*.

83. See again, the *Chicago Tribune*, *Cincinnati Post*, and *New Orleans State*, September 29, 1920.

84. See "This Is the Truth," by Shoeless Joe Jackson as told to Furman Bisher, *Sport*, October 1949.

85. "This Is the Truth," 13.

86. Months prior to the trial, Judge William E. Dever had rendered a significant pretrial ruling in Black Sox defense favor, denying a prosecution motion for an indefinite continuance of the proceedings. The short peremptory trial date then set by Dever prompted State's Attorney Crowe to administratively dismiss the original indictments returned in the case, and re-present the matter to the grand jury for superseding charges.

87. This sensitivity and desperate reaction to pre-series fix rumors was a stunning departure from events recounted in Jackson's sworn April 1923 civil case deposition. Then, Jackson had claimed to be oblivious to the series corruption until Lefty Williams informed him about it several nights after the series was over.

88. "This Is the Truth," 14. A number of witnesses were presented at the criminal trial by the Gandil defense. None of the accused players testified before the jury at trial, but Jackson, Eddie Cicotte, and Lefty Williams did take the stand out of the jury's presence in support of the unsuccessful defense motion to suppress their grand jury testimony.

89. "This Is the Truth," 14.

90. "This Is the Truth," 83.

91. Lamb, *Black Sox in the Courtroom*, 89–90.

92. "This Is the Truth," 83.

93. "This Is the Truth," 83.

94. Under then-applicable Illinois criminal law, the offense of conspiracy was committed the moment that two or more persons agreed to commit an unlawful act. No action (overt act) needed be taken by the conspirators in furtherance of their plan for the crime to have been committed. See *People v. Lloyd*, 304 Ill. *23, 136, N.E.* 505 (Ill. Supreme Ct. 1922). Given that, the purported abandonment of the plot to throw the World Series by Jackson (or any of the other Black Sox defendant) had no legal effect. Nor did the criminal law principle of renunciation apply once a bet on the Series outcome had been placed by an in-the-know gambler with some unsuspecting White Sox backer. At that moment, the crime of conspiracy was irrevocably committed.

95. Donald Gropman, *Say It Ain't So, Joe! The True Story of Shoeless Joe Jackson* (New York: Citadel Press, 3rd ed., 2001), 185–90.

96. Gene Carney, "Comiskey's Detectives," *Baseball Research Journal*, Vol. 38, No. 2 (Fall 2009), 108–16.

97. For a session-by-session account of developments during the first Cook County grand jury investigation of the fix, see again, Lamb, *Black Sox in the Courtroom*, 29–79.

98. As per notes of the Cicotte interview taken by Austrian now reposed in the Chicago History Museum's Black Sox archive (Box 1/Folder 2).

99. For further demolition of the argument that Jackson's grand jury testimony was false and implanted in his mind by others, see Craig R. Wright, "The Austrian Conspiracy, " www.BaseballsPast.com, 2015.

100. "This Is My Story of the Black Sox Series," by Arnold (Chick) Gandil, as told to Mel Durslag, *Sports Illustrated*, September 17, 1956.

101. JTT, page 599, et seq. (Allen); JTT, Page 648, et seq. (Brigham). During his testimony, Allen recited the 128 or so answers that Jackson had denied giving to the grand jury during his testimony earlier in the civil trial.

102. JTT, page 1169 et seq. (deposition of bank teller John J. Cornell admitted in evidence).

# An Examination of MLB Play Call Challenges

Anne C. Marx Scheuerell and David B. Marx

The replay review system has changed Major League Baseball. The goal of the instant replay system was to reduce the impact of umpire error, while minimizing the time needed to review plays. In this paper we will examine the effects that replay review has had on the game and its strategies.

Major League Baseball (MLB) was the last of the four major US sports to implement a replay review system. Opposition to replay review included arguments that "bad calls" are traditionally part of America's national pastime, and concerns over game delays and the limitations of instant replay technology.[1] Despite strong resistance, MLB implemented a limited replay review system in 2008.[2] The initial system mandated that umpires on the field select play calls to be reviewed rather than team managers. The limited replay review system was in effect through 2013.

In January 2014, MLB announced an expansion of the replay review system.[3] The expanded version extended play challenges to team managers and increased the types of plays that may be reviewed.[4] The new rules, which are still in effect as of this writing, allow each team manager two challenges to start each postseason game, divisional or wild card tie-breaker game, and one challenge to start every other game including the All-Star Game. If a challenge is upheld, the manager retains the ability to challenge another play call, but never more than two in a regular season game.[5] The umpire crew chief also has the discretion to review a potential home run call at any time during a game. Beginning in the eighth inning, a crew chief may initiate a play call review of any other reviewable call if the team manager has no challenges remaining. To accommodate the expected increase in play call challenges, seven minor league umpires were promoted to the major leagues and the Replay Operations Center was established.[6]

The new rules brought about changes in the staffing at the team level as well. MLB authorized teams to hire video review coordinators. A review coordinator would quickly assess footage from multiple camera angles and counsel team managers whether to challenge a play.[7] The review coordinator is largely invisible to spectators, but two additional changes are noticeable to those watching a game. First, the "dirt-kicking, cap-flipping, vein-popping argument" that has been part of baseball's tradition of challenging play calls has been replaced by a modern watch party, as predicted before the 2014 season by Paul White in *USA Today*.[8] Second, base running is arguably more physical as "the swipe, pop and phantom tags are disappearing because they are less efficient at guaranteeing contact with the runner."[9]

For sabermetric enthusiasts, of course, a new replay review system means new measures of performance for replay review analysis. In the spring 2015 issue of the *Baseball Research Journal*, Gil Imber presented three new measures of performance including the Review Affirmation Percentage (RAP), Team Success Percentage (TSP), and Manager's Challenge Success Percentage (MCSP). RAP is the percent of play calls affirmed and thus not overturned. RAP includes analysis of play calls reviews challenged by both umpires and team managers. TSP is the percent of play calls overturned, regardless if the play call review was challenged by umpires or a team manager. MCSP is the percent of play calls overturned when the play call was challenged by the team manager.[10]

## PURPOSE OF THE STUDY

The purpose of this study was to examine MLB play call challenge data (RAP, TSP, and MCSP) in relation to a variety of variables. Data from play call challenges (N = 1352) during the 2015 MLB season were analyzed across the 30 MLB teams, the types of play calls reviewed (home run, ground rule/automatic double, fan interference, stadium boundary calls, force play, tag play, fair/foul on balls hit in the outfield, trap play in outfield only, batter hit by pitch, timing play. touching a base, passing runners, and record keeping), umpire positions, and innings the play was challenged. Specific areas examined included the relationships between the MCSP and teams, RAP and types of play calls, RAP and umpire positions, and RAP and the inning the play was challenged.

## METHOD

Data from play call challenges during the 2015 MLB regular season (N = 1352) were obtained from baseballsavant.com in January of 2016. Specific play call challenge variables included MLB team challenger, the types of plays reviewed (catch or drop, fair or foul on balls hit in the outfield, fan interference, ground rule/automatic double, hit by pitch, home run, home-plate collision, play at first, record keeping, rules check, stadium boundary, tag play, tag-up play, timing play, touching a base, and trap play), position of the umpire making the call (first base, second base, third base, and home plate), and the inning the play was challenged (1, 2, 3, 4, 5, 6, 7, 8, and 9 +). Once the data were coded, entered and cleaned (duplicated challenges were excluded), they were analyzed using Statistical Analysis Software (SAS). A variety of analyses was used to generate descriptive data and examine trends related to MCSP and MLB teams, RAP and types of play challenges.

## RESULTS

### MCSP and Teams

Of the 1352 play call challenges, 50.74% were overturned (TSP = .5074; RAP = .4926). The umpires challenged 172 play calls, more than any individual team. However, the umpires had the highest RAP of .7126. It is important to note umpire challenges apply to all games, while the manager challenges only apply to that team's games. Therefore, although the umpires are over four times higher than the team average, they are only about 1/7 of the total number of challenges. The Rays challenged the most play calls of any team (n = 53) and the Tigers challenged the least (n = 27). The mean of number of challenges per team was 44.61. The Yankees had the largest percent of play calls overturned (75%; MCSP = .75) and the Rays had the fewest (32.08%; MCSP = .3208). The mean MCSP was .5440 (see Table 1).

A Chi-square was conducted to examine the differences in MCSPs among MLB teams. MCSPs did statistically differ among MLB teams, $X2$ (30, N = 1352) = 86.25, p = < .0001. As shown in Table 1, The Yankees, Mariners, Diamondbacks, Royals, and Twins were more likely to have a play call overturned than the Rangers or Rays.

A correlation analysis examined the relationship between the number of play calls challenged and MCSP values. The number of play calls challenged by a team were moderately negatively correlated with MCSP (r = -.495). Therefore, the analyses indicated the more plays a team challenged the lower the MCSP value.

**Table 1. Frequency and Percent of Team Challenging Play Call Being Overturned**

| | Overturned | | |
| Challenging Team | No (%) RAP | Yes (%) MCSP | Frequency (n) |
|---|---|---|---|
| Umpire | 71.26 | 28.74 | 174 |
| Rays | 67.92 | 32.08 | 53 |
| Red Sox | 59.62 | 40.38 | 52 |
| Rangers | 67.31 | 32.69 | 52 |
| Astros | 50.00 | 50.00 | 50 |
| Blue Jays | 58.00 | 42.00 | 50 |
| Cubs | 42.86 | 57.14 | 49 |
| Rockies | 48.94 | 51.06 | 47 |
| Braves | 50.00 | 50.00 | 46 |
| Pirates | 45.45 | 54.55 | 44 |
| Dodgers | 56.82 | 43.18 | 44 |
| Twins | 35.71 | 64.29 | 42 |
| White Sox | 50.00 | 50.00 | 42 |
| Padres | 54.76 | 45.24 | 42 |
| Royals | 35.00 | 65.00 | 40 |
| Angels | 40.00 | 60.00 | 40 |
| Giants | 43.59 | 56.41 | 39 |
| Mariners | 28.95 | 71.05 | 38 |
| Phillies | 36.84 | 63.16 | 38 |
| Mets | 44.74 | 55.26 | 38 |
| D-backs | 33.33 | 66.67 | 33 |
| Cardinals | 51.52 | 48.48 | 33 |
| Yankees | 25.00 | 75.00 | 32 |
| Marlins | 38.71 | 61.29 | 31 |
| Reds | 38.71 | 61.29 | 31 |
| Orioles | 43.33 | 56.67 | 30 |
| Brewers | 46.67 | 53.33 | 30 |
| Nationals | 56.67 | 43.33 | 30 |
| Indians | 46.43 | 53.57 | 28 |
| Athletics | 48.15 | 51.85 | 27 |
| Tigers | 59.26 | 40.74 | 27 |
| **Total** | **50.74** | **49.26** | **1352** |

RAP and Type of Play Call Reviewed

Seventy-three percent of play calls reviewed were either tag plays (40.75%) or plays at first (32.32%). During the 2015 MLB regular season, there was only one automatic double reviewed and two timing plays reviewed. The type of play call most frequently overturned was fan interference (66.66%; RAP = .3333). Rules checks, timing plays, and automatic double types of plays were not overturned during the 2015 regular season.

A Chi-square was used to examine the statistically significant differences in RAP values among types of play calls reviewed. RAPs did statistically differ by type of play reviewed, $X2$ (16, N = 1352) = 94.28, p = < .0001.

As shown in Table 2, play calls on fan interference, plays at first, force plays, and hit by pitch were more likely to be overturned than rules check, timing rule, automatic double, home-plate collision, or tag up play calls.

**Table 2. Frequency and Percent of Types of Play Reviewed and Overturned**

| | Overturned | | |
|---|---|---|---|
| | No (%) | Yes (%) | |
| Type of Play | RAP | TSP | Frequency (n) |
| Tag Play | 54.63 | 45.37 | 551 |
| Play at 1st | 36.38 | 63.62 | 437 |
| Home Run | 69.81 | 30.19 | 106 |
| Force Play | 47.89 | 52.11 | 71 |
| Hit by Pitch | 48.44 | 51.56 | 64 |
| Home-plate Collision | 92.59 | 7.41 | 27 |
| Fair or Foul | 52.38 | 47.62 | 21 |
| Catch or Drop | 61.11 | 38.89 | 18 |
| Trap Play | 54.55 | 45.45 | 11 |
| Tag-up Play | 81.82 | 18.18 | 11 |
| Fan Interference | 33.33 | 66.67 | 9 |
| Record Keeping | 83.33 | 16.67 | 6 |
| Touching a Base | 83.33 | 16.67 | 6 |
| Rules Check | 100.00 | 0.0000 | 6 |
| Stadium Boundary | 60.00 | 40.00 | 5 |
| Timing Play | 100.00 | 0.00 | 2 |
| Automatic Double | 100.00 | 0.00 | 1 |
| **Total** | **50.74** | **49.26** | **1352** |

RAP and Umpire Position

The position of the umpire that was reviewed the most frequently was first base (39.94%). A Chi-square examined the differences between RAP values among umpire positions. RAP values did statistically differ among umpire positions, $X2$ (3, N = 1352) = 50.31, p = < .0001. Umpires positioned at first base (RAP = .3981) were more likely to be overturned than umpires positioned at third base (RAP = .6529) or home plate (RAP = .6053; see Table 3).

**Table 3. Frequency and Percent of Position of Umpire Being Overturned**

| | Overturned | | |
|---|---|---|---|
| Position | No (%) | Yes (%) | |
| of Umpire | RAP | TSP | Frequency (n) |
| First | 39.81 | 60.19 | 540 |
| Second | 53.62 | 46.38 | 414 |
| Home | 60.53 | 39.47 | 228 |
| Third | 65.29 | 34.71 | 170 |
| Total | 50.74 | 49.26 | 1352 |

RAP and Inning of Play Call

More plays were reviewed during the seventh inning (n = 189) in the 2015 regular season than any other inning. The fewest number of plays—119—were reviewed during the fourth inning. Plays reviewed in the first inning had the highest percent of calls overturned (66.01%; RAP = .3399) and plays reviewed in the eighth inning had the lowest percent of calls overturned (53.33%; RAP = .6467; see Table 4). A Chi-square indicated RAP values did statistically differ among innings the play call was reviewed, $X2$ (8, N = 1352) = 44.96, p = < .0001. Play calls challenged in the first, second, or third inning were more likely to be overturned than plays challenged in the eighth or ninth. (See Table 4).

**Table 4. Frequency and Percent of Inning Play was Challenged and Overturned**

| | Overturned | | |
|---|---|---|---|
| | No (%) | Yes (%) | |
| Inning | RAP | TSP | Frequency (n) |
| 1 | 33.99 | 66.01 | 153 |
| 2 | 44.72 | 55.28 | 123 |
| 3 | 42.54 | 57.46 | 134 |
| 4 | 47.06 | 52.94 | 119 |
| 5 | 51.63 | 48.37 | 153 |
| 6 | 49.29 | 50.71 | 140 |
| 7 | 55.03 | 44.97 | 189 |
| 8 | 64.67 | 35.33 | 167 |
| 9 | 60.92 | 39.08 | 174 |
| **Total** | **50.74** | **49.26** | **1352** |

A logistical regression analysis examined the relationship between the inning the play was challenged and RAP values. The regression model was adjusted for MLB team and umpire position. What inning the play call was challenged significantly predicted RAP scores, t(1317) = -6.19, p < .0001. The inning of a challenge also explained a significant proportion of variance in RAP scores, $R2$ = 0.1358, F(1,1317) = 38.27, p < .0001.

## DISCUSSION

Our 2015 MLB replay review data analyses bear similarities to analyses of the 2014 replay review data. Imber stated that based on the 2014 MLB replay review data, "the more reviews experienced by a given team, the greater the chance that some of these reviews were unsuccessful and/or frivolous." Similarly, this study indicated a negative correlation (r = .495) such that the more play calls a team challenged, the lower the team's MCSP value—and thus, lower the likelihood the review would be overturned. In both the 2014 and 2015 regular seasons, the umpires had the highest RAP at .769 and .7126, respectively. These trends may in part be due to the choice of teams to request a review from the umpire rather than use a manager's challenge. Teams more successful at getting umpires to initiate a play call review would have a lower frequency of manager play call challenges. Moreover, it may be assumed that teams would be more likely to request the umpire initiate a review rather than use a manager's challenge when the play call in question is indeed very questionable.

Another trend from the 2014 MLB regular season that carried over to 2015 was that the RAP increased as the game progressed. There are several possible reasons for this. Umpires may have improved as each game advanced. Managers' judgment in challenging play calls may have gotten poorer as each game continued. However, the most likely reason is that to use a manager challenge early is the game is a greater risk than using one later in the game. Play challenges can also be used as part of a strategy to provide more time for a pitcher during high leverage situations in the game.

The MLB replay review system has changed some aspects of America's favorite pastime. It has added a new element to team strategy, new team staff positions, and new data to be analyzed. Data from the 2015 MLB regular season indicated RAP is impacted by team, type of play call, umpire position, and most statistically significantly, inning the play was challenged. Teams should continue to invest in understanding and maximizing the opportunities presented by the replay review system. ∎

## Notes

1. Zachary D. Rymer, "Breaking Down the Pros and Cons of Instant Replay in MLB." *Bleacher Report.* October 03, 2017. Accessed September 19, 2018. http://bleacherreport.com/articles/1156392-breaking-down-the-pros-and-cons-of-instant-replay-in-mlb.
2. Associated Press. "MLB Approves Replay in Series That Start Thursday." ESPN. August 27, 2008. Accessed September 17, 2018. http://www.espn.com/mlb/news/story?id=3554357.
3. Paul Hagen, "Expanded replay approved, to begin this season." MLB.com. January 16, 2014. Accessed February, 2015 from http://m.mlb.com/news/article/66737912/mlb-approves-expandedinstant-replay-beginning-with-2014-season.
4. MLB Replay Review Regulations. (n.d.) Accessed February 25, 2019. http://m.mlb.com/official_rules/replay_review.
5. Hagen, MLB.com, 2014.
6. Gil Imber, "Confirmed: MLB Hires 7 New Umpires to Full-Time Staff," Close Call Sports & Umpire Ejection Fantasy League. Accessed September 19, 2018. http://www.closecallsports.com/2014/01/mlb-hires-umpires-baker-blaser-rackley.html.
7. B. Walker, "Replay Wizards Becoming Key Positions on MLB Teams." Spokesman.com. March 21, 2014. Accessed September 19, 2018. http://www.spokesman.com/stories/2014/mar/22/replaywizards-becoming-key-positions-on-mlb-teams/.
8. Paul White, "How Instant Replay Will Truly Change Baseball," *USA Today.* February 28, 2014. Accessed September 19, 2018. http://www.usatoday.com/story/sports/mlb/2014/02/27/how-instantreplay-will-change-baseball/5879639.
9. David Manel, "How Has Instant Replay Changed Baserunning?" Bucs Dugout. May 20, 2015. Accessed September 19, 2018. http://www.bucsdugout.com/2015/5/20/8626635/tagging-sliding-replay.
10. Gil Imber, "Reviewing Instant Replay: Observations and Implications from Replay's Inaugural Season." *Baseball Research Journal* 44, no. 1 (2015). Accessed September 19, 2018. https://sabr.org/research/reviewing-instant-replay-observations-and-implications-replay-s-inauguralseason.
11. Imber, "Reviewing Instant Replay," *BRJ*, 2015.
12. Imber, "Reviewing Instant Replay," *BRJ*, 2015.

# File and Trial

*Examining Valuation and Hearings in MLB Arbitration*

## Navneet S. Vishwanathan

The 2018 season was certainly an interesting one in the American League East. The Boston Red Sox put forward a historically strong championship team and the New York Yankees followed up their 2017 ALCS campaign with a wild-card finish. However, off the field and in the conference room, the excitement of the division began well before Opening Day. Here, in the realm of arbitration, three cases illustrate the peculiarities of a financial system suffused with new trends, uncertainty, and risk aversion.

On January 31, Red Sox outfielder Mookie Betts won his arbitration hearing, securing him the highest salary ever awarded for a first-time arbitration-eligible player at $10.5 million. That was $3 million more than the Red Sox' bid, and a whopping $9.5 million raise from Betts's 2017 salary.

Two weeks later, in a contentious hearing on February 15, Marcus Stroman lost his case against the Toronto Blue Jays, resulting in a 2018 salary of $6.5 million, $400,000 less than what he'd filed for.

And in a forgotten headline, on February 6, Jonathan Schoop and the Baltimore Orioles managed to overcome their $1.5 million gulf in salary filings without an arbitrator, settling on an $8.5 million salary for 2018.

These cases represent the three possible outcomes of the MLB arbitration process: a player winning the hearing, a team winning the hearing, and a mutually agreed upon settlement prior to a hearing. However, the likelihood of each outcome varies significantly based on salary filings and player performance. This study seeks to examine this system and arrive at conclusions about whether players and teams with high gaps in filings are more or less likely to follow the arbitration process through to a hearing.

Delving a step deeper into the salary filings themselves, Betts, Stroman, and Schoop may have filed for salaries substantively different from what their skill sets were worth a mere 10 years ago. Given the recent proliferation of advanced metrics in baseball, the evaluation of talent has changed significantly. This study further examines whether compensation and skill premiums for particular aspects of a player's game have changed over time.

On these two general points of inquiry, this study builds a comprehensive picture of the MLB arbitration process. By understanding how the arbitration process affects incentives for negotiation and settlement, it applies economic logic of contract theory to a controlled environment of arbitration. And by examining trends in valuation and compensation, the study draws conclusions about how baseball's information revolution affects bargaining for contracts and salary. Ultimately, this reveals two conclusions: risk aversion from players and teams in arbitration hearings, and the proliferation of advanced metrics and skill-based valuation of players as reflected in compensation.

## MLB ARBITRATION OVERVIEW

Before discussing the data and model strategy, it is important to examine the arbitration system, whose design significantly affects salary filings and the incentive structure for players and teams. There are two major components to consider: eligibility standards for arbitration and the arbitration procedure itself.

Arbitration dates to the 1973–74 offseason. Under current rules, players with between three and six years of service time are eligible to have their salaries decided by arbitration. Two major exceptions to this eligibility window exist. First, any player with more than six years of service time can elect to engage in the arbitration process with a consenting team. However, since these players are also eligible for free agency, they rarely opt for arbitration and instead negotiate contracts directly with teams. A notable exception was David Ortiz, who in 2012 elected to enter arbitration with the Red Sox rather than exploring the free-agent market.

The more important exception to the eligibility standards is the class of players known as "Super Twos." Players in the top 22 percent of service time for those between two and three years of service time are eligible for arbitration one year early, for a total of four years. Super Twos are often the top young performers in the league and are rewarded with a bonus year of arbitration eligibility. Entering arbitration one year earlier can have multiplicative effects on earnings in subsequent years, and thereby may affect the incentives of the player.

Turning from eligibility to process, Major League Baseball's arbitration system can be classified as a "final-offer arbitration" (FOA) system. In this format, both parties submit a bid or proposal to resolve a dispute and present evidence in favor of their valuation. The arbitrator then chooses one of the two bids and cannot derive a value in between the bids. This feature distinguishes MLB's arbitration system from others such as the National Hockey League's, where arbitrators are free to select either bid or assign any value in between. As a result of MLB's final-offer system, bids are often significantly less extreme, since presenting an outlier bid would likely result in losing the entire difference between the two bids rather than the difference with a midpoint.

In terms of process, eligible players and teams unable to come to terms by a mid-January deadline enter the filing period. Here, teams and players are still able to negotiate contracts, but must first file salary figures that constitute their bids in a potential arbitration hearing. If the parties are still unable to reach an agreement after filing, they proceed to a hearing, but remain free to settle at any point before it commences.

In this ultimate phase, players and teams present their respective cases in front of a panel of three arbitrators using admissible evidence such as quality of performance—as measured by both publicly and non-publicly available data, comparisons to previous salary, comparison to like arbitrations, and injury history. Arbitrators then render a decision within 24 hours.

Given these rules, arbitration provides a clearly controlled and regulated laboratory for studying the changes in valuation patterns and effects of contract theory in baseball. With most players signing one-year deals, the confounding effects of multi-year agreements, incentive based bonuses, opt-out clauses, and perks such as no-trade clauses are removed. In arbitration, value is directly linked to performance and the perceived ability to sustain that performance in the future.

## MLB PERFORMANCE AND EVALUATION TRENDS

Complementing this understanding of the MLB arbitration system are important trends and transformations in the thought around evaluation and performance measurements in baseball. Here, the post-*Moneyball*

environment and the information revolution have brought about many changes.

Three emergent categories in this transformation are advanced metrics, batted-ball data, and Statcast. The first of these was the earliest entrant into the baseball information revolution, gaining prominence in the late 20th century and producing hallmark sabermetric statistics. The main achievement of these advanced metrics was removing bias from conventional measures and isolating the individual contributions of players. This has led to more precise evaluation of talent levels and the underlying skills possessed by baseball players.

The second and third classes of data—batted-ball information and Statcast data—consist of information on player and ball movement during games. These statistics do not evaluate the outcomes of any given play but instead provide data on a player's strength, speed, and skills. These metrics further divorce skills from outcomes and are particularly relevant for arbitration cases as players and teams may be able to point to underlying skills (or defects) as indicators of a player's value rather than using outcome-oriented data that may be biased by the presence of other players in data events. In contrast to sabermetrics, the availability of Statcast data is highly regulated and asymmetrical. While some Statcast information is publicly available, a large number of data and measurements are only available to teams. Therefore, Statcast is not admissible in arbitration hearings and is not used in this study.

Nonetheless, the impact of Statcast data on baseball trends is important to note. Since Statcast was introduced in 2015—in the middle of this dataset—it provides a natural experiment for changes in player performance and valuation due to changes in the data landscape. As an example, the Statcast metric "Launch Angle" measures the angle of a batted ball. With the increasing availability of these data and research showing fly balls to be more productive in run-scoring, many hitters have altered their swings to add loft—a trend that is perceptible in the non-Statcast measure fly-ball rate. Thus, while Statcast data are not used in this study, the impact of Statcast may be observed through other metrics that reflect changes in player behavior.

## LITERATURE REVIEW

By and large, the previous literature that drives this study falls into two major categories: models for evaluating free-agent contracts based on performance statistics and evaluations of the FOA system.

## Modeling Compensation with Metrics

Wasserman (2013) examined non-performance indicators of free-agent compensation such as player-agent influence, market size, and month of signing. In this study, Wasserman controlled for player performance using an aggregate measure of player value—Wins Above Replacement (WAR)—and found that performance is significant in predicting salary at the 1 percent level in all regressions. Building upon this work and breaking down WAR into its component measures would show which metrics are better indicators of compensation, yielding a more robust examination of the correlations between performance and compensation. In addition, breaking down WAR into component parts would allow this study to trace changes in valuation and compensation of various skills over time.

In this realm, Pollack (2017) has examined the relationship between various metrics and compensation. Pollack's approach was novel in that it examined only arbitration contracts and free-agent contracts signed the year previous to their inclusion in the dataset, thereby isolating the year-over-year change in salary. In this study, Pollack found a significant relationship for on-base percentage and isolated power with compensation. Furthermore, by examining the individual annual cross sections for the effects of OBP and ISO, Pollack found that OBP's effect on salary relative to ISO had grown over time, evidencing a more analytic approach to compensation, as OBP is heralded as the poster-child of the *Moneyball* revolution. Extending this work to arbitration salaries and isolating the effects of more advanced metrics such as weighted runs created plus (wRC+) could reaffirm Pollack's conclusion.

## FOA and Alternative Dispute Resolution

The second body of literature relevant to this study situates the MLB arbitration system in the context of other alternative dispute resolution (ADR) mechanisms. Scholars such as Carrell and Manchise (2013) compare FOA to more traditional interest arbitration methods, citing the advantages of FOA in promoting compromise and early settlement due to the winner-take-all structure. The arbitration hearing presents the evident risk of losing the entire difference between salary bids rather than settling on a midpoint.

Monhait (2013) builds on these claims, pointing to the effectiveness of the FOA system at inducing settlement as evidenced by the fact that from 1974 to 1993, only 9 percent of eligible players completed the process with a hearing. The frequency has been even lower in recent years, with only 2.5 percent of players who filed for arbitration going to a hearing in 2011 and no players entering a hearing in 2013.

Twenty years earlier, Burgess and Marburger (1993) found that team victories in arbitration hearings led to salaries 9 percent lower than comparable players who settled, and that player victory led to salaries 14 percent higher than comparable players who settled. This theory adds to Carrell and Manchise's argument that the potential to lose salary through an arbitrated decision may nudge the sides toward early settlement.

The two main claims made by this paper are anchored by key texts in the previous literature. First, recognizing that sabermetrics have influenced the thoughts of negotiators and valuation of players, this study demonstrates that the effect of advanced metrics on salary has grown in recent years. Second, while large gaps in salary filings reflect large gaps in valuation and longer roads to compromise, I argue that given the constraints of FOA, players entering a hearing bear the risk of losing large sums of money and therefore settle early when the difference in bids grows.

## DATA OVERVIEW

The data drawn for this study consist of pooled cross-sectional data aggregated from two major sources—MLB Trade Rumors and Fangraphs—and contains arbitration filing information and performance indicators for all players who filed contract figures for arbitration in a seven-year period from 2011 through 2017. The performance statistics are lagged one year, such that a player's value in year $t$ will be evaluated using performance in year $t-1$. While considering career averages for statistics is an alternate option for evaluation, arbitration-eligible players often face higher variation in year-over-year playing time. As such, the best indicator of a player's projected usage during the span of the one-year arbitrated contract is his usage in the preceding year. Overall, this creates a population of 269 players used in the analysis: 146 pitchers and 123 batters.[1] The majority of players in the population are only present for one year and do not reenter the arbitration process. Only nine players entered the arbitration process the traditional-maximum three times and no players reached the Super Two maximum of four arbitration filings.

The variables contained in the data consist of descriptive variables—Name, Year, Team, and Position—and filing data taken from MLB Trade Rumors' annual arbitration tracker, which aggregates arbitration filings and settlements. These filing variables contain both the Team Filing and Player Filing, as well as Midpoint, Settlement Amount, Bid Difference, a binary variable for arbitration hearings, Hearing Outcome, Salary in year *t-1*, Service Time, and a binary variable for Super Two status.

The performance metrics themselves are drawn from Fangraphs and contain four main categories. First are traditional counting statistics such as at-bats and hits for batters, and innings pitched and strikeouts for pitchers. The second group consists of rate statistics, which are averages such as ERA or weighted averages such as slugging average. The third group consists of sabermetrics that employ advanced mathematical methods in their calculation. These include weighted on-base average (wOBA) for hitters and batting average on balls in play (BABIP) for pitchers. The final group consists of batted-ball data such as ground-ball percentage and contact rate. Ultimately, this yields a set of 59 variables for pitchers and 43 variables for hitters.

### Summary and Descriptive Statistics

Table 1 and Table 2 compare salary filing, settlement information, and select performance metrics for pitchers and hitters, respectively. Generally, the group of hitters has slightly higher salary filings and settlements than pitchers, with the mean settlement for hitters being just over $4 million and the mean settlement for pitchers at $3.7 million. Both groups had average bid differences of around $1 million and settlements for either group were just below the midpoint between the two bids (i.e. closer to the team filings). In addition, both groups had mean service times of around 3.6 years, indicating that the average player is entering the arbitration process for the first or second time. This comes as no surprise given that players with more service time may have signed long-term contracts; teams sought to avoid incremental annual raises and players sought long-term guarantees of money.

In terms of performance, the group of players filing for salary arbitration exhibits noticeable variation from average players. Pitchers have pitched to an ERA of 3.19 and an ERA- of 80.33. As such, the mean pitcher in the population has an ERA 19.77 percent better than the league-average pitcher.[2] In terms of WAR, this sums to 1.67 wins above a replacement-level player over the course of a season.

The average hitter has a triple-slash line (average/on-base average/slugging average) of .268/.334/.432 and a wRC+ of 109.4, indicating performance 9.4 percent better than the average major-league hitter. These hitters have produced a mean WAR of 2.6, commensurate to a solid starting player. Clearly, the average

player entering the filing period of the arbitration process is better than the average MLB player. This may be a case of selective sampling, since only good players are tendered contracts and offered the option to enter arbitration. However, it could also be an indication that better players are relatively more willing to challenge their teams and seek higher salaries rather than settling early.

Table 3 examines the group of players who entered an arbitration hearing. Here, pitchers followed the arbitration process to completion more frequently than hitters: 21.23 percent of pitchers in the population went to arbitration hearings, compared to 11.29 percent of hitters. Pitchers also lost their hearings more frequently than hitters, only winning 13 of the 31 cases (42 percent), while hitters won seven of 14. The average award in these cases was $3.4M for pitchers and $4.2M for hitters. When compared to the entire group of players who exchanged salary figures, the mean settlement through hearings for pitchers was roughly $300,000 lower than the overall mean settlement. For hitters, the hearing settlements were roughly $200,000 higher than the overall mean.

## EMPIRICAL CONSIDERATIONS AND MODEL DESIGN

Given various qualities of the data such as small sample sizes, repeated cross sections, and potential for omitted variable bias, many considerations must be made in developing an effective empirical strategy and in designing a model. Considering these factors, the first two models below analyze why players and teams choose arbitration hearings over settlement, and the final model attempts to identify growing skill premiums and the dollar-value of performance indicators.

### Predicting Likelihood to Enter Arbitration Hearing

For the FOA models, particular considerations must be made for the independent variable, as there are multiple methods for constructing the regressor. First, the absolute difference in bids can be useful in determining how larger differences and a perceived gulf in filings impact hearing likelihood. However, this introduces bias from large contracts, which naturally have larger gaps in salary filings. This bias can be controlled through the inclusion of a dummy variable for the size of the contract.

To address additional omitted variable bias, further control variables are placed for performance—assuming that the quality of performance affects a player's arbitration incentives—and for Super Two status—assuming that the level effects of early arbitration have an effect as well. This yields the following model, where the probability of a hearing is dependent on the coefficient $\beta_1$ multiplied by the absolute difference between bids plus the effects of the controls:

$$\Pr(H = 1) = \beta_{0+}\beta_1|Bid_{player} - Bid_{team}| + \beta_2 Midpoint + \beta_3 WAR + \beta_4 SuperTwo + \varepsilon$$

Alternatively to the absolute difference regressor, using a relative independent variable that measures the bid difference relative to the size of the contract combines the effects of contract size and bid difference into one variable. The controls for WAR and Super Two status remain, yielding the following model:

$$\Pr(H = 1) = \beta_{0+}\beta_1\left(\frac{|Bid_{player} - Bid_{team}|}{Midpoint}\right) + \beta_2 WAR + \beta_3 SuperTwo + \varepsilon$$

### Relationships between Measures of Player Value and Salary Filing

For the performance metric valuation models, the high level entry and exit of players between each annual cross section necessitates considerations in the empirical approach. Table 4 illustrates the two main problems with conducting regressions at an annual cross section level to measure changes over time. First, compared to pooled data, each individual year may not have enough observations to provide insight on the relationships between performance and salary. Second, inconsistent variation in mean filing between years may surround the data in too much random noise to decipher trends. The peak mean filing was in 2016 at $5.66 million and the lowest was the next year, 2017, at $3.92 million. A remedy to these problems is to use three-year rolling periods as opposed to annual cross sections. This method allows proper analysis by creating a larger sample size in each period and also tunes out sample-related noise by pooling adjacent years together.

Furthermore, the risk of multicollinearity between independent variables must be considered as well. As players with strong performance in some areas likely have strong results in others, using multiple performance variables in the same regression may bias coefficients and reduce significance. As an example, a player with low ERA would likely also have a low FIP (fielding independent pitching). Including both of these variables in the same regression would dilute the effects of either measure on salary and reduce the accuracy of the model.

In order to isolate the values of individual metrics and skills, each independent variable must be tested for its effect on salary in separate regressions. This comes with some limitations, as the explanatory power of each coefficient may not be precise. However, by comparing the fit, standard errors, and coefficients for each independent variable across regressions, the model can provide some insight on which metrics are more relevant in determining salary than others.

These two major considerations produce the following model, where a regression for each individual performance metric S is repeated five times, restricting each iteration to a different three-year rolling period in the data set:

$$Settlement_i = \beta_0 + \beta_1 S_i + \beta_2 Service + \beta_3 Positional + \varepsilon$$

Here, the dependent variable being considered is not either bid, but rather the settled or arbitrated salary. The model allows us to measure whether $\beta_1$—the dollar value of a one-unit increase in performance metric $S$—has changed over time. If the literature is true, then the $\beta_1$ and statistical significance for advanced metrics are expected to rise in more recent periods.

To address omitted variable bias in these regressions, controls are placed for service time and for positional adjustments. Since players generally receive strong raises for each year regardless of their performance, players with more service time will naturally have higher salaries, and controlling for this in model becomes crucial.

For positional controls, certain positions are frequently paid more lucratively than others. For example, while starting pitchers and relief pitchers may have similar levels of performance as measured by ERA, the starting pitcher would be compensated more due to his higher utilization. In addition, certain forms of production are more valuable from one position than another. Since most first and third basemen have higher offensive profiles, each marginal unit of offensive production is less valuable from these positions.

The most effective method to create these positional controls is to create a dummy variable for relief pitchers in the pitcher regressions and a dummy variable for defense-premium positions in the hitter regressions. Here, the selected defense-premium positions are catcher, second base, and shortstop. While center field is also considered a defense-first position, many outfielders play games at multiple outfield positions and therefore the entire group of outfielders is not considered defense-premium.

## RESULTS

Testing these models, the results indicate strong risk aversion by both teams and players, significantly affecting the likelihood to enter an arbitration hearing. In addition, the results show the proliferation of advanced analytics and skill-based over outcome-based valuation of major-league players.

### Examining Likelihood to Go to Hearing

As seen in Table 5, both models—measuring the bid difference either relative to contract size or in absolute terms—demonstrate highly significant negative coefficients, indicating that players with large gaps in salary filings are less likely to enter hearings. In fact, in the aggregate sample of players, an increase of $100,000 in bid difference reduces the likelihood of a hearing by 2.7 percent and a 1 percent increase in bid difference to midpoint ratio decreases the likelihood of a hearing by 1.1 percent. These figures present an incredibly significant effect considering only 16.73 percent of players in the sample even made it to a hearing. Quite evidently, teams and players are incredibly risk-averse and fear losing the arbitration hearing and being forced to agree to a suboptimal salary. Therefore, the incentive to settle is driven up by higher bid differences.

Furthermore, in the aggregate sample, an increase in filing midpoint by $100,000 increases hearing likelihood by 0.56 percent. As such, all else equal, players with higher filing midpoints are more likely to head to a hearing. By contrast, WAR has a negative coefficient. Therefore, while WAR indicates that better players are less likely to head to a hearing, the positive coefficient on midpoint states that "better" players are more likely to head to a hearing.

Though these indicate opposite effects, considering the effect of a high midpoint with WAR constant and vice versa, the theory provides explanatory qualities. A player with a high bid that inflates the midpoint—holding performance constant—is more likely to head to an arbitration hearing. Most likely, the group captured here is players with poor levels of performance but an aggressive salary filing—an easy candidate to be challenged in a hearing. By contrast, an increase in WAR—holding contract size constant—makes players less likely to go to an arbitration hearing. This likely indicates that good players are privileged during the arbitration process, given more time and effort in negotiations, and offered more opportunities to settle early.

The final variable of interest in these regressions is the control for Super Two status. The models indicate that Super Two status increases the likelihood of hearings substantially, by 14.3–16.9 percent, depending on the model. As such, these young players seem more likely to challenge their teams on salary evaluations. This too comes as no surprise since challenging a team in a player's first (and bonus) year of arbitration eligibility can lead to significant level effects in subsequent arbitration hearings. A salary increase from the league minimum of $545,000 to even $1 million can snowball into much larger raises in the following years.

Interestingly, Super Two pitchers are even more likely to enter an arbitration hearing, 18.9–24.5 percent more likely than non-Super Two pitchers. One likely explanation is that pitchers are far more susceptible to injury and therefore are more likely to be non-tendered in subsequent periods. As a result, pitchers may challenge their teams more while their performance is commensurate to a higher salary, securing earnings in the immediate term.

As a final robustness check on the effect of salary filings and bid differences on likelihood to enter trial, the initial specifications were tested with an alternative performance control, seen in Table 6. FIP for pitchers and wRC + for hitters were chosen as metrics related to and as components of WAR, but still incomplete measures of total performance since they do not aggregate other factors of performance measurement like WAR does. With these controls as well, the coefficients on the variables of interest retain their signs, significance, and relative size. Even with alternative and incomplete controls, the effect of risk aversion continues to dominate the decision on early settlement versus an arbitration hearing.

### Factors Affecting and Correlated with Filings

Examining the salary filings themselves, players and teams seem to be incorporating more skill-based evaluations, using advanced metrics to determine player value. For both hitters and pitchers, conventional measures of value are slowly being replaced by sabermetric and batted-ball alternatives that emphasize more precise evaluations of talent rather than evaluation of outcomes. The results from the regression here are displayed in a line graph in order to demonstrate the changes in coefficients over time and to allow comparison of the compensation effects of various metrics. Graphs 1 and 2 illustrate the relationship of select metrics with salary over time. The vertical position of each point shows the dollar value per unit of production for the given metric—its value—while the size of the point shows the statistical significance of these metrics—the accuracy in predicting salary.[3] Essentially, metrics with a high statistical significance are linked closely to salary and are useful tools for predicting salary; metrics with high dollar values are worth more per unit.

For pitchers in particular, the evidence points toward the fact that traditional measures of pitcher success and durability such as innings pitched, wins, and ERA have fallen in prominence compared to alternatives such as FIP and true ERA (tERA).

As seen in Graph 1, the relationship between innings pitched and salary decreases over the periods examined with each additional inning being worth $23,460 in the first rolling period but only $15,770 in the last period, representing a 33 percent decline. In addition, the significance of the coefficients drops as well from above 99 percent significance initially to 90 percent significance at the end.

This decline in the relationship between IP and salary can perhaps be attributed to the growing dominance of relievers and short leashes on starting pitchers. As dominant relievers such as Dellin Betances, Zack Britton, and Kenley Jansen have entered the sample of arbitration-eligible players, the emphasis on innings pitched and workhorse-style durability has waned in favor of effectiveness in run prevention. And while relievers are still compensated at a lower level than starting pitchers, their influence on the game's strategy—leading to shorter starts and more "bullpenning"—has manifested in a reduction of the effect of IP on salary.

In addition to this, other traditional metrics of pitcher value—wins and ERA—have seen middling and inconsistent relationships with salary in the rolling periods. These metrics have seen their relationship with salary vary inconsistently between periods with total insignificance in some years and strong relationships in others without any distinct pattern. As such, while wins and ERA may have some influence on salary, there is a possible indication that other factors and measures may have a more influential effect.

What then has replaced IP, wins, and ERA? Alternatives such as FIP and tERA.[4] FIP only takes into account the factors a pitcher can control, excluding all cases in which the fielders interact with the outcome of a play—thereby acting as a more skill-oriented version of ERA. While FIP was significant in the earliest period, its significance grew from 95 percent initially to above 99 percent in the final period, evidencing an increasingly strong relationship with salary. Much more starkly, the compensation for a one-unit change in FIP changed from $665,375 in the earliest period to $1,299,270 in the ultimate period:

nearly double the effect. By comparison, the effect of a unit change in ERA—measured on the same scale as FIP—was level at around $750,000 across all rolling periods.

True ERA (tERA) attempts a similar method of evaluation but instead of entirely ignoring fielding, it incorporates effects of batted-ball data, crediting pitchers who are able to produce weak contact—thereby representing an even more skill-oriented version of FIP. Here, the effect of tERA makes a more remarkable climb than FIP, beginning at 90 percent significance and a $467,407 effect per unit on settlement and ending at a 99 percent significant, $1,087,499 effect per unit. As such, pitcher skills such as inducing groundballs and producing popups have been compensated well, even when conventional and biased measures of success may not indicate value. Teams have begun to compensate the peripherals and potential for success rather than the incidence of success itself.

For hitters as well, the movement away from traditionally valued statistics is evidenced in trends. Examining the traditional triple-slash statistics, each demonstrates a different impact on salary. In Graph 2, batting average showed insignificant coefficients in any given period and revealed relatively smaller coefficients, evidencing that high-average hitters are not compensated strongly. On-base average factors in walks and hit-by-pitches and is compensated slightly more per one-standard deviation change. OBA is also significant at least at the 90 percent level, reflecting the post-*Moneyball* evaluation of players in which OBA has replaced AVG as the conventional measure of offensive prowess. Finally, slugging average evidences the strong relationship between compensation and power. In the first period, SLG was compensated at $1,397,602 per standard deviation, nearly twice the value of a unit of OBA or AVG. Clearly, power hitters are valued strongly; this has not changed dramatically over the course of time.

In fact, alternative methods for evaluating power hitters—or even potential power hitters—have become more significant in salary settlements. Fly balls are highly valuable for hitters and hitting the ball in the air consistently is a mark of a highly skilled player. Fly balls are more likely to fall for an extra base hit or home run, and even in the worst-case scenario where they result in an out, fly balls can still drive in runs via sacrifice flies. As such, fly-ball rate can be used as a proxy for run-producing potential even when SLG might not capture the actualized run production. As seen in Graph 2, Fly-ball rate has made a dramatic change in correlation with salary. Initially, FB% had weak correlations and insignificant coefficients, with a 1 percent increase equating only $94,503 in additional salary. However, in the most recent period—and post Statcast introduction—a 1 percent increase in FB% resulted in a $606,693 rise in settlement and is significant at the 95 percent level. This follows a similar pattern to the tERA trend where teams and players are able to isolate and effectively leverage tools that are correlated with success even when this success hasn't been measured.

The fly-ball rate case itself may be a manifestation of a trend in baseball data in the Statcast era, the "fly-ball revolution." Beginning with the introduction of Statcast, the compensation for higher fly-ball rates began to take off. Recently, high profile names such as J. D. Martinez and Justin Turner made marked differences in their career paths by adding loft to the ball; fly balls are in vogue in baseball. Increased compensation for fly-ball heavy hitters through the arbitration process is the most recent manifestation of this. Even though the Statcast measure cannot be deployed in an arbitration hearing, its effect can be felt through proxies such as fly-ball rate, furthering evidence of the growing impact of advanced metrics and modern strategies on salary.

## Conclusions

Clearly, when it comes to arbitration hearings, risk aversion seems to be a dominant factor in considering whether to head to an arbitration hearing or settle early. Teams and players are unwilling to risk the difference between their bids when this gap increases and are thus brought together toward early settlement. This stands as a testament to the success of the final-offer arbitration system in promoting compromise. And while controversial hearings—such as those of Stroman in 2018 and Betances in 2017—characterized by passive-aggressive Twitter rants and inflammatory media statements will always occur, these are by and large an exception to the trend in arbitration. The arbitration system promotes a convergence in bids, and when this convergence doesn't exist, compromise becomes all the more important. Good players are privileged with greater emphasis on striking accord early, outlandish bids are challenged, and young players are ready to take risks. All evidence a healthy and functional system.

Furthermore, in terms of the proliferation of advanced metrics and analysis in the evaluation of players, the general buckets of valuable skills have not changed: run prevention for pitchers and power for hitters are still valued at a premium. However, the tools and measures used to evaluate these skills have certainly changed over time. Less of a premium is being placed on outcome and more on ability. And with increased tools to measure these capabilities, players are being rewarded for the potential to achieve even when the actual achievement may not reach commensurate levels. Relief pitchers are being rewarded for their effectiveness at higher rates despite limited innings pitched. Batters are being rewarded for factors correlated with power rather than the true incidence of power itself. Clearly, both teams and players are becoming much smarter in their evaluation and in their presentation of cases to arbitration panels.

Revisiting the three cases above—Betts, Stroman, and Schoop—the implications of the AL East's arbitration story lines are evident. Betts was not the most likely candidate to head to an arbitration hearing; the $3 million difference between Betts and the Red Sox was incredibly high and reflected an enormous risk for either party entering a hearing. Furthermore, as one of the best right fielders in the American League, Betts's case likely drew significant attention from Boston and was unlikely to hurtle toward a hearing. The predicted path for Betts was likely closer to Schoop's one-year deal or a long-term contract that bought out his arbitration eligibility. By contrast, Stroman may represent the classic arbitration case: a low-risk hearing for either party, bargaining over a small fraction of their bids. And while Stroman expressed his frustration on Twitter following the hearing, history shows that the Stromans of the world will likely end up there again. Ultimately, the final-offer arbitration system does its job. Those who disagree widely tend to work toward compromise, while those who disagree only a little take a chance and roll the dice. ∎

## Works Cited in Literature Review

Tyler Wasserman, "Determinants of Major League Baseball Player Salaries," *Surface* (Spring 2013), https://surface.syr.edu/honors_capstone/99/.

Brian Pollack, "What Gets Paid? Analyzing the Major League Baseball Contract Market" (honors thesis, Duke University, 2017), https://dukespace.lib.duke.edu/dspace/bitstream/handle/10161/14325/Pollack2017.pdf?sequence=1.

Michael Carrell and Louis Manchise, "At Impasse? Consider Final Offer Arbitration ," *The Negotiator Magazine*, December 2013–January 2014, http://negotiatormagazine.com/pages.php?a=AR637&p=1.

Jeff Monhait, "Baseball Arbitration: An ADR Success," *Journal of Sports and Entertainment Law* 4, 2013. http://harvardjsel.com/wp-content/uploads/2013/06/Monhait.pdf.

Paul L. Burgess and Daniel R. Marburger, "Do Negotiated and Arbitrated Salaries Differ under Final-Offer Arbitration?" *Industrial and Labor Relations Review* 46, no. 3, April 1, 1993, https://doi.org/10.1177/001979399304600307.

Table 1.  Pitchers Summary

| n | Pitchers 146 | | | |
|---|---|---|---|---|
| | Mean | St. Dev | Minimum | Maximum |
| Player Filing | $4,519,623.00 | $3,092,767.00 | $875,000.00 | $21,500,000.00 |
| Team Filing | $3,448,904.00 | $2,358,718.00 | $725,000.00 | $17,000,000.00 |
| Settlement | $3,786,983.00 | $2,380,395.00 | $800,000.00 | $11,325,000.00 |
| Bid Difference | $1,070,719.00 | $937,014.70 | $50,000.00 | $5,500,000.00 |
| Service Time | 3.65 | 0.97 | 2.13 | 6.13 |
| AVG | 0.229 | 0.036 | 0.119 | 0.305 |
| ERA | 3.19 | 1.02 | 0.00 | 6.15 |
| Kper9 | 8.59 | 2.51 | 0.00 | 17.67 |
| WAR | 1.67 | 1.46 | -0.60 | 7.30 |
| ERA- | 80.33 | 25.00 | 0.00 | 140.00 |

Table 2.  Hitters Summary

| n | Hitters 123 | | | |
|---|---|---|---|---|
| | Mean | St. Dev | Minimum | Maximum |
| Player Filing | $4,796,748.00 | $2,646,750.00 | $1,000,000.00 | $12,000,000.00 |
| Team Filing | $3,623,618.00 | $2,176,230.00 | $700,000.00 | $11,350,000.00 |
| Settlement | $3,984,462.00 | $2,364,090.00 | $700,000.00 | $10,550,000.00 |
| Bid Difference | $1,173,130.00 | $754,985.70 | $200,000.00 | $3,400,000.00 |
| Service Time | 3.58 | 0.90 | 2.13 | 5.17 |
| AVG | 0.268 | 0.028 | 0.174 | 0.359 |
| OBP | 0.334 | 0.031 | 0.216 | 0.414 |
| SLG | 0.432 | 0.069 | 0.197 | 0.633 |
| WAR | 2.60 | 2.07 | -1.30 | 8.80 |
| wRC+ | 109.40 | 24.51 | 8.00 | 179.00 |

Table 3.  Arbitration Hearing Summary

| | Pitchers | Hitters | Overall |
|---|---|---|---|
| n | 146 | 123 | 269 |
| Hearings | 31 | 14 | 45 |
| % Hearings | 21.23 | 11.38 | 16.73 |
| Player Victory | 13 | 7 | 20 |
| Team Victory | 18 | 7 | 25 |
| Player Victory % | 41.94 | 50.00 | 44.44 |
| Mean Settlement | $3,409,355.00 | $4,191,071.00 | $3,591,630.00 |

Table 4.  Mean Player Filing by Year

| | n | Mean Player Filings |
|---|---|---|
| 2011 | 33 | $4,982,576.00 |
| 2012 | 44 | $4,844,889.00 |
| 2013 | 35 | $4,172,143.00 |
| 2014 | 39 | $4,391,667.00 |
| 2015 | 55 | $4,467,727.00 |
| 2016 | 34 | $5,663,088.00 |
| 2017 | 29 | $3,915,517.00 |
| Total | 269 | $4,679,207.00 |

**Table 5. FOA Regressions**

### Probability of Hearing (Probit —Marginal Effects)

| | Dependent variable: Hearing | | | | | |
|---|---|---|---|---|---|---|
| | **Pitchers** | | **Hitters** | | **Total** | |
| (Bid Dif/Mid)*100 | -0.012*** | | -0.009*** | | -0.011*** | |
| | -0.012 | | -0.019 | | -0.01 | |
| Bid Dif/100K | | -0.036*** | | -0.018*** | | -0.027*** |
| | | -0.039 | | -0.041 | | -0.027 |
| Mid/100K | | 0.006*** | | 0.005*** | | 0.006*** |
| | | -0.009 | | -0.01 | | -0.007 |
| WAR | -0.023 | 0.005 | -0.031** | -0.036** | -0.035*** | -0.032** |
| | -0.104 | -0.125 | -0.102 | -0.112 | -0.069 | -0.078 |
| Super Two | 0.245*** | 0.188** | 0.099 | 0.100 | 0.169*** | 0.143** |
| | -0.368 | -0.367 | -0.47 | -0.467 | -0.283 | -0.281 |
| Constant | 0.113 | -0.144** | 0.097 | 0.141** | 0.115** | -0.672*** |
| | -0.346 | -0.308 | -0.509 | -0.415 | -0.28 | -0.237 |
| Observations | 146 | 146 | 123 | 123 | 269 | 269 |
| Log Likelihood | -59.275 | -58.198 | -32.264 | -34.301 | -93.075 | -95.238 |
| Akaike Inf. Crit. | 126.551 | 126.395 | 72.529 | 78.601 | 194.149 | 200.476 |

Note: *p<0.1; **p<0.05; ***p<0.01

**Table 6. FOA Robustness Check**

### Probability of Hearing (Alternative Controls—Marginal Effects)

| | Dependent variable: Hearing | | | |
|---|---|---|---|---|
| | **Pitchers** | | **Hitters** | |
| (Bid Dif/Mid)*100 | -0.011*** | | -0.009*** | |
| | -0.012 | | -0.017 | |
| Bid Dif/100K | | -0.033*** | | -0.016*** |
| | | -0.038 | | -0.038 |
| Mid/100K | | 0.006*** | | 0.004*** |
| | | -0.009 | | -0.01 |
| FIP | 0.081** | 0.063 | | |
| | -0.181 | -0.184 | | |
| wRC+ | | | -0.002** | -0.002* |
| | | | -0.008 | -0.009 |
| Super Two | 0.205** | 0.157* | 0.070 | 0.077 |
| | -0.379 | -0.377 | -0.48 | -0.46 |
| Constant | -0.229 | -0.375** | 0.283* | 0.035 |
| | -0.72 | -0.737 | -0.997 | -0.805 |
| Observations | 146 | 146 | 123 | 123 |
| Log Likelihood | -57.71 | -57.041 | -32.694 | -35.567 |
| Akaike Inf. Crit. | 123.42 | 124.083 | 73.387 | 81.134 |

Note: *p<0.1; **p<0.05; ***p<0.01

**Graph 1. Pitcher Compensation Trends**

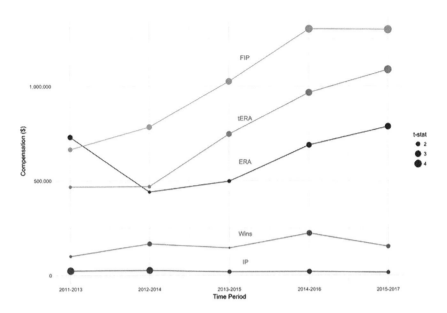

**Graph 2. Hitter Compensation Trends**

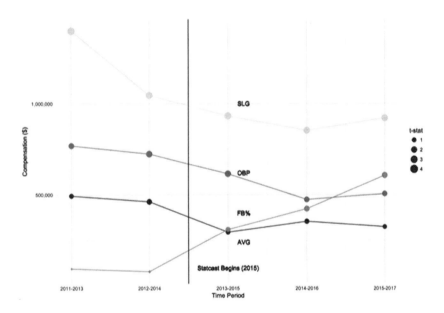

## Notes

1. Jarrod Parker (Oakland, 2015) was omitted from the analysis despite filing for salary arbitration and losing his hearing against the Athletics since Parker underwent Tommy John surgery and did not play in 2014, the year preceding his arbitration hearing. David Ortiz (Boston, 2012) was omitted since he did not enter the arbitration process as a conventionally arbitration-eligible player but as a free-agent who elected arbitration over entering free-agency.

2. 100 (Indexed League Average ERA-) - 80.33 (ERA- for population) = 19.77%.

3. For rate statistics, one unit of production is equal to a one standard deviation change in the metric.

4. While both tERA and Skill Interactive ERA (SIERA) incorporate the effects of batted-ball data in their evaluation of pitchers, tERA is used in this analysis over SIERA since SIERA is applied in more prognostic and predictive contexts while tERA is used to evaluate past performance compared to a traditional ERA.

# Team Batting Average

## *A Comprehensive Analysis*

### Douglas Jordan and David Macias

It's July 1 of any year. Your favorite team has played about half the season and has been struggling at the plate recently. The team batting average (BA) is .234 compared to the league average of .246. This solitary datum indicates that the team's BA is well below the league average. But what is the history of team BA over the course of the season? Has the team been consistently below average or is this a result of their recent struggles at the plate?

One of the primary results of the analysis done for this paper is to show what happens to team BA over the course of a season and to see if there are any league-wide similarities over the course of a season. Once this analysis is complete, we will be able to establish how many games into the season are necessary to draw a conclusion about a team's batting ability.

At the beginning of a season, people will sometimes say it's too early to draw any conclusions about a team. For example, on April 12, 2018, with the San Francisco Giants' record at 5–6, Grant Cohn wrote, "It's way too early to make statements etched in stone about the Giants."[1] But just 17 days later when the Giants' record was 13–14, C.W. Nevius stated, "[D]on't tell us it is early. If last year taught us anything, it is that the way a team starts a season can be an excellent predictor of how it ends a season."[2] How long does it take to be able to draw a reasonable conclusion? Does it require 50 games, 40 games, 20 games, or is it even fewer? The surprising conclusion from this analysis is that at the 16-game mark (roughly 10 percent of the season) you can be fairly certain whether a team will be weak-hitting or strong-hitting for the entire season.

## METHODOLOGY

Retrosheet provides game logs for every MLB game played during a season. These game logs provide hitting, pitching, and fielding data for both teams, which include hits and at-bats for each team for the game. In order to perform the analysis in this paper we wrote a Visual Basic program to extract hits and at-bats from the Retrosheet data for each game during a season. The

data were aggregated game by game. This allowed team BA to be calculated after every game and a season-long series of team BA to be constructed. MLB data for the five years 2013–17 were used to provide the data for the analysis. The final team BA for every team, for each year, was compared with the final team BA shown in Baseball-Reference.com in order to ensure that the calculations were accurate. No discrepancies were found.

## RESULTS: PART 1

The data described above are used to produce a graph of a team's BA as the season progresses. Figure 1 shows the plots for four randomly chosen NL teams in 2017.

Team BA varies considerably over the course of a season. The Giants' BA declined consistently over the first 35 games of the season before bottoming at .225, and then climbing thereafter to finish at about .250. Philadelphia's BA peaked at .260 at game 34, then declined to .240 over approximately the next 20 games, before finishing at .250. Seeing how team BA changes through a season is interesting, but those raw data can be used to answer more interesting questions. The team BA at the end of the season is the most accurate representation of how they batted in aggregate. We can use the data to find out how quickly teams approach their final season BA. To do that, the difference between the team BA at any point in the season and the final team BA is calculated. The results for the same four teams in Figure 1 are shown in Figure 2.

The graphs shown in Figure 2 are all within about five points of the final team BA by game 120 of the season, and three of the four are within five points by game 100. Except for the Cubs, the Figure 2 curves are roughly flat after game 100, which suggests that team BA for most teams doesn't change too much after that point of the season. However, four teams is too small a sample to draw any general conclusions, so this analysis is repeated for all MLB teams for 2017. The results are shown in Figure 3.

The results shown in Figure 3 clarify the smaller sample result in Figure 2. In 2017, team BA rose from game 20 to game 70 for MLB. For MLB as a whole,

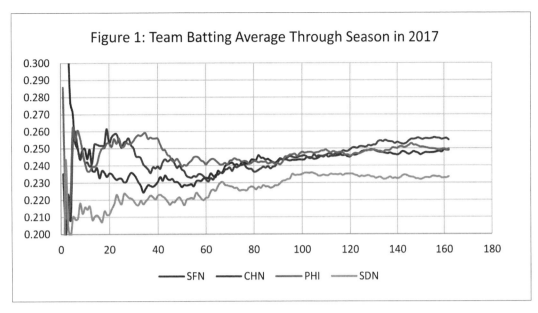

Figure 1: Team Batting Average Through Season in 2017

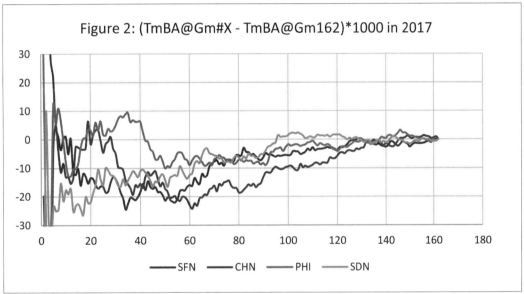

Figure 2: (TmBA@Gm#X - TmBA@Gm162)*1000 in 2017

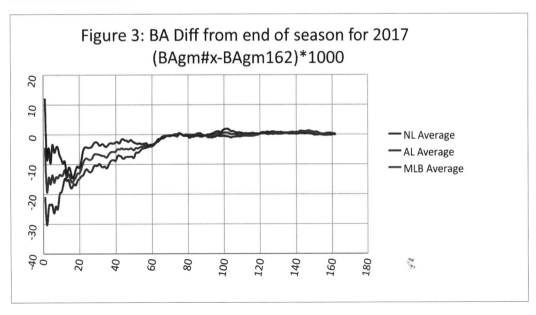

Figure 3: BA Diff from end of season for 2017
(BAgm#x-BAgm162)*1000

team BA rose by about 13 points from game 20 to game 70. Thirteen points is a large increase. On average, team BA improved significantly until about halfway through the season. Of course, this is only one year's results. Does the same thing happen in other years? Figure 4 shows what happened in MLB overall for the years 2013–17.

Figure 4 shows that the general trend of team BA increasing over the first half of the season also occurs in 2013–17. In addition, the tendency increases from 2013–17. The increase in team BA over the first half of the season is larger in 2017 than in any of the other years.

This result matters because people may draw erroneous conclusions if they don't know that team batting averages tend to rise until about mid-season. For example, in an article about no-hitters written roughly one-quarter of the way through the 2018 season, Dave Sheinin states, "Meantime, the league wide batting average of .245 (down 10 points from 2017 and 26 points from 1999) is at a 46-year low."[3] Sheinin is comparing end of season MLB baseball batting averages with an early season MLB batting average. Based on the result of this paper's analysis, it's very likely that the MLB batting average at the end of the 2018 season would be higher than .245, which would refute the point Sheinin is trying to make.

Finally, the Figure 4 result provides an answer to the perennial question of whether pitchers or hitters have an advantage early in the season. Jason Catania explored this question at the beginning of the 2014 season and concluded, "So while you might have expected pitchers to have an advantage early on relative to the rest of the season…the results don't always bear that out, at least in recent years."[4] In contrast to what Catania found, Figure 4 shows (at least recently) that pitchers have an advantage over hitters in terms of batting average during the early stages of a season.

## RESULTS: PART 2A

There is another interesting question that can be examined, given the time series of team BA that was used to generate the previous results: How many games into the season does it take to determine a team's batting prowess? Obviously, a game or two is not sufficient, but how many games into the season are required to draw a reasonably accurate conclusion about whether a team will be a strong- or weak-hitting team over the course of the season? "Common wisdom" has said that it can take 30–40 games to know the true character of a team. Those numbers are anecdotal. What do the actual data say?

To analyze this question, we compared team batting averages to the league average at 16-game intervals through the first half of the season. Sixteen games is chosen because it represents about 10 percent of the season. Those differences are compared to the difference from the league batting average at the end of the season. For example, in 2017, the Giants were batting .233 after 16 games, while the NL overall batting average was .240. At the end of the season, the Giants were batting .249 while the NL overall batting average was .254. The differences between these pairs of numbers, –.007 and –.005, are multiplied by 1000 to become one point in Figure 5. The same analysis is done for all fifteen NL teams for 2013–17 to generate the 75 datum points shown in Figure 5. The same analysis is done separately for the AL (because of the designated hitter) with the results shown in Figure 6.

A linear regression is run to establish the relationship between team BA differences at game 16 and team BA differences at the end of the season. The regression lines are the dotted lines in the two figures, with the equations and regression coefficients shown in the upper right corner of each figure. The coefficients of 0.26 for the NL and 0.21 for the AL show two things. First, the relationship between the differences in team BA at game 16 and team BA at game 162 is positive, so a higher (lower) team BA difference at game 16 will tend to indicate a higher (lower) team BA difference at game 162. The magnitude of the coefficients indicates that if the team BA at game 16 is 10 points above (below) the league average, then the best estimate of team batting average at game 162 will be 2.6 (NL) and 2.1 (AL) points above (below) the league average at game 162. The t-statistic associated with the NL coefficient of 0.26 is 4.8 and the t-statistic associated with the AL coefficient of 0.21 is 4.6. Both of these t-statistics are statistically significant at the one percent level, and indicate that there is a strong relationship between the difference in BA at game 16 and the difference in BA at game 162. In other words, looking at a team's BA compared to the league average at game 16 of the season can give you a pretty good idea of how the team's BA will be compared to the league at the end of the season. To see the diagnostics associated with the regressions, contact the author for figures.

## RESULTS: PART 2B

The fact that there is a statistically significant relationship between team BA differences at games 16 and 162 is important, but not very useful in practice. However, it would be useful to know how likely it is that a weak (strong) hitting team at game 16 will be a weak

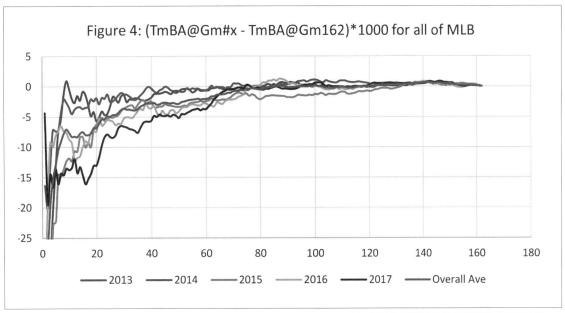

Figure 4: (TmBA@Gm#x - TmBA@Gm162)*1000 for all of MLB

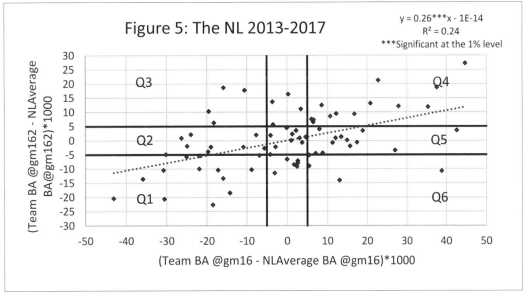

Figure 5: The NL 2013-2017

$y = 0.26{***}x - 1E{-}14$
$R^2 = 0.24$
***Significant at the 1% level

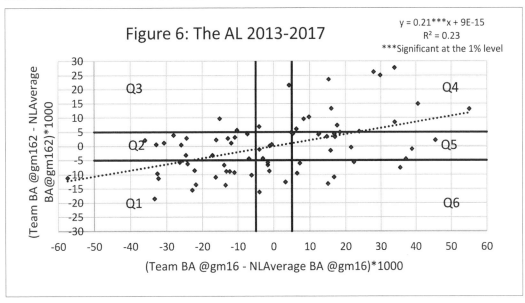

Figure 6: The AL 2013-2017

$y = 0.21{***}x + 9E{-}15$
$R^2 = 0.23$
***Significant at the 1% level

(strong) hitting team through the rest of the season. The data in Figures 5 and 6 allow us to answer that question. We ignore teams whose BA is within five points of the league average at game 16 (those between the two heavy vertical lines). These teams are hitting near the league average, so for one of them to finish the season above or below the league average would not be very surprising.

That leaves Figures 5 and 6 divided into six quadrants that are labeled Q1, Q2 etcetera. The points in Q1 represent teams that were more than five points below the league average at game 16 and were more than five points below the league average at the end of the season. For these teams, their performance at game 16 accurately predicted their below average performance at game 162. Points in Q3 represent teams that were batting more than five points below the league average at game 16 but are more than five points above average at season's end. These teams saw significantly improved batting performance over the course of the season. Similar statements can be made for the teams in Q4 and Q6 except that teams in Q6 saw significantly worse batting performance as the season progressed.

The numbers of teams in each quadrant allows us to assess a probability that a team that is in Q1 or Q4 at game 16 will stay there. For example, in Figure 5, there are 26 teams who were batting more than five points below the league average at game 16. Thirteen of those teams were also batting five points or more below league average at game 162. The analogous numbers for the AL in Figure 6 are 32 and 16. Combining the data for the two leagues together yields a total of 29 out of 58 teams that remained in Q1

between game 16 and game 162. This is exactly half, or 50 percent of the teams. The combined numbers for both leagues in Q4 are 26 out of 60, or 43 percent. These results show that a below-average batting average team at game 16 has a 50 percent chance of being a below-average batting average team for the whole season. The data in Q4 show that above-average hitting teams at game 16 have a 43 percent chance of staying above-average for the whole season. It's also important to note that a below-average hitting team at game 16 has only a 6 out of 58 chance, roughly 10 percent, of ending the season with a BA more than five points above the league average. An above-average hitting team at game 16 has a 10 out of 60 chance, 17 percent, of hitting more than five points below average by the end of the season.

These results suggest that weak or strong hitting teams at game 16 tend to stay that way. But what happens as the season progresses? Data that are applicable at only one point in the season aren't very useful. Therefore the analysis just described was also done at the 32, 48, 64, and 80 game marks of the season. The results are shown in Figure 7.

Figure 7 shows what happens as the season progresses. The Q1 and Q4 results show that the percentages of weak (strong) hitting teams that stay that way over the course of the season increase as the season progresses. For example, in Q1, 70 percent of the teams that are hitting poorly at game 64 of the season will stay that way, compared against 50 percent at game 16. Only two out of 57 teams—3.5 percent—that were hitting below average at game 64 ended the season more than five points above the league average. The Q3 results as a group show that the chances of a

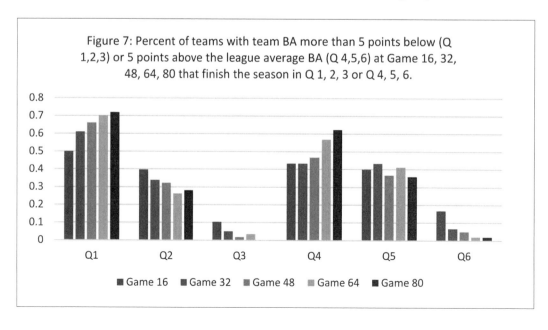

Figure 7: Percent of teams with team BA more than 5 points below (Q 1,2,3) or 5 points above the league average BA (Q 4,5,6) at Game 16, 32, 48, 64, 80 that finish the season in Q 1, 2, 3 or Q 4, 5, 6.

weak hitting team improving to hit five points or more above the league average by the end of the season start at ten percent and decline as the season progresses. It is interesting to compare the Q1 and Q4 results as groups. The lower percentages in Q4 show that it is more likely that teams that are hitting well early in the season will see deteriorating hitting performance. The slightly higher percentages in Q6 as a group compared with Q3 tell the same story.

**CONCLUSION**

Data for 2013–17 show that team batting averages tend to rise over the first half of the season for MLB as a whole (Figure 4). The difference between team BA and the league average at games 16, 32, 48, 64, and 80 is plotted against the difference between team BA and the league average at the end of the season (Figures 5, 6). The results show that there is a statistically significant relationship between these two differences, even at game 16 of the season. In other words, it only takes about 10 percent of the season to get a reasonably good idea if a team is going to be a strong- or weak-batting average team for the whole season. Finally, Figure 7 shows that a team that is batting at least five points below (above) the league batting average at game 16 has a 50 percent (43 percent) chance of hitting more than five points below (above) the league average at the end of the season. ■

**Notes**

1. Grant Cohn, "Missed Opportunity," *The Press Democrat* (Santa Rosa, CA), Sports section, 1, April 12, 2018.
2. C. W. Nevius, "Creaky Giants ship continues to take on water," *The Press Democrat* (Santa Rosa, CA), Sports section, 1, April 29, 2018.
3. Dave Sheinin, "No-hitters (and near-misses) show how MLB is changing—but is it for the better?" *Washington Post*, May 11, 2018. https://www.washingtonpost.com/news/sports/wp/2018/05/11/no-hitters-and-near-misses-show-how-mlb-is-changing-but-is-itfor-the-better/?utm_term=.cc69f31525f1.
4. Jason Catania, "Do Hitters or Pitchers Have the Upper Hand Early in the MLB Season?" April 1, 2014, https://bleacherreport.com/articles/2013296.

# World Series Game Situation Winning Probabilities: Update

## Douglas Jordan

This is a brief update to the article, "World Series Game Situation Winning Probabilities: How often do teams come back from behind?" that appeared in the Fall 2014 *BRJ*. The original paper calculated the probabilities of winning the World Series for all possible game combinations; the update includes data for the five World Series played in 2014–18. Table 1 contains both the original results through the 2013 season, and additional analysis which includes the results for the next five seasons.

**Table 1. Historic Probabilities of Winning for Different World Series Game Situations**

| World Series game situation | Team is | Number of times the team wins WS (to 2013 / to 2018) | Total number of times the WS has stood at this game situation (to 2013 / to 2018) | Percentage of times the team wins the WS given the game situation (to 2013 / to 2018) |
|---|---|---|---|---|
| 1–0 | Ahead | 67 / 70 | | 63.8 / 63.6 |
| 1–0 | Behind | 38 / 40 | 105 / 110 | 36.2 / 36.4 |
| 2–0 | Ahead | 41 / 43 | | 80.4 / 81.1 |
| 2–0 | Behind | 10* / 10* | 51 / 53 | 19.6 / 18.9 |
| 3–0 | Ahead | 24 / 24 | | 100 / 100 |
| 3–0 | Behind | 0 / 0 | 0 / 24 | 0.0 / 0.0 |
| 2–1 | Ahead | 55 / 58 | | 67.9 / 67.4 |
| 2–1 | Behind | 26 / 28 | 81 / 86 | 32.1 / 32.6 |
| 3–1 | Ahead | 38 / 40 | | 88.4 / 87.0 |
| 3–1 | Behind | 5 / 6 | 43 / 46 | 11.6 / 13.0 |
| 3–2 | Ahead | 41 / 43 | | 68.3 / 68.3 |
| 3–2 | Behind | 19 / 20 | 60 / 63 | 31.7 / 31.7 |

\* These ten teams are the: Yankees in 1956, 1958, 1978, 1996; Dodgers in 1955, 1965, 1981; Pirates in 1971; Royals in 1985; Mets in 1986

To summarize the data in the table succinctly: a team that leads the World Series by one game (1–0, 2–1, or 3–2) wins the series approximately two-thirds of the time. A team that leads by two games (2–0 or 3–1) wins the Series roughly 80 percent of the time. This means that it is vitally important for the team that lost Game 1 to win Game 2. History shows that it is very difficult to come back from a 2–0 deficit. The same reasoning applies to Game 4. Game 4 is almost a must-win game for the team that is behind 2–1 in order to avoid falling into a 3–1 hole. Only six teams (see the earlier paper for the list) have ever won the World Series after being down 3–1.

World Series results from 2014–18 illustrate these two ideas. The Mets (2015) and Dodgers (2018) lost the first game of the Series and then failed to win Game 2. Both lost in five games. The Giants (2014) and Dodgers (2017) won Game 4 to tie the Series at two games each. Each of those World Series went the full seven games which gave both of those teams a good chance to win. The Giants did prevail in 2014 while the Dodgers lost to the Astros in 2017.

What impact have the World Series results from 2014–18 had on the data presented in the 2014 article? The biggest change is that the chance of winning for a team that is behind 3–1 increased from 11.6 percent to 13.0 percent. This 12 percent (1.4/11.6) increase in the percent chance of winning is a result of the Cubs coming from behind 3–1 to win the World Series in 2016. The Cubs were only the sixth team in history (out of 46) to come back from that deficit to win. But it was a close call for the Cubs. They won Games 5 and 7 by one run and Game 7 went 10 innings. The other fairly large change is in the 2–0, 0–2 situation. Both the Royals and Red Sox (in 2015 and 2018 respectively) won the first two games and then went on to win the championship. This increases the percentage of teams that have won when being ahead 2–0 from 80.4 percent to 81.1 percent and decreases the percentage of winning for teams that are behind 0–2 from 19.6 percent to 18.9 percent.

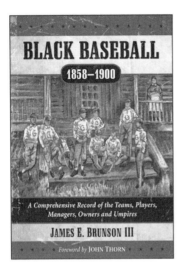
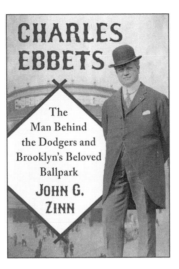
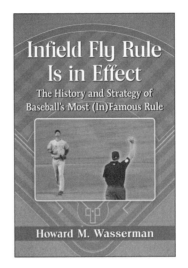
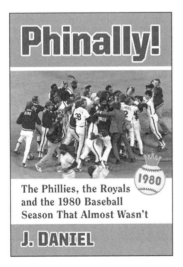

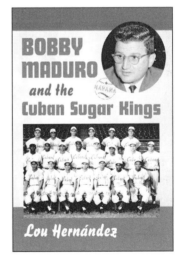

# American League or National League

## *Who Owns New York City?*

### Dusty Turner and Gabriel B. Costa

In the spring of 2017, Quinnipiac University put out a poll that led the media to proclaim that New York was (back to being?) a "National League city" because, although the poll showed the Yankees holding a 48–43% preference among fans upstate, in the city the poll swung 45–43% in favor of the Mets.[1] At about the same time, a local sports radio talk show host made a comment to the effect that, while the Yankees presently "owned" New York, that was not always the case and that in times past, New York had been a "National League" city. Setting aside for a moment that the Quinnipiac poll had a margin of error greater than the 2-percent Mets lead that led to the proclamation, this got us to thinking about whether there was some way to measure when The Big Apple was indeed dominated by fans of the Senior Circuit and when fans of the American League (read: Yankees) were in the majority.

We will investigate this question with both subjective and quantitative approaches. We will take a look at temporal (historical), spatial (geographical), and social (Twitter) aspects of this issue. We will then consider some objectively measurable quantities (victories, attendance figures, head-to-head competitions, social buzz, etc.) to arrive at a plausible conclusion.

### HISTORY AND SUBJECTIVE ANALYSIS

In 1903 three major league teams played within the five boroughs which now comprise New York City. The Giants, Yankees (also known as the Highlanders), and the Dodgers (also called the Robins and the Superbas) all vied for local fans. John McGraw ruled his "Jints" with an iron hand and won a number of pennants and a World Championship (1905). Whether the Dodgers (one pennant) or the Yankees (no pennants) were the second-favorite team in town is immaterial. The New York Giants ruled New York. *From 1903 till 1919, New York was a National League City.*

At that point, one could not easily envision McGraw's Giants succumbing to any challenge in the foreseeable future. In fact, these very Giants would win four successive pennants (1921–24) with world titles in 1921 and 1922. (Who could have predicted that they would not win another World Series for over three decades?)

But Babe Ruth ushered in the Roaring Twenties and his 1920 Yankees would draw over 1,000,000 fans, in the Giants' own Polo Grounds, no less. The Bambino would hit 54 home runs, outhomering 14 of the remaining 15 Major League teams. Ruth did not dominate the sport; he transcended the game. He did even better in 1921, and everybody wanted to see The Babe.

The die was cast. McGraw wanted the Yankees to leave the Polo Grounds, which they did in 1923 for a grand new stadium which would only solidify the position of the Yankees in the hearts of New Yorkers.

Then came Lou Gehrig. In 1925, the Iron Horse began a streak without missing a game for a decade and a half. In 1936, Joe DiMaggio came aboard, and would lead the Yankees to four straight world titles. Even with the likes of Carl Hubbell and Mel Ott… *from 1920 till 1939, New York was an American League City.*

From 1940 through the late 1950s, the three New York teams dominated post-season play, especially the Dodgers and the Yankees. The Bombers were nearly unbeatable in October. And heated debates on street corners throughout the boroughs about the three New York City center fielders—Willie, Mickey, and The Duke—were reflective of the passion New Yorkers had for baseball. During this period, one is tempted to say that New Yorkers were really aligned with their boroughs, giving the National League a 2–1 edge over the Junior Circuit. However, the attendance figures don't tell the whole story, especially in light of the fact that the Dodgers and Giants would soon abandon New York for greener pastures. For now, let's say that *New York was pretty much split on this question from 1940 till 1957.*

The year was 1958. With the Dodgers now in Los Angeles and the Giants now in San Francisco, *New York was clearly an American League City from 1958 till 1961*, with the Yankees winning three Pennants and two World Series in these four years.

The same was also true in both 1962 (Yankees were

World Series winners against the Giants) and 1963 (they lost the World Series to the Dodgers)...and possibly in 1964 (and they lost again, this time to the St. Louis Cardinals). *New York was still an American League City.* This was true even though the National League had returned to New York with the birth of the Mets in 1962.

But 1964 was also a year of transition. The Yankees fired manager Yogi Berra after losing the World Series (after which Berra promptly went to the Mets). The Yankees were getting old with icons like Mickey Mantle and Whitey Ford showing signs of their age. The hallowed House That Ruth Built, Yankee Stadium, was also showing its age, while the New Breed (as the Mets were called) moved from the venerable Polo Grounds to Shea Stadium, a ballpark with no posts or girders to obstruct the vision of the fans.

As time went on, the Mets were slowly getting better and better, while the Yankees kept getting worse and worse. The Amazin's (as the Mets were also called) won the World Series in 1969, under the tutelage of Dodgers legend Gil Hodges and nearly won another world title in 1973 under Yankees icon Yogi Berra. *From 1965 till 1973, New York was a National League City.*

But the pendulum was swinging back because of a bombastic shipbuilder by the name of George M. Steinbrenner. The Boss would become the principal owner of the Yankees and would not quit until his Bombers were back on top of the heap. From 1973 thru 1981, the Yankees won four pennants and two World Championships. His "Bronx Zoo" teams—Billy Martin, Thurman Munson, Reggie Jackson, et al provided fodder for the back page of the *New York Daily News* virtually every day, and twice on Sundays. In a journalistic sense, the Mets did not even exist. *From 1974 till the early 1980s, New York was an American League City.*

The pendulum came back again in the early 1980s. With superstars like Dwight Gooden, Darryl Strawberry, Keith Hernandez and Gary Carter, the Mets would win the World Series in 1986. They owned New York, not only that year, but for the next few years as well. However, they were to win no more pennants until 2000. The Yankees actually had the best record in the major leagues for that decade. However, neither New York team wore the world crown from 1987 onwards...so, primarily based on the second half of the decade, *New York was a National League City from 1982 until 1989.*

Over the next seven years, the Mets finished only once with a winning season (1990). The Yankees did not start out well, but they began to turn the corner in 1993, and actually led the American League East division in 1994, only to be stymied by a work stoppage. The tide was turning back to the American League. However, at this point, let us say that *New York was pretty much split on this question from 1990 till 1995.*

All of this was to change in 1996. George Steinbrenner was still at the controls and players like Derek Jeter, Mariano Rivera, Jorge Posada and the like would bring a new era of winning to the Yankees. They would win World Series titles in 1996, 1998, 1999, 2000, and 2009.

Regarding the 2000 Series, New York would host a Subway Series for the first time since 1956. The Yankees went on to defeat the Mets in five games, with most media reporting that there *seemed* to be more Yankees fans at Shea Stadium than Mets followers at Yankee Stadium.[2]

In any event, *from 1996 to the present, New York is an American League City.*

The following table summarizes our *subjective* calculations:

**Table 1. New York City Preferences**

| Years | City Preference | Years |
|---|---|---|
| 1903–1919 | NL | 17 |
| 1920–1939 | AL | 20 |
| 1940–1957 | Even | 18 |
| 1958–1964 | AL | 7 |
| 1965–1973 | NL | 9 |
| 1974–1981 | AL | 8 |
| 1982–1989 | NL | 8 |
| 1990–1995 | Even | 6 |
| 1996–2017 | AL | 22 |

Note that from a geographical point of view, the boroughs of Queens and Brooklyn seem to be Mets territory while the Bronx, Staten Island, and Manhattan have more Yankees rooters. Long Island pretty much belongs to the Mets while southern Connecticut and northern New Jersey is saturated with Bombers. Measuring fanship by ticket sale location versus team predominantly preferred on Facebook yields slightly different results, but the map below depicts the general fanship borders by borough.[3,4]

**Figure 1. New York City Map Showing Stadiums and their Proximity to Each Borough**

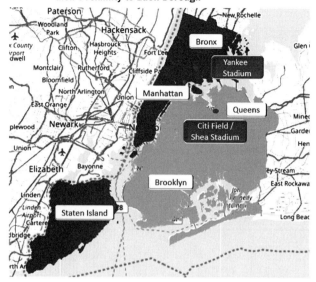

## QUANTITATIVE ANALYSIS

It is time now to switch gears and to crunch the numbers. From this quantitative approach, we will not only consider the "league-wise head-to-head" win-loss records of the four teams in question (New York Giants, Brooklyn Dodgers, New York Yankees, and New York Mets), but also attendance figures. While fans do not always turn out for a winner, history has clearly indicated that when teams win, they are more likely to draw more fans than when they lose.

It pretty much follows, then, that if a team is better on the field and more fans are coming to the home field of the better of two teams (or the best out of three teams), it seems plausible to conclude that the league which is represented by this team is the preferred league in the city.

The Win-Loss records of the teams in question were easy to obtain.[6] The following three tables reveal how the New Yorkers performed on the field.

**Table 2. Pennants and World Series**

| Years | Team | Pennants | World Series |
|---|---|---|---|
| 1903–1957* | NY Giants | 15 | 4 |
| 1903–1957 | BRK Dodgers | 9 | 1 |
| 1903–2017 | NY Yankees | **40** | **27** |
| 1962–2017 | NY Mets | 5 | 2 |

*No World Series in 1904 or 1994.

**Table 3. Yankees vs NY National League in World Series**

| Opponent | World Series Won | World Series Lost |
|---|---|---|
| NY Giants | 4 | **2** |
| BRK Dodgers | **6** | 1 |
| NY Mets | 1 | 0 |

**Table 4. Interleague Play**

| Team | Wins | Losses |
|---|---|---|
| NY Yanees | **66** | 46 |
| NY Mets | 46 | **66** |

If New Yorkers love a winner, then, based on the data above, the Big Apple is clearly an American League city.

We next took a look at the attendance figures. Unlike the Win-Loss records, the attendance figures were much harder to analyze due to a number of factors, especially when trying to compare the National League versus the American League. Both leagues changed from counting *turnstile numbers* to counting *ticket sales*, but the AL made this change in 1966, the NL not until 2000.[7]

Most probably, all things being equal, the National League's method of reckoning would have given them a figure *less* than what would have been reported for the American League. For example, if, in 1990, the Mets reported 2,000,000 as their season's attendance and the Yankees reported the same number, chances are the Mets would have sold more than 2,000,000 tickets. But by how many? That's the question.

What we decided to do was to *adjust* National League attendance figures from 1967 through 1992, by multiplying them by a generous factor of 1.1. So, in the example above, the 1990 Mets would have had an *Adjusted* Attendance of 2,000,000 x 1.1 = 2,200,000. This would mean that 200,000 tickets went unused.[8]

The following tables summarize the New York City attendance figures from 1903 through 1957, (Giants, Dodgers, and Yankees) and from 1962 through 2017 (Mets and Yankees).[9]

**Table 5. New York City Attendance Figures, 1903–57**

| Team | Attendance | Years Leading City in Attendance |
|---|---|---|
| NY Giants | 42,831,882 | 17 |
| BRK Dodgers | 38,939,115 | 5 |
| NY Yankees | **53,164,456** | **33** |

**Table 6. New York City Attendance Figures, 1962–2017**

| Team | Attendance 1962–66 | Attendance 1967–92 | Adjusted Attendance 1967–92 | Attendance 1993–2017 | Attendance 1962–2017 | Years Leading City in Attendance |
|---|---|---|---|---|---|---|
| NY Yankees | 6,446,332 | 47,195,703 | 47,195,703 | **81,708,642** | 135,350,677 | **35** |
| NY Mets | **7,436,317** | **49,826,917** | **54,809,609** | 61,880,514 | 119,143,748 | 21 |

These numbers pretty much speak for themselves, no?

A final comment about league preference: the fact is that from 1903 through 1957, the National League played approximately twice as many games as the Yankees did in New York City, because there were two National League teams in residence. This would seem to give an enormous edge to the Senior Circuit…yet, the numbers do not seem to bear this out.

To be sure, there have been ebbs and flows, and there were times when McGraw's Giants and the Amazin' Mets owned the city, but by and large—both on the field and in the stands—it seems that for a majority of seasons, a majority of New Yorkers preferred the American League. This has been especially true in recent times. The last time the Mets outdrew the Yankees was in 1992, even though they won the National League pennant in 2015. And with the 2018 Yankees boasting several media-friendly, marketable stars such as Aaron Judge and Giancarlo Stanton, we don't see the trend changing for the foreseeable future.

### SOCIAL MEDIA ANALYSIS

Another element we'd like to discuss is the social media aspect of fanship. Which team generates a larger buzz in social media? When a team is discussed on social networking websites, is it generally positive or negative? Using specialized software we were able to quantify and analyze Twitter discussions of the current New York teams.

Using the *rtweet* package in *R* we conducted the following analysis on tweets from October 13, 2018, through October 23, 2018, by searching terms "New York Yankees" and "New York Mets."[10,11] During this time period, both teams were out of the playoffs and looking towards their offseason. The search terms include both the city name and the mascot as to eliminate superfluous tweets when the terms "Yankees" or "Mets" would be used out of the context of baseball. We are assuming that if a tweet contains one of these search terms, then it represents a fan of that specific team expressing their feelings about their team. We are assuming outside actors to be very limited.

**Figure 2. The New York Yankees Generate a Larger Twitter Buzz than Their National League Counterpart**

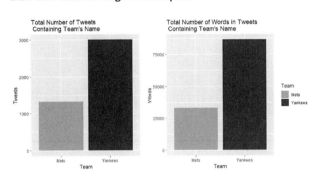

At first glance, we can see there is a clear favor in mass of tweets favoring the Yankees. More people are tweeting about the "New York Yankees" than the "New York Mets."

Taking a deeper look, when people tweet about these teams, what is their sentiment?

**Figure 3. Yankees Fans Generate More Emotion in Their Tweets than the New York Mets**

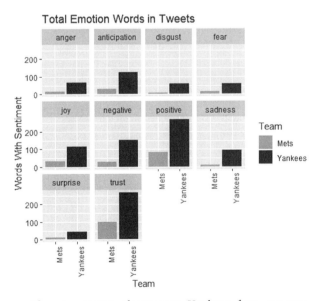

The raw counts show more Yankees fans expressing more emotion towards their team, but that is a factor of having more tweets about the Yankees. Let's look at emotion words per tweet about that team.

**Figure 4. Tweets Involving the Yankees Involve More Negative Emotions than the Mets**

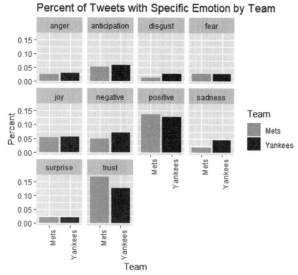

*Who owns New York? From his debut in 1946 until his death in 2015, Yogi Berra owned New York no matter which borough he was playing or managing in.*

Figure 4 reveals some very interesting points. While the Yankees tweet more about their team, on average, the Yankees fans are more negative towards the Yankees than Mets fans toward the Mets. The Yankees fans express more sadness, anger, and distrust towards their team while the Mets fans express more trust. Although the Yankees fans are more active on Twitter, they are more negative and pessimistic than their Mets fan counterparts.

Based on this analysis, we consider the current social landscape of both teams to be close. However, due to the overwhelming mass of tweets which include the term "New York Yankees" both negative and positive, the scale slides in favor of the Yankees "owning" New York.

### CONCLUSION

New York City's storied history of great American and National League baseball give each league claim to be the apple of the Big Apple's eye. Throughout the last century plus, both leagues have fought on the diamond, in World Series, in fan attendance, geography, and even most recently, social networking Web sites. We've analyzed each area and we tip the scales in favor of New York being an American League City. ∎

### APPENDIX: ALL-TIME TEAMS

As an addendum to this discussion, we would like to present a comparison between an All-Time Yankees Team and an All-Time New York City National League Team.

We made our selections and evaluations using the following guidelines:

- We took the liberty of moving some players to a different position (e.g., leaving Joe DiMaggio in center field while stationing Mickey Mantle in left field).

- We considered players' records for only the years they played in the Big Apple (1903 through 2013). For example, Sandy Koufax would make an All-Time Los Angeles Dodgers team, but not its Brooklyn counterpart.

- We gave the edge to one player over another only if we felt it was clear that he was truly superior to the other.

- We picked two catchers for each team.

- We chose a pitching staff composed of five starting pitchers and one reliever.

**TABLE 7. The All-Time Teams**

| Position | Yankees | NYC NL | Edge | Comments |
|---|---|---|---|---|
| 1B | Lou Gehrig | Bill Terry | Yankees | The Iron Horse was the greatest first baseman ever and the consummate clean-up hitter. |
| 2B | Tony Lazzeri | Jackie Robinson | NL | Had Robinson Cano stayed in New York, he may well have been the greatest keystone sacker to ever play there. |
| SS | Derek Jeter | Pee Wee Reese | Yankees | Jeter may well be the second greatest shortstop ever, ranking behind only Honus Wagner. |
| 3B | Graig Nettles | David Wright | Even | A-Rod has too much baggage. |
| C | Yogi Berra Bill Dickey | Roy Campanella Mike Piazza | Even | NL tandem has edge in power, but AL has edge in hitting, fielding and rings. |
| LF | Mickey Mantle | Duke Snider | Even | Mickey over Duke…but not by that much…call it a push. |
| CF | Joe DiMaggio | Willie Mays | Even | Only Solomon could determine which one rates over the other. |
| RF | Babe Ruth | Mel Ott | Yankees | Melvin was the Master, but there was/is only one Sultan. |
| SP | Jack Chesbro Whitey Ford Lefty Gomez Red Ruffing Andy Pettitte | Dwight Gooden Carl Hubbell Christy Mathewson Tom Seaver Dazzy Vance | NL | AL has four Hall of Famers with Pettitte a possibility… but NL staff composed of Big Six, The Meal Ticket and Tom Terrific gets the nod. |
| RP | Mariano Rivera | John Franco | Yankees | Nobody is close to the Great Mariano. |
| MGR | Joe McCarthy | John McGraw | Even | Can't do better than these two icons. |

Prediction: Because of superior hitting and Mariano, the Yankees would defeat NYC NL in a seven-game Series, 4–2.

# Notes

1. "New York Fans In Yankees State Of Mind, Quinnipiac University Baseball Poll Finds; But Teams Are Close In New York City." March 31, 2017. https://poll.qu.edu/new-york-state/release-detail?ReleaseID=2447.

2. Lapointe, Joe. "Baseball: Subway Series; Strangers in a Strange Land: Yankee Fans at Shea." *The New York Times*. October 26, 2000. Accessed February 22, 2019. https://www.nytimes.com/2000/10/26/sports/baseball-subway-series-strangers-in-a-strange-land-yankee-fans-at-shea.html.

3. Tom Giratikanon, Josh Katz. "Up Close on Baseball's Borders." *The New York Times*. April 24, 2014. Accessed February 22, 2019. https://www.nytimes.com/interactive/2014/04/23/upshot/24-upshot-baseball.html.

4. "Infographics: Where Mets and Yankees Fans Live." *Vivid Seats*. Accessed February 22, 2019. https://www.vividseats.com/blog/infographics-where-mets-and-yankees-fans-live.

5. Joe Cheng, Bhaskar Karambelkar and Yihui Xie (2018). Leaflet: Create Interactive Web Maps with the JavaScript 'Leaflet' Library. R package version 2.0.0. https://CRAN.R-project.org/package=leaflet

6. "MLB Stats, Scores, History, & Records." https://www.baseball-reference.com/.

7. Belson, Ken. "The Official Attendance Can Become Empty of Meaning." *The New York Times*. September 22, 2012. Accessed February 25, 2019. https://bats.blogs.nytimes.com/2012/09/22/the-official-attendance-can-become-empty-of-meaning/.

8. Is 1.1 a reasonable guess? Clearly this factor could be raised or lowered. Our strong suspicion is that it should be lowered to perhaps 1.05. In any case, for the sake of argument, all Adjusted comparative National League seasonal attendance figures (from 1903 through 1999) were multiplied by 1.1.

9. Baseball Almanac, http://www.baseball-almanac.com/teams/laatte.shtml.

10. Michael W Kearney (2018). rtweet: Collecting Twitter Data. R package version 0.6.7 Retrieved from https://cran.r-project.org/package=rtweet.

11. R Core Team (2018). R: A language and environment for statistical computing. R Foundation for Statistical Computing, Vienna, Austria. URL https://www.R-project.org/.

# Philadelphia in the 1881 Eastern Championship Association

## Robert D. Warrington

The Eastern Championship Association (ECA) was formed in 1881 by baseball clubs from New York, Pennsylvania, and Washington, DC. Two teams from Philadelphia were among its members, including the first one with the nickname Phillies. The Association had an unsettled existence—reflecting the institutional instability that afflicted organized baseball in the final quarter of the nineteenth century—and lasted only one year. Nevertheless, it served as a critical steppingstone in returning Philadelphia ball clubs to a professional league structure, from which they had been excluded since 1876. This article briefly describes the formation of the Association, but focuses on the members from Philadelphia—in particular, the Phillies.

### A NEW BASEBALL ASSOCIATION APPEARS

The ECA was founded on April 11, 1881, at a meeting in New York City attended by representatives of several major independent baseball clubs. The organization was intended to be "a paying circuit for the clubs named between New York and Washington."[1] Those present were William W. White of the Nationals of Washington, Louis H. Mahn of the "new Boston nine," William Barnie of the Atlantics of Brooklyn, John Kelly of the New York team, and James Mutrie of the Metropolitans of New York.[2] In addition, the Athletic club of Philadelphia sent a message heartily endorsing the Association and pledging to join it.[3]

The impetus for the ECA was based on several factors, one of which was captured by the *Philadelphia Inquirer* newspaper in an article that supported the city's participation in the Association:

> Not since the old Athletic Club was expelled from the [National] league during the Centennial year has baseball been so popular in this city. Many attempts have been made in the past five years to revive the old-time interest, but all have proved partial failures, simply because there was no recognized association outside of the league for the club to connect itself with. This want has been supplied this season

by the organization of the Eastern Championship League....[4]

Owners of the independent clubs who established the ECA believed that without a league structure within which to compete, people would regard their seasons as nothing more than a succession of individual games. The Association provided a forum to crown a champion, and the anticipation of the best record gaining that title made each win count toward a greater goal.[5] Every ECA club wanted to bring home a championship, and owners judged the excitement of such a competition would convince people who lived in the cities they represented to show their support by becoming paying customers at the turnstiles.

The ECA, it is important to note, was not a rebel movement formed to challenge the National League's monopoly on major league status; instead, it was intended to cooperate with the League to make clubs in both organizations more profitable. The major advantage in becoming an adjunct to, rather than a rival of, the NL was that it allowed games to be scheduled between Association and League teams. Staging these games in ECA cities exposed NL baseball to wider audiences—especially in the larger metropolitan areas represented only in the Association—and held the prospect of potentially lucrative paydays. ECA fans, it was judged, would be especially eager to cheer on their hometown crews if the opponents to be vanquished were major league teams.

### THE ASSOCIATION EXPERIENCES A SHIFTING STRUCTURE

In addition to creating the ECA, representatives at the inaugural meeting established arrangements for operating the new organization:

- The schedule would run from April 20 through October 1.

- Applications for membership would be accepted until May 15.

- Association teams would play 12 games against each other—six apiece at each home ballpark.

- If a club dropped out before the season concluded, none of the games it played against other Association members would count in determining the champion.

- So long as doing so did not prevent them from fulfilling their 12-game obligation to the ECA, member teams could also play games against NL opponents, college teams, independent clubs and "commercial nines."[6]

- The "Mahn dead ball"—named after Boston's Louis H. Mahn—would be used in all games between Association teams.[7]

The need for a provision governing what to do if a team disbanded before the season's end was well founded. As was characteristic of baseball organizations 1869–1900, the ECA's size and membership fluctuated as the season progressed.[8] Initially, it consisted of six teams, three from New York City—Metropolitans, Quicksteps, and New Yorks, the Atlantics from Brooklyn, the Nationals from Washington, DC, and the Athletics from Philadelphia.[9]

Attrition set in by mid-June, caused by clubs being unable to maintain their financial solvency. The Nationals disbanded, citing "lack of interest" among fans, and were replaced by a team in Albany, New York.[10] The New Yorks dropped out next and were replaced by the Domestics of Newark, New Jersey. Additional changes in ECA membership occurred over time.[11]

### THE ATHLETICS UNSETTLED ENTRY INTO THE ECA

The name "Athletics" goes back to the origins of baseball in Philadelphia.[12] The semi-professional versions of the team played between 1860 and 1870, compiling a record of 298–40.[13] They evolved into the all-professional Athletics that represented the city in the 1871 National Association (NA)—a club that won the pennant—and the NL's 1876 Athletics, which were booted from the league after refusing to make their final western trip to cut their financial losses.[14] The Athletics club of 1881 was the latest iteration with that moniker and it emerged from the debris of the previous Athletics team that had folded during the summer of 1880. Restructured into a new organization in September 1880, the club was at that time the most well-known independent club in Philadelphia.[15]

The ECA was eager to have Philadelphia represented among its members, and the Athletics were quickly granted admission. It was announced in mid-April that the club would play home games at Oakdale Park, Charles "Chick" Fulmer would be the team's manager, and he would be assisted by Charles Mason. Both men began recruiting players, according to one newspaper report, and the Athletics planned to take the field in May.[16]

Chick Fulmer plays an intriguing role in the somewhat convoluted evolution of Philadelphia's relationship with the ECA. Journeying through a nomadic baseball career, Fulmer was a member of teams based in 10 different cities. His stops included Philadelphia, where he was on the roster of the NA's Athletics 1873–75. Never a great player but certainly a capable one, especially defensively, Fulmer was courted by clubs seeking to upgrade their capabilities.[17]

But the Athletics were not alone among Philadelphia's independent clubs with an eye on joining the Association to increase their legitimacy and profitability. In early May, a newspaper report disclosed rumors that another team was being organized in the city to play in the ECA.[18] Two weeks later, an article appeared stating the Athletics were being reorganized, and in what turned out to be more than just a coincidence, Chick Fulmer did not appear in any games played by the Athletics in early and mid-May.[19] The *New York Clipper* brought these threads together in a late May report:

> The Athletics have secured exclusive use of Oakdale Park for four days each week, the Olympics practicing every Tuesday and Friday. Brouthers and Hays of the Brooklyn Atlantics are wanted by the Athletics to strengthen them. All communications for the Athletics should be addressed to H.B. Phillips, manager, 258 N. Ninth Street, Philadelphia. Charley Fulmer has organized a strong nine that will probably play at Twenty-Fourth Street and Ridge Avenue, and be known as the Philadelphias. Fulmer's team includes Caperoon, pitcher; O'Brien, catcher; Householder, Fulmer and Fouser on the bases; Myers, shortstop; and Luff, Berklebach, and Landis in the outfield. A series of exciting games may be looked for between these rival nines.[20]

Fulmer had returned to his peripatetic ways by severing ties with the Athletics and forming his own team to compete in the Association. His decision compelled the Athletics to reorganize by combining with a "prominent"—albeit unnamed—club "so as to present a representative nine able to hold their own with the best organizations in the country."[21] The Athletics also needed a new manager, and the position went to Horace Phillips.[22]

While he was well acquainted with switching teams, the reasons for Fulmer's about-face are not entirely clear. Several possibilities exist. He may have undertaken the move to gain greater leverage with the Athletics' owners—Bill Sharsig and Charles Mason—over the operation of the team and/or distribution of profits from games.[23] Fulmer also may have savored an opportunity to help operate a franchise from the front office, not just manage players on the field. Alternatively, he may have believed having a second Philadelphia team in the Association would allow, as the newspaper article noted, "a series of games between these rival nines." They could be scheduled to fill open dates during the season, converting incomeless days into potentially profitable ones by attracting large numbers of paying customers to watch an intra-city rivalry.

Whatever Fulmer's motives, his reported flirtation with leading the Philadelphias was brief and ended abruptly. On May 30, the Athletics played the Nationals at Oakdale Park, and in a report recapping the game, "The Athletics were strengthened by Charles Fulmer, who played second base and will captain the nine hereafter. The Athletics won by a score of 6 to 2."[24] For reasons that remain unclear, he returned to the Athletics and played for the team the rest of the season. But his position with the club was diminished. The mid-April newspaper report had stated Fulmer would be the manager while the late-May report indicated his role was as team captain. Phillips would manage the Athletics with Mason as assistant manager.[25] That arrangement continued throughout the season.

### THE PHILLIES EMERGE, BUT NOT FOR LONG

Fulmer's relationship with the Philadelphias was over, but the club was not finished, and an opportunity to join the ECA still beckoned. Some of the players identified as those Fulmer was recruiting still wound up on the team and formed the nucleus of its roster. They were Henry Myers, Jack O'Brien, Frank Berkelbach, and Doc Landis. Myers also served as team manager.[26] Landis played for the Athletics earlier in the season and then switched to the Philadelphias.[27] Another former player, Charlie Waitt, was mentioned as possibly involved in organizing the team.[28]

Although not a member of the ECA, the Philadelphias played their first game against the Association's

Nationals on June 6, 1881. It took place at Oakdale Park—the Athletics' home ballfield—as one of two games. The Nationals played the Philadelphias in the morning, and the Athletics in the afternoon.[29]

A newspaper report on the Philadelphias' game called them a "new club."[30] Another acknowledged the club had been reorganized with a new lineup:

> The Philadelphia Club has recently been reorganized with the following nine: Sweeney, pitcher; O'Brien, catcher; Shetzline, Reynolds and Dixon on the bases; Myers, shortstop; Barber, Birchall and Landis in the outfield; with Lomas, tenth man and change-pitcher. The Philadelphias played their opening game on the morning of June 6th at Oakdale Park; the Washingtons then defeating them after a close and exciting contest by a score of 5 to 3.[31]

The fact the Athletics permitted the Philadelphias to use their ballpark indicated they were not opposed to a second Philadelphia-based team joining the ECA once Fulmer had returned. The financial benefits of an intra-city rivalry still applied. Games between the Athletics and Philadelphias might draw sizable crowds when no other games were scheduled.[32] The use of Oakdale Park by the Philadelphias also reflected the fact the club was still searching for a home ballpark, but it was a quest that would be resolved within the month.

Cordial relations between the Philadelphias and Athletics were again in evidence on June 11 when members of the former stepped in to help stage a game against the latter. Circumstances surrounding the hastily arranged contest were described in the *New York Clipper*:

> The threatening aspect of the weather on June 11th caused the non-appearance of the Metropolitans of this city in Philadelphia, when they were booked to play the Athletics. A large assemblage had gathered at Oakdale Park and the Athletics arranged to play a picked nine, including six of the new Philadelphia Club. Billy McLean acted as umpire, and a close contest was anticipated, but the Athletics won easily, the figure being 14–1.[33]

The Philadelphias did not have to wait long to enter the ranks of the ECA. A newspaper article reported in mid-June:

The Philadelphia Cub, including such well-known players as Sweeney, O'Brien, Shetzline, Reynolds, Dixon, Myers, Barber, Lomas and Landis, have been admitted into the Eastern Championship Association, taking the place of Louis H. Mahn's Boston team. The Philadelphias secured the grounds at Twenty-Fourth Street and Ridge Avenue, where many improvements will be made, including a new grandstand and fence. Their opening game with the Atlantics of Brooklyn June 17th was postponed on account of rain.[34]

The ballpark at "Twenty-Fourth Street and Ridge Avenue" was named Recreation Park. The location had been used to play baseball since the Civil War, and would figure prominently in Philadelphia baseball in the years ahead.[35,36]

With their game on June 17 rained out, the Philadelphias' first game as a member of the ECA was against an Association opponent—the Quicksteps of New York—and was played at Recreation Park on June 24.[37] In addition to being the club's inaugural ECA game, it was remarkable for another reason. Although heretofore called the Philadelphias in newspaper reporting, an article in the next day's *Philadelphia Inquirer* describing the contest unveiled the club's nickname—a moniker that was far more portentous for the history of baseball in Philadelphia.

The initial game for the Eastern baseball championship between the Philadelphia and New York Clubs was played at Twenty-fourth Street and Ridge Avenue yesterday afternoon in the presence of about five hundred people. Contrary to general expectation, the Philadelphias won the contest after outplaying their opponents at all points. The Philadelphia club has just been organized and, considering that this is the first game they have played against a good club, and that they did not have their full nine in the field, the victory is all the more creditable…Two bases on called balls and an error of Tracy gave the "**Phillies**" [emphasis added] an unearned run in the second inning….[38]

This author believes this represents the first time the "Phillies" nickname appears in newsprint linked with a Philadelphia professional baseball team. Another Philadelphia baseball club would form in 1882 and make a far more enduring claim to the nickname, but the 1881 ECA team was the first to have the

"Phillies" moniker applied to it, and thereby claim an important niche in the city's baseball history. Newspaper reporting of the period often identified longstanding clubs by their team names rather than by the cities they represented. In the ECA, these included theAtlantics of Brooklyn, Athletics of Philadelphia, and Nationals of Washington. Newly-formed clubs, however, were initially identified by adding an 's' to the names of their home cities to make them easy to recognize, distinguish them from other teams playing in the cities, and because they had not acquired their own names. Such Association teams were the Albanys, New Yorks, and Philadelphias.[39] As nicknames for such clubs became better known, they appeared in newspaper game coverage for identification purposes. Consequently, the use of "Phillies" in the article, especially with quotations around the word, shows it was a nickname for the Philadelphia Club, and undoubtedly would have appeared more frequently in newspaper coverage had the team continued to exist.[40] (The club is referred to as the Phillies through the remainder of this article.)

The Phillies got off to a victorious start as a member of the Association, beating the Quicksteps by a 10–1 score. The Athletics played the Quicksteps the next day and defeated them 10–5 at Oakdale Park.[41]

The second contest pitting the Phillies against an ECA opponent occurred on July 2, when the team visited the Polo Grounds in New York to take on the Metropolitans. It was a lopsided affair with the home team pummeling the visitors, 18–4. The Metropolitans scored nine runs off Landis over three innings, and then added the same tally off Lomas during the rest of the game. Over 1,200 spectators watched the contest.[42]

The New Yorkers went first to the bat, and after two men were out a base hit by Foster and a two-baser by Poorman earned a run, the only one they obtained in the game. For the home team Myers went to first base on called balls, Shetzline made a two-base hit and Landis a single, three runs being made before the side was disposed of, one of which was earned. Two bases on called balls and an error of Tracy gave the "Phillies" an unearned run in the second inning, and in the third single hits by O'Brien, Reynolds and Slater a two-baser by Lomas and an error of Leary gave them four more runs, three of which were earned. Myers, Landis and Sweeney batted well in the sixth inning and earned two more runs, which were the last made. Landis' pitching was the feature of the contest. To-day the New Yorkers play the Athletics at Oakdale Park. The score was

*First use by a newspaper of 'Phillies' as a nickname for a baseball club in Philadelphia.* Philadelphia Inquirer, *June 25, 1881.*

PHILADELPHIA INQUIRER

81

The next recorded games played by the Phillies took place in Baltimore on July 4 and 5. The club's opponent were "a local nine," and the visitors won both games. Landis pitched for the Phillies in the first game, and Lomas occupied the pitcher's box in the second contest.[43]

And then the Phillies were gone, relocated to a new city. The *New York Clipper* reported the abrupt transfer in this manner:

Baltimore, MD will be represented on the ballfield during the remainder of the season by a strong professional team managed and captained by Henry Myers, with its headquarters at Newington Park. The Philadelphia nine has been transferred bodily to Baltimore and strengthened by some prominent local players. The new team, including Caperoon, pitcher; Whiting, catcher; Sweeney, Shetzline and Barber on the bases; Myers, shortstop; and O'Rourke, Morgan and Landis in the outfield, played their opening game on July 14th with the Peabodys—the amateur champions of Baltimore. The professionals secured a signal victory the figure being 8 to 1 in their favor.[44]

None of the reports on the Phillies' departure from Philadelphia offered an explanation for the move, but the reasons almost certainly mirror those of other ECA clubs that disbanded after a short period of time—financial insolvency.[45] The Nationals had disbanded on June 11 because, according to one newspaper account, "it was impossible to arrange sufficient games to prove pecunarily [*sic*] profitable."[46] During the approximately one month between the Phillies' entrance into the Association and their relocation to Baltimore, the club was able to play only three games against Association opponents—the Nationals, Quicksteps, and Metropolitans—the contest against the Atlantics having been rained out. Other than two games against an amateur team in Baltimore, the club was inactive.

The Phillies, moreover, were clearly overshadowed by the Athletics in scheduling games.[47] The Athletics played four games against ECA opponents and two more against an NL club over seven days in late June, and four of them were held in Philadelphia. With the exception of the Quicksteps—who played the Phillies on June 24 and the Athletics on June 25—the other clubs visiting the city played only the Athletics.

The Athletics also consistently drew larger crowds. For example, the National League Bostons opposed the Athletics at Oakdale Park on June 22 and 23. The first game drew 4,000 customers, while the second

attracted 3,000 fans, dwarfing the number of seats the Phillies were able to fill in their home games against Association opponents.[48] The Phillies, moreover, were idle on those dates. Why Boston and other NL clubs that visited Philadelphia for two-game sets versus the Athletics would not or could not split the series—one game each against the Athletics and Phillies—isn't clear, but it unquestionably contributed to the latter's financial woes.

The Phillies also encountered difficulties scheduling games against other ECA teams. For example, on July 4, while the Phillies were playing a game against an amateur club in Baltimore, the Athletics had two games against the Association's Atlantics. The first game was held in the morning and took place at the West Chester fairgrounds. It attracted "a large crowd." The afternoon duel occurred at Oakdale Park and was watched by 3,000 spectators.[49] Again, it is uncertain why Brooklyn was unable to play one game versus the Phillies and the other against the Athletics—as the Nationals had done on June 6—especially on a holiday likely to attract a large number of spectators to the ballpark.

Another contributing factor to the Phillies' demise probably was that Philadelphia's fan base was inadequate to support two baseball franchises profitably. Clearly, the Athletics were the premier team in the city that drew marquee opponents and attracted the biggest crowds. Just as the New Yorks folded after they did not compete successfully for fans with the Metropolitans, the Phillies disbanded after they were similarly disadvantaged. In all likelihood, the Phillies, like the Nationals, were not "pecunarily [*sic*] profitable."

Baltimore did not escape the Phillies' fate.[50] The club played its last game on August 27, 1881, and did not finish the season.[51] Earlier in the month, Myers left as manager of the Baltimore team, shifting to the Providence Grays of the NL.[52] That arrangement, however, lasted only a short period, and Myers returned to the Baltimore club to help it reorganize.[53]

### DISTINGUISHING THE PHILLIES FROM THE ATHLETICS
The ECA's Phillies team is mostly lost to history; indeed, some baseball reference sources do not acknowledge the club's existence, listing only the Athletics as Philadelphia's entry in the Association. For example, Baseball-Reference.com does not identify the Phillies as one of the ECA's clubs in 1881, and assigns all the players who were with the team as having been on the Athletics' roster.[54] These oversights are likely attributable to the Phillies' brief existence, but they

have unquestionably contributed to the club's obscurity in Philadelphia's baseball past.

What is certain is that the Phillies and Athletics were separate teams. The sequence of games on June 24 and June 25 against the Quicksteps illustrate the presence of the two clubs in the Association. Newspaper articles recapping the games identify the Quicksteps' opponent on June 24 as the Phillies and June 25 as the Athletics. The first game was played at Recreation Park—home of the Phillies—and the second at Oakdale Park—home of the Athletics.[55]

In addition, when the Phillies were at the Polo Grounds playing the Metropolitans on July 2, the Athletics were at home on the same day playing the Atlantics at Oakdale Park.[56] Lineups of the Phillies and the Athletics for their games that day show the clubs had entirely different rosters:

| Phillies' Lineup<br>July 2, 1881 | Athletics' Lineup<br>July 2, 1881 |
| --- | --- |
| Henry Myers, SS | Jud Birchall, LF |
| John Shetzline, 2B | Sam Weaver, RF |
| Doc Landis, P | Henry Luff, CF |
| Ed Whiting, C | Eddie Fusselback, C |
| Jerry Sweeney, 1B | Chick Fulmer, 2B |
| Frank Berkelbach, LF | Cub Stricker, SS |
| Dixon, 3B | Joe Battin, 3B |
| Lomas, CF | Charlie Householder, 1B |
| Charlie Barber, RF | Gid Gardner, P |

Numerous newspaper accounts also confirm Philadelphia had two clubs in the ECA during the 1881 season. For example, the *New York Clipper* ran an article July 9 identifying the seven clubs in the Association as the Metropolitans, New Yorks and Quicksteps of New York, the Albanys of Albany, the Atlantics of Brooklyn, and the Athletics and Philadelphias of Philadelphia.[57] While there was a small amount of player crossover between the Phillies' and Athletics' clubs—Landis played for both teams—that was consistent with the frequent movement of players among NL and ECA teams in 1881.

### THE HAMILTON DISSTON CLUB

As noted, when the Phillies folded and the franchise transferred to Baltimore, most of the players went, too.[58] Some, however, subsequently departed Baltimore either of their own accord or were released and returned to Philadelphia. Fortuitously, yet another club was being organized in the city where they could ply their trade. According to a newspaper article reporting the development:

A new professional club to represent Philadelphia has lately been organized, and will be called the Hamilton Disston in compliment to one of the most popular young men of the Quaker City. John J. Ryan, a well-known veteran who had figured prominently in past seasons with the Bostons and Louisvilles will captain the new nine, and Charles E. Gross Jr. will act as manager. Negotiations are now pending to lease the ground at Twenty-Fourth Street and Ridge Avenue and put it in first-class condition. The Disstons will open with the following nine: Lomas, pitcher; Whiting, catcher; McCartney, Reynolds and Meyerle on the bases; Greenwood, shortstop; and Ryan, Slater and Berklebach [sic] in the outfield. The management will improve the nine as occasion offers. All clubs visiting Philadelphia are requested to communicate with Chas. E. Gross Jr., 659 North Thirteenth Street, in regard to dates.[59]

Lomas, Whiting, Slater, and Berkelbach had previously played for the Phillies. Despite the description of the Disstons as "professional," however, they were really an amateur team that played amateur opponents. For example, the club played its first game on August 4, defeating the Graffley amateur club by a score of 11 to 9.[60] There is no evidence to indicate the Disstons lasted past the 1881 season.

### BEYOND THE ECA

When the ECA season concluded, the Athletics finished in second place behind the New York Metropolitans. Overall, the club played 92 games and finished with a 42–50 record.[61] These figures include games against clubs in the Association and NL, and contests against college, commercial, and independent teams. During their brief existence, the Phillies played only five games, going 1–2 against Association opponents, and 2–0 versus an independent club in Baltimore.

The Association lasted only one season. Rumors that it would disband began as early as July.[62] The ECA's shaky financial foundation and revolving-door membership contributed to its demise, as did the fact the more powerful clubs—the Metropolitans and Athletics—sought major league status by joining the NL or aligning with an organization that would rival that League. After its application for admittance to the NL was rejected, the Athletics joined the new American Association (AA) for the 1882 season.[63] The AA was organized in November 1881, and challenged the NL's monopoly on major league status, a step the

ECA was neither designed for nor capable of doing.[64] The Phillies were reconstituted—now under the leadership of H.B. Phillips and A.J. Reach—and admitted to the NL-affiliated League Alliance in 1882.[65] The move served as a prelude to the club's ascension to the NL the next year.[66]

Despite its short-lived existence, the ECA provided a critical steppingstone in transitioning the structure of baseball in Philadelphia from a loose aggregation of independent teams into a league organization. It welcomed the original "Phillies" franchise in 1881, and while that team experienced a fleeting existence and is little remembered, it served as the forerunner of a club with the same nickname that was established the following year and continues to this day. ∎

## Notes

1. "An Eastern Championship," *New York Clipper*, April 16, 1881. "Playing circuit" is subject to interpretation. It most likely meant the league was intended to be profitable. Spectators would pay an admission fee to watch games, and players would receive salaries. Whether all players' salaries were guaranteed or dependent on ticket gate revenue for each game is unclear.

2. "Baseball Men in Council," *The New York Times*, April 12, 1881. These cities were for a variety of reasons unrepresented in the National League. David Nemec, *The Beer and Whisky League* (New York: Lyons & Burford Publishers, 1994), 16.

3. *New York Clipper*, April 16, 1881.

4. "The Championship," *Philadelphia Inquirer*, July 28, 1881. Baseball was frequently spelled as two words in the nineteenth century, including in the article as it appeared in the Inquirer. To ensure consistency in this text, the contemporary spelling of baseball is used throughout, as it is for other words that were spelled differently over a hundred years ago. Shortstop, for example, is spelled as one word in this text, although it was hyphenated in the 1880s.

5. What exactly a club would receive for winning the ECA championship was not decided at the initial meeting. Presumably, a handsome trophy would be awarded. In early July, the Mayor of Albany, NY, a city represented in the Association by the Albanys, announced he would award a gold ball to the champion team, although whether this prize was intended to complement an Association trophy was not made clear. "BASEBALL," *New York Clipper*, July 9, 1881.

6. "Commercial Nines" were teams sponsored by businesses. For example, the Rosenberg Manufacturing Company sponsored a baseball team, as did the August, Bernhelm, and Baner Company, both located in Brooklyn, NY. "BASEBALL," *New York Clipper*, July 9, 1881.

7. *New York Clipper*, April 16, 1881.

8. David Nemec, *The Great Encyclopedia of 19th Century Major League Baseball* (New York: Donald I. Fine Books, 1997), 165. Nemec notes, "Between 1869 and the close of the nineteenth century nearly 900 professional baseball franchise were launched; more than three-quarters of them went belly up in two years or less and only 50 lasted as long as six years."

9. *The New York Times*, April 12, 1881.

10. https://en.wikipedia.org/wk/1881_in_baseball.

11. *Philadelphia Inquirer*, July 28, 1881.

12. The lineage of various franchises that claimed the name Philadelphia Athletics, and machinations involving the 1881 version before its entry into the ECA is covered in, John Shiffert, *Base Ball in Philadelphia: A History of the Early Game, 1831–1900* (Jefferson: McFarland & Company), chapters 4–9.

13. Ibid., 42.

14. David Jordan, *The Athletics of Philadelphia: Connie Mack's White Elephants, 1901–1954* (Jefferson: McFarland & Company, 1999), 8–9.

15. Shiffert, *Base Ball in Philadelphia*, 97.

16. "BASEBALL," *New York Clipper*, April 23, 1881.

17. Charles F. Faber, "Chick Fulmer," *Baseball Biography Project*, https://sabr.org/bioproj/person/309302d5.

18. "BASEBALL," *New York Clipper*, May 7, 1881.

19. "BASEBALL," *New York Clipper*, May 21, 1881.

20. "BASEBALL," *New York Clipper*, May 28, 1881. The inclusion of Fouser's name in the article is odd. Bill Fouser was an infielder/outfielder who played in 21 games for the Athletics of the NL in 1876. That was the extent of his major league career. His name is never mentioned again in connection with the Philadelphias. https://www.baseball-reference.com/players/f/fousebi01.shtml.

21. *New York Clipper*, May 21, 1881.

22. *New York Clipper*, May 28, 1881.

23. Shiffert, *Base Ball in Philadelphia*, 97.

24. "BASEBALL," *New York Clipper*, June 4, 1881.

25. Mason is identified as assistant manager in a newspaper article that describes improvements to Oakdale Park that were carried out under his supervision. "BASEBALL," *New York Clipper*, July 23, 1881.

26. "New York Defeated," *Philadelphia Inquirer*, June 25, 1881; *New York Clipper*, July 9, 1881.

27. Landis had pitched for the Athletics in a game May 9 against the Metropolitans. In addition to pitching, Landis played the outfield. "BASEBALL," *New York Clipper*, May 14, 1881. Caperoon pitched for the Athletics but did not play for the Philadelphias. *New York Clipper*, May 14, 1881. He did pitch, however, for the Baltimore club after the Philadelphias' franchise was relocated to that city. "BASEBALL," *New York Clipper*, August 13, 1881.

28. *New York Clipper*, May 7, 1881. Charlie Waitt was an outfielder and first baseman who played in the National Association (1875), National League (1877, 1883) and American Association (1882). In 1883, he was on the Phillies, but his tenure with the club lasted one game. www.baseball-reference.com/players/w/waittch01.shtml.

29. "Baseball," *Philadelphia Inquirer*, June 6, 1881. Washington defeated the Athletics 8–0 in the afternoon.

30. "Baseball," *Philadelphia Inquirer*, June 7, 1881.

31. "BASEBALL," *New York Clipper*, June 11, 1881. The inclusion of Birchall's name on the Philadelphias' roster is a mistake. Jud Birchall played for the Athletics during the 1881 season.

32. There is no evidence the Philadelphias and Athletics ever played a game. It is unclear why such a contest was never scheduled, but several factors may account for it, including, the Philadelphias' brief existence and the availability of other clubs to visit the city for games. Despite the potential appeal of an intra-city Philadelphia ballgame, playing other clubs, especially those in the NL, was almost certainly judged to draw a larger crowd.

33. "BASEBALL," *New York Clipper*, June 18, 1881. In another example of cooperation between the two clubs, Frank Berkelbach, an outfielder for the Philadelphias, was selected by the Athletics to umpire one of their home games against the Albanys on July 9, 1881. The home team won the closely-contested affair 7–6. "Baseball," *Philadelphia Inquirer*, July 11, 1881.

34. *New York Clipper*, June 25, 1881. The statement that the Phillies replaced Boston is odd. Boston was never part of the Association. While Boston's Louis Mahn attended the inaugural meeting of the ECA, it was to advance his baseball interests by having the Association adopt his ball for use in games, which it did. Mahn tried the same tactic later that year when he attended a meeting on November 2, 1881, called to organize the American Association. Other attendees soon discovered that Mahn was not there to enroll a Boston entry, but instead, to advocate for the use of his ball in games played by the new league. The American Association did, nevertheless, agree to have Mahn's sporting goods company supply baseballs for its games. Nemec, *Beer and Whiskey League*, 21–23.

35. Recreation Park had been used as a ballfield by independent clubs for years, and it continued to be so even after the Philadelphias selected it as their home. For example, while the Philadelphias were in Baltimore playing "a local nine," the Graffley and Mailineaux amateur nines played a game of baseball at Recreation Park on July 4th. "Baseball," *Philadelphia Inquirer*, July 4, 1881.

36. Rich Westcott, *Philadelphia's Old Ballparks* (Philadelphia: Temple University Press, 1996), 9–14. Westcott provides an overview of the history of Recreation Park, calling it the "Birthplace of the Phillies."

37. The Philadelphias had played the Nationals on June 6th, but that took place before the former had been admitted to the ECA. The game against the Atlantics, which would have been the Philadelphias first contest against an Association opponent after joining the ranks of the ECA was, as noted, rained out.

38. "Baseball," *Philadelphia Inquirer*, June 25, 1881. The Phillies used two substitute players in their lineup because, as stated in the article, "they did not have their full nine in the field." The substitutes were Slater and Reynolds—their first names are unknown—who according to available records played in that game and never again in the ECA. https://www.baseball-reference.com/register/league.cgi?id=9a276014.

39. The long-lived Metropolitan baseball club was identified by its full nickname, "Metropolitans," and also by a shortened version of same, "Mets." Both were used interchangeably in reporting on the club's games. For examples of "Mets" appearing in newspaper accounts, see *New York Clipper*, May 7, 1881, June 18, 1881, July 23, 1881, August 27, 1881, and September 17, 1881.

40. The NL Philadelphia baseball club was referred to as the "Philadelphias" and the "Phillies" in newspaper coverage of games during the team's inaugural season in the league (1883). *Philadelphia Inquirer*, various dates.

41. "Baseball," *Philadelphia Inquirer*, June 27, 1881.

42. *New York Clipper*, July 9, 1881.

43. "BASEBALL," *New York Clipper*, July 16, 1881.

44. *New York Clipper*, July 23, 1881.

45. The *Inquirer* reported, "The Baltimore Club has recently organized and is composed entirely of Philadelphia players under the management of Henry Myers, formerly of the Athletic and Philadelphia Clubs." "Badly Beaten," *Philadelphia Inquirer*, July 21, 1881.

46. *New York Clipper*, June 18, 1881.

47. Ironically, 73 years later in 1954, it would be the Philadelphia Athletics who relocated to another city (Kansas City) because of a shaky financial foundation, and the fiscally solid Phillies who remained. There was also a belief among some American League owners and league president William Harridge that Philadelphia no longer had a sufficient fan base to support two major league teams—the same thinking that may have contributed to the transfer of the ECA's Phillies to Baltimore in 1881. See Robert. D. Warrington, "Departure Without Dignity: The Athletics Leave Philadelphia," https://sabr.org/research/departure-without-dignity-leave-Philadelphia.

48. "BASEBALL," *New York Clipper*, July 2, 1881. The Phillies drew only 500 spectators to their game against the Quicksteps at Recreation Park on June 24th. *Philadelphia Inquirer*, June 25, 1881.

49. "Baseball," *Philadelphia Inquirer*, July 5, 1881.

50. When the Baltimore club was established, it was announced that its headquarters would be at the Newington Park ballfield, and that E. W. Gardner would be its business agent. A newspaper article praised Gardner, saying his appointment "should be a guarantee that the affairs of this new professional organization should be attended to in an efficient manner." But the club lasted just over a month in the ECA. *New York Clipper*, July 23, 1881

51. "BASEBALL," *New York Clipper*, September 3, 1881.

52. "BASEBALL," *New York Clipper*, August 20, 1881.

53. "BASEBALL," *New York Clipper*, September 10, 1881. After Myers returned to Baltimore, he became the team's player/manager when it was a member of the American Association in 1882. In addition to Myers, others who had played for the Phillies in 1881 were on the Orioles' roster in 1882: John Shetzline, Doc Landis, and Ed Whiting. Nemec, *Great Encyclopedia*, 190.

54. https://www.baseball-reference.com/register/league.cgi?id=9a276014

55. *New York Clipper*, June 11, 1881.

56. *New York Clipper*, July 9, 1881.

57. *New York Clipper*, July 9, 1881.

58. All but two of the players who were in the Phillies' lineup for the game on July 2nd were in Baltimore's lineup for the club's first game on July 20th against, appropriately enough, the Athletics. The exceptions were Doc Landis and Lomas. They were replaced in the lineup by John Caperoon and John O'Rourke. Caperoon had been mentioned as one of the players being recruited for the Philadelphias by Chick Fulmer. The Athletics won by a score of 15–4. *Philadelphia Inquirer*, July 21, 1881.

59. "Baseball in Philadelphia," *New York Clipper*, August 6, 1881.

60. *New York Clipper*, August 13, 1881.

61. "BASEBALL," *New York Clipper*, December 17, 1881.

62. "BASEBALL," *New York Clipper*, July 30, 1881.

63. For more information about the Athletics 1881 season, its role in the creation of the American Association, and team manager Horace B. Phillips, see Brock Helander, "Prelude to the Formation of the American Association," https://sabr.org/research/prelude-formation-american-asociation.

64. Nemec, *Beer and Whiskey* League, 21–22.

65. Al Reach is an important figure in early organized baseball and in Philadelphia's baseball history. For a biographic sketch of Reach's career as a baseball player, sports manufacturing entrepreneur and Philadelphia Phillies' president, see, Rich Westcott and Frank Bilovsky, *The Phillies Encyclopedia*, 3rd edition (Philadelphia: Temple University Press, 2004), 365–67.

66. *New York Clipper*, December 17, 1881.

# Barney Dreyfuss Buys Pittsburgh

## Bob Bailey

As the story goes, in 1899 Barney Dreyfuss purchased the Pittsburgh National League club, arranged a trade with the team he previously owned, the Louisville Colonels, and spirited away all of Louisville's best players, including Honus Wagner, Fred Clarke, and Rube Waddell. This established the Pirates as one of the dominant National League teams for more than a decade.

Several elements of the story are true. However, the acquisition of the team was much more complicated, as Dreyfuss was a minority stockholder until 1901. Dreyfuss had developed a strategy that included disposing of his stock in the Louisville club and entering into an unusual agreement with the Colonels that gave him complete control of the players under contract and on reserve. His ability to control the final disposition of Louisville stars like Wagner and Clarke had given Dreyfuss the leverage he needed to make a deal for another club. But the deal with Pittsburgh did not initially give Dreyfuss full ownership of the Pirates.

During much of the 1890s the National League struggled. The advent of the 12-club league in 1892, coupled with the economic downturn in the United States in 1893, cut revenues, consigned too many teams to be out of the pennant-chase by July, and, in general, depressed profits in the baseball world.

By 1899, the issue of dropping franchises from the league to return to an eight-team circuit had been discussed for several years.[1] Club owners saw this downsizing as the path to profitability, but worried about the cost of cutting out four franchises. When the National League and American Association merged after the 1891 season, four teams were contracted, and the surviving clubs had to finance the payouts to the departing clubs for several seasons.[2]

Louisville was one of the weaker franchises in the NL. After the Colonels' pennant-winning year of 1890, the team struggled mightily, never finishing higher than ninth in the 12-team league during the 1890s. Their total NL record for the period was 419–683–22, a .380 winning average, and their average finish was 39 games behind the pennant winner.

The club was reputed to be bankrupt in 1895. It needed a loan of $4,000 from the National League to open the season (the loan was repaid in July).[3] About this time Dreyfuss, a new investor in the Colonels, joined the Louisville board of directors. A 30-year-old bookkeeper for the Bernheim Bros. Distillery Company in Louisville, Dreyfuss was a cousin of Isaac Bernheim, founder of the company, and had emigrated from Germany in 1883.[4]

We do not know the level of Dreyfuss's investment in the Louisville club, but it was sufficient to earn him a seat on the board.[5] He was named board secretary at the close of the 1895 season.[6] About the same time Dreyfuss joined the board of directors, the club hired a local newspaper man, Harry Pulliam, to serve as club secretary. By January 1897, Pulliam ascended to the club presidency, with Dreyfuss serving as secretary/treasurer. Dreyfuss and Pulliam became fast friends, which would be central to Dreyfuss's acquisition of Pittsburgh and Pulliam's assuming the presidency of the National League in 1902. In December 1897, Dreyfuss left the Louisville board, pleading the crush of business as a whiskey merchant forced his hand.

Early in 1898, Dreyfuss attempted to acquire enough stock to assume control of the club. He claimed that the Colonels owed him $8,000 for funds he had advanced to keep the team afloat and he wanted full payment in cash or all the treasury stock the club still held, which would have given him full control. Majority owner Thomas Hunt Stuckey offered Dreyfuss an alternate settlement that did not involve any treasury stock, and Dreyfuss accepted. Establishing his claim from the club and receiving less than a full settlement may have given Dreyfuss the idea to leverage the team's debt to him into his control of players' contracts when he sought another franchise.[7]

Dreyfuss was aware that the NL was looking at reducing the size of the league from 12 clubs to eight and that Louisville would be a prime target for elimination. Perhaps he believed that the NL agreement, which ran until 1902, would protect his investment or lead to a substantial payment for the franchise if the league acted to eliminate teams before 1902. Or he may have seen some potential value in controlling an NL franchise if he were to seek to purchase another club.

In March 1898, the Louisville papers reported that Dreyfuss was interested in buying the St. Louis club. Owner Chris Von der Ahe was mired in financial and legal problems but still sought $95,000, a price Dreyfuss deemed excessive.[8] This is the earliest indication that Dreyfuss wanted to stay in the baseball business, regardless of location.

The United States entered the Spanish-American War in April 1898. Although the conflict only lasted a few months, the war depressed baseball attendance and curtailed revenues.[9] Speculation about contraction and Louisville's reported loss of $13,000 in 1898 led G.A. Van Der Beck of Detroit to make a run at acquiring the Colonels. The papers were full of stories about the negotiations. There are notes that Louisville carried a debt of over $30,000 and that the owners were seeking $50,000 for the club. At the same time, Van Der Beck was negotiating to buy the Cleveland club, another candidate for elimination. It was said Van Der Beck was never serious about purchasing Louisville and used the club as a tool to improve his position in the Cleveland negotiations.[10] In the end, Van Der Beck was not successful in either negotiation.

Although Dreyfuss was on and off the Louisville board several times at his own request, he often represented the club at league business meetings.[11] He represented Louisville at the National League annual meeting in December 1898. He appeared to be more convinced than ever that Louisville would not be part of the league by 1900, and there were reports Louisville was receiving offers to sell players to teams like Philadelphia, Chicago, and New York.[12] The Louisville directors, however, believed they could navigate through the coming storm and announced they were keeping the club in Louisville and trying to sell stock to raise capital. But the sale raised only a few thousand dollars in subscriptions and was canceled in February.[13]

We can speculate that Dreyfuss viewed the actions of the Louisville board as ineffective as he resumed the club presidency in mid-February.[14] He had been the de-facto president, dealing with player contracts and league activities, since the end of the 1898 season. He announced that that club was no longer for sale and began working in earnest to prepare for the 1899 season.[15] He signed several players and made plans with the owners of Eclipse Park, who were also members of the team's board of directors, to upgrade the Colonels' home field.[16]

Dreyfuss was blindsided at the National League meeting in late March when the league approved the 1899 schedule. It removed 11 Sunday home games in Louisville that had been on the earlier draft schedule. Dreyfuss was furious. Suddenly, Louisville's schedule was littered with Monday or Friday doubleheaders. Sunday games were the lifeblood of many teams. Dreyfuss speculated about the animus displayed by Jim Hart of Chicago, John Brush of Cincinnati, and Frank Robison of Cleveland since he had opposed their effort to give Cleveland control of the St. Louis franchise. He was probably right, but some sportswriters speculated that this also may have been an effort to undermine Louisville so that the Colonels might voluntarily withdraw from the league.[17]

We need to remember that this was the era of syndicate baseball ownership, meaning owners could have investments in multiple franchises in the same league. Today, baseball rules and antitrust legislation prevent such a situation on the same scale, but in the late 1890s Baltimore and Brooklyn had interlocking directorates and common ownership and Cleveland's Robison brothers controlled both the Cleveland and St. Louis franchises.[18]

Through April, Dreyfuss battled with Hart and Brush to restore the Sunday dates. In the end, he recovered most of the Sunday games, but it had to have been clear to Dreyfuss that the future of the Colonels in the National League was dim.[19] The team did poorly in the early going, and at the end of June they were in 10th place, 23 games out. They climbed to ninth place in July, 21 games behind Brooklyn, but troubles continued to mount. During a severe electrical storm on August 12, the Colonels' ballpark burned to the ground. The club was forced to play its games on the road, which did not help its financial position. Louisville played well in the second half, ending with a 75–77 record, still 28 games behind pennant-winning Brooklyn.

Louisville may have been a bereft franchise in the standings, but its roster contained assets coveted by other clubs. The Louisville outfield boasted two future Hall of Famers. Player/manager Clarke patrolled left field while Wagner often played in right when he wasn't covering third base. Clarke had joined the team in 1894 from the Savannah club. His manager and teammate was John McCloskey, a well-traveled Louisville native who undoubtedly told Dreyfuss and Pulliam about the outfielder. By 1897, Clarke was the Colonels' manager. He was an average fielder but he batted .334 as a Colonel. Wagner was acquired from Paterson in the Atlantic League in 1897 after being scouted by Pulliam, Louisville's president.[20] Wagner batted .322 for Louisville and showed good power and speed.

Others on the Louisville team were also sought by other teams. Tommy Leach and Claude Ritchey covered the left side of the infield and batted around .300 most seasons. Pitcher Deacon Phillippe won 21 games in 1899, his first season in the majors, and Bert Cunningham was a reliable starter coming off a 28-win season in 1898. Late in the season, Louisville reacquired Waddell, who had a fastball that would ultimately take him to the Hall of Fame, though in Louisville he was just a package of potential.

With a roster like that, why could the Colonels never break into pennant contention? The local owners never fully capitalized the club to compete and rarely had any management with much baseball experience. If money and baseball business acumen were the keys to success, Louisville was 0-for-2. Since joining the National League in 1892, the Colonels had been consistent in getting off to poor starts. Except for 1897, they were never over .500 through May. But in 1898 and 1899 they played better than .600 ball the last two months of the season (September and October). These strong finishes may have given Dreyfuss hope that if he could keep the core of players together, he might be able to fashion a winning club.

But with the end of the 1899 season, Dreyfuss had several problems to solve. He had to figure a way to use the coming elimination of the Louisville franchise to his advantage and he needed to discover a way to leverage the Louisville player assets. Dreyfuss devised a strategy to give himself control of the Louisville players and began a search for a new franchise.

Over the prior year Dreyfuss had assumed the presidency of the Colonels at least twice and now, in early 1899, he again relinquished that position. Pulliam became president, briefly, but Dreyfuss retained an officer position as vice president and treasurer. This kept him on the club's board and gave him some control over finances.[21] Why Dreyfuss ceased being club president so many times is not known. But in a family history written by Dreyfuss's cousin, Isaac Bernheim, he reports that "upon the urgent advice of physicians, he voluntarily relinquished his position and disposed of his interest in the firm [Bernheim Bros. Distilling Co.] to take up an occupation less confining."[22] It is not clear what illness caused Dreyfuss to leave the family business but he focused his future efforts entirely on staying in the baseball business.

Dreyfuss later reported that on October 31, 1899, he sold his stock in the Louisville club and severed his connections with the team. Also on that date, Dreyfuss and the Louisville club came to an agreement dealing with control of the Louisville players' contracts and reserve rights, which had been established in the reserve rule in 1879. Teams retained sole negotiating rights for a player's services even after a contract expired. A document discovered in the Dreyfuss file at the National Baseball Library details an option Dreyfuss purchased from the Louisville club on the day he divested of his stock.[23] The option gave Dreyfuss a 60-day window in which he would have the right to direct the club to "sell, assign and transfer to [Dreyfuss]…each and all of the contracts of whatever kind it has with base ball players, including all its rights of whatever kind to reserve for its use the services of base ball players."[24] Dreyfuss now controlled how and where the Louisville club could trade, sell, or release any of the players named in the option. He had the ability to move Louisville players to any team he might acquire. The option's cost to Dreyfuss was only $50, but if he exercised it he further agreed to pay off $25,000 of debt the Louisville club owed. A little over $20,000 was to pay off bank loans that were due and $4,750 was for personal loans the club owed. Of that amount, $1,750 was owed to Dreyfuss himself.[25]

The document gave Dreyfuss control of Fred Clarke, Honus Wagner, Charlie Dexter, Dummy Hoy, Fred Ketchum, Mike Kelley, Claude Ritchey, Billy Clingman, Tommy Leach, Chief Zimmer, Tacks Latimer, Tom Messitt, Bert Cunningham, Deacon Phillippe, Rube Waddell, Walt Woods, Harry Wilhelm, Pete Dowling, Bill Magee, and Patsy Flaherty.

Louisville clearly needed cash anywhere it could find it. If Dreyfuss exercised his option, the club would be able to cover a large portion of its debt. But the loans listed on the option document did not cover any amounts the club had incurred during operations in 1899, nor obligations to smaller merchants in Louisville. Paying off the banks, however, would give the club some wiggle room in dealing with any 1899 deficit.

As Dreyfuss searched for a National League ballclub to buy, the option agreement protected him from having Louisville sell any player out from under him. There had been inquiries over the past several years from a number of clubs about purchasing a number of Louisville players, but no club seemed to be ripe for purchase.[26] As Dreyfuss surveyed the baseball landscape he focused on Pittsburgh as his primary target.

The controlling partner of the Pirates franchise was W. W. Kerr, the son of a physician and former Pittsburg mayor. His main occupation was as a bookkeeper and

*Barney Dreyfuss bought 47 percent of the Pirates, partly with money and partly by delivering the Louisville Colonels' best players to Pittsburgh.*

clerk at Arbuckle & Co., a coffee roasting firm that later merged with Maxwell House. In *Pittsburg City Directories* Kerr is consistently listed as a clerk but he probably occupied a more prominent role, as his sister was married to the owner.

Kerr got involved with baseball in 1890 and ultimately became the controlling partner of the Pirates with Philip Auten of Chicago. Through the 1890s, the club was a middle-of-the-pack team and there were rumblings that Kerr might be looking to sell. In September 1899, Kerr had been quoted as saying, "If I wasn't in base ball you can bet that I wouldn't go in it under the present conditions."[27] With his full control of the Louisville players, Dreyfuss offered $70,000 for full ownership of the Pittsburgh franchise. In early November 1899, the sporting press reported that the deal was done.[28] But by November 11, it was dead. Now Kerr only wanted to sell a minority share of the Pirates and retain a controlling interest. This was contrary to a recent *Sporting Life* report that Kerr desired to be rid of the day-to-day responsibilities of club presidency.[29] He may have sensed that adding players like Wagner, Clarke, and Phillippe would move the Pirates into pennant contention. But Dreyfuss was looking for a deal that would include no partners, so he declined.[30] Dreyfuss had talks with Jim Hart of Chicago and John Brush of Cincinnati about buying them out, but they were only interested in acquiring some of the Louisville players.[31]

Kerr soon decided to take another opportunity to secure the Louisville players and he approached Dreyfuss in early December with an offer to sell just under half of the outstanding stock in the Pittsburgh club to Dreyfuss, who, having no other candidates for a baseball acquisition, agreed.[32] It was actually a two-part deal. In the first transaction, Louisville assigned the rights to all of its reserved players to Pittsburgh in exchange for Dreyfuss's payment of $25,000 (per the October 31 agreement). The Pirates, in turn, gave Dreyfuss 150 shares of stock in the club for his part in delivering the players to Pittsburgh. In the second agreement, Dreyfuss paid the Pirates $21,330 for an additional 323 shares of stock. In the end, Dreyfuss ended up paying about $98 per share for 473 shares in the Pittsburgh club, estimated at about 47 percent of the outstanding stock.

So for $46,330 Dreyfuss obtained just under a half interest in the Pirates and allowed the Colonels to retire the bulk of their debt. Pittsburgh got a roster that would be a powerhouse for over a decade and Dreyfuss got to stay in baseball. Several weeks later, at the annual meeting of the Pittsburgh club, the sale was completed and Dreyfuss was elected president.[33] He understood that he was not purchasing a controlling interest, stating upon the announcement of the deal, "I will not have control. I am a partner."[34]

As the clubs were closing the deal it apparently became clear that the parties had forgotten something. By releasing all its reserved players to Pittsburgh, Louisville no longer had a team. The franchise owned no players. This appears to be the motivation for structuring the various deals as a trade: The Pirates tossed four players back to the Colonels. While Pittsburgh gained the rights to all of Louisville's former players, it sent infielders George Fox, Art Madison, and John O'Brien, and 25-year-old rookie pitcher Jack Chesbro to Louisville. Except for Chesbro, none ever again appeared in the major leagues. Chesbro would develop into a Hall of Fame pitcher with five 20-win seasons, but in 1899 he was just a throw-in.

About a month after the deal, National League president Nick Young notified the Louisville club that according to NL records, the team had no players. This may have been an effort to push Louisville out of the league quickly and have one fewer team to compensate, but Pulliam would have none of it. He told the Louisville newspapers that there was a side arrangement with Pittsburgh that some of the excess players the Pirates received would be returned to Louisville before the season started. The Colonels also drafted several players from the Western League, Interstate League, and New York State League. While there is no evidence that Louisville ever signed these players, the club could make an argument that it controlled at least 10 players.[35]

In the end, Louisville kept up appearances sufficiently to receive a $10,000 payment from the National

League to fold the franchise. In March 1900, the NL also paid Cleveland $25,000, Baltimore $30,000, and Washington $46,500 to exit from the league. Louisville's lower payment reflects the fact that the team did not own its ballpark, and that the players under the club's control didn't impress anyone. Louisville assigned Jack Chesbro's contract back to Pittsburgh.[36]

Before the start of the 1900 season, Dreyfuss brought in Pulliam to serve as the Pittsburgh club's secretary.[37] Pulliam replaced Frank Balliet, co-owner Phil Auten's nephew, who had held the position for several seasons.[38] The Pirates made a major jump in 1900, climbing to second place in the standings and earning a reported $40,000 profit.[39] This was quite a contrast to just a year before, when Kerr had been quoted in *Sporting Life* saying that the Pirates would struggle to turn a profit in 1899.[40]

But all was not well with senior management. Kerr and Auten, although majority stockholders, had deferred to Dreyfuss, the largest single shareholder, as president when he brought Pulliam from Louisville. The Kerr-Auten contingent now felt it could reestablish its authority and reinstate Balliet.

Throughout November and December 1900, Kerr had released a series of comments to the press that Pulliam was leaving the Pittsburgh club to join the Chicago organization. He never stated it as fact, just as his "understanding." He also reported that Pulliam had already resigned from his position with the Pirates.[41]

These press reports were merely a prelude to the Pittsburgh club's annual meeting in Jersey City on December 11, 1900. During that meeting, Kerr and Auten declined to reelect Pulliam as secretary, though they did not formally propose another candidate.[42] The meeting was adjourned without taking any other actions. Before the end of December, stories were making the rounds that Dreyfuss was about to be dumped as president at a director's meeting on January 12. Kerr was quoted saying that Dreyfuss "has been a little bit out of line lately."[43]

Kerr had liked being in charge of the club before the coming of Dreyfuss, but he was never able to develop a competitive team. In the five seasons before Dreyfuss arrived with a passel of Louisville players, Pittsburgh never finished above sixth place, finishing an average of 25 games out of first. Kerr had a quirk of not wanting to remain at a game if the Pirates were losing.[44] Now that they were one of the stronger National League teams, he was ready to reassume the leadership position. Kerr stated several times during

this internal battle that others could have done what Dreyfuss did in elevating the Pirates to contender status and making the club a substantial profit.[45]

The January 12, 1901, meeting was a disappointment to Kerr and Auten. Dreyfuss, as president and presiding officer, refused to recognize any motions for business to be transacted. He agreed with the lawyer he had retained that the meeting notice had been legally defective, so no business could be completed. The business to be completed was Dreyfuss's ouster.[46] Kerr and Auten sued in New Jersey court (the Pittsburgh club was incorporated in New Jersey) to force Dreyfuss to call a meeting and transact business. Club attorney Norman Rowe attempted to get a single New Jersey Supreme Court judge to issue the order to force a meeting and was rebuffed. He was told to take the case before the full state Supreme Court in Trenton.[47]

Taking the battle to Trenton would cost the Kerr faction at least another month. Even if it successfully raised the issue before the court, Dreyfuss would have the opportunity to respond, take depositions, prepare his case, and generally take up a good bit of time. The legal maneuvering would probably last into the fall.[48] Kerr apparently had no stomach for a drawn-out fight and within two weeks Dreyfuss had secured Kerr's option to purchase the majority holdings of Kerr and Auten. There was also a rumor floating around that the American League was about to place a new team in Pittsburgh, and the Kerr-Auten faction may have feared sharing the city with another team.[49]

By late February, Dreyfuss exercised his option, acquiring the majority holdings of Kerr and Auten along with the 35 shares held by John Tener and his brother, which had been acquired around 1890. Dreyfuss paid Kerr and Auten a reported $66,150 to become the sole owner of the Pirates. Adding up the $21,330 Dreyfuss paid in 1899, the $66,150 he paid for the remaining outstanding stock, and his $25,000 payment to Louisville for control of the club's player contracts, Dreyfuss acquired the Pittsburgh club for $112,480.[50]

It is not entirely clear what Kerr's motivation was for giving up the fight. The potential of a protracted legal battle lasting into the latter part of the year may have been a factor. And the coming expiration of the 1892 National League-American Association pact in the fall may have caused him to wonder if his stock's value might fall in such an uncertain market.

Whatever his reasons, Kerr was now out of baseball. At the end of 1902, Pulliam was elected president of the National League. Dreyfuss would own the Pirates until his death in 1932. During the next 30 years, the Pirates won six pennants and two World

Series, and they finished second in the National League seven times. Dreyfuss was at the center of the rapprochement of the National and American leagues in 1903 and was a key organizer of the first AL-NL World Series that year. In 1909, he built Forbes Field, considered a massive project at the time, and was involved in the Federal League War, the investigation of the 1919 Black Sox Scandal, and the move to install Kenesaw Mountain Landis as baseball commissioner. His baseball management career was celebrated in 2008 with his induction into the National Baseball Hall of Fame. ■

## Notes

1. *Courier-Journal* (Louisville), June 10, 1895; February 24, 1898; December 14, 1898; *The Sporting News*, Dec 31, 1898; "Baseball: League-Association," *New York Clipper*, November 9, 1895; "Louisville Not to be Dislodged," *Sporting Life*, July 13, 1895; "Hub Happenings," *Sporting Life*, December 24, 1898; John B. Foster, "The Big Team Shift," *Sporting Life*, December 24, 1898; John J. Saunders, "Louisville Lines," *Sporting Life*, December 31, 1898; "Editor 'Sporting Life,' Which Way Out?" *Sporting Life*, November 12, 1898.
2. Bob Bailey, "The Forgotten War: AA-NL 1891," *The National Pastime* 19 (1999); "Baseball: A Twelve Club League," *New York Clipper*, December 26, 1891.
3. *Courier-Journal*, March 5, 1895; July 29, 1895.
4. Jeff Youngblood, *The Early Life and Times of Barney Dreyfuss*, unpublished monograph, 2002, Barney Dreyfuss File, Baseball Hall of Fame.
5. *Courier-Journal*, March 18, 1895.
6. *Courier-Journal*, November 11, 1895; December 27, 1895.
7. *Courier-Journal*, February 1, 1898.
8. *Courier-Journal*, March 1, 1898.
9. *Courier-Journal*, June 16, 1898; Elmer. E. Bates, "Bates Budget," *Sporting Life*, August 27, 1898.
10. *Courier-Journal*, December 1, 1898; December 2, 1898; December 3, 1898; December 4, 1898; December 5, 1898; December 6, 1898; December 15, 1898; December 27, 1898.
11. *Courier-Journal*, February 17, 1899.
12. *Courier-Journal*, January 1, 1899.
13. *Courier-Journal*, February 1, 1899.
14. *Courier-Journal*, February 17, 1899.
15. *Courier-Journal*, February 28, 1899.
16. *Courier-Journal*, March 9, 1899; March 10, 1899; March 19, 1899.
17. *Courier-Journal*, March 27, 1899.
18. Bill Lamb, "John Day," SABR BioProject, https://sabr.org/bioproj/person/c281a493; David Quentin Voigt, *American Baseball: From the Gentleman's Sport to the Commissioner System* (University Park, PA: Pennsylvania State University

Press, 1983), 166; Harold Seymour and Dorothy Seymour Mills, *Baseball: The Early Years* (New York: Oxford University Press), 1960, 238.
19. *Courier-Journal*, April 11, 1899; April 12, 1899; April 13, 1899; John J. Saunders, "Mad Louisville," *Sporting Life*, April 8, 1899.
20. *Courier-Journal*, Jun 3, 1897; June 5, 1897; July 16, 1897.
21. "Pulliam Pulled," *Sporting Life*, February 25, 1899; John J. Saunders, "Saunders' Story," *Sporting Life*, February 25, 1899.
22. Isaac Wolf Bernheim, *The Story of the Bernheim Family* (Louisville, KY: John P. Morton & Co., 1910), 65.
23. Dreyfuss-Benswanger Papers 1886–1971, Baseball Hall of Fame, BA MSS 186.
24. Option document in Dreyfuss-Benswanger Papers.
25. Agreement dated October 31, 1899 between the Louisville Base Ball Club and Barney Dreyfuss, Dreyfuss-Benswanger Papers.
26. "That Big Deal," *The Sporting News*, February 5, 1898.
27. Circle, "Pittsburg Points," *Sporting Life*, September 23, 1899.
28. "Dreyfuss Has It," *Sporting Life*, November 4, 1899.
29. Circle, "Pittsburg Points," *Sporting Life*, November 25, 1899.
30. "Dreyfus Done," *Sporting Life*, November 11, 1899.
31. "Best Players of Louisville to Come Here," *Pittsburg Dispatch*, December 9, 1899; "Caught on the Fly," *The Sporting News*, December 16, 1899; "News and Comment," *Sporting Life*, December 16, 1899.
32. "Up to Dreyfuss," *Sporting Life*, December 9, 1899; Pittsburg-Louisville-Dreyfuss Sale Documents Dated December 5, 1899 in Dreyfuss-Benswanger Papers.
33. Circle, "Pittsburg Points," *Sporting Life*, January 6, 1899; "Dreyfus' Delight," *Sporting Life*, January 13, 1900.
34. Circle, "Proud Pittsburg," *Sporting Life*, December 16, 1899.
35. "Circuit Reduction," *Sporting Life*, March 17, 1900.
36. John J. Saunders, "Louisville Roused," *Sporting Life*, January 6, 1900.
37. Circle, "Pittsburg Points," *Sporting Life*, February 24, 1900; "News and Comments," *Sporting Life*, March 17, 1900.
38. Circle, "Pittsburg Points," *Sporting Life*, December 23, 1899.
39. Francis C. Richter, "Dreyfuss Dumped," *Sporting Life*, December 29, 1900.
40. "News and Comment," *Sporting Life*, September 2, 1899.
41. A.R. Cratty, "Doyle Is Wanted," *Sporting Life*, November 24, 1900; A.R. Cratty, "The Annual Meet," *Sporting Life*, December 8, 1900; A.R. Cratty, "Pittsburg Points," *Sporting Life*, December 22, 1900.
42. A.R. Cratty, "Pittsburg Points," *Sporting Life*, December 22, 1900.
43. Richter, "Dreyfuss Dumped," *Sporting Life*, December 29, 1900, 7."
44. Circle, "Pittsburg Points," *Sporting Life*, May 27, 1899; "News and Comment," *Sporting Life*, November 18, 1899.
45. A.R. Cratty, "Angry Owners," *Sporting Life*, December 29, 1900.
46. Francis C. Richter, "Doughty Dreyfuss," *Sporting Life*, January 26, 1901; A.R. Cratty, "Pittsburg Points," January 26, 1901; "Dreyfuss' Deed," *Sporting Life*, January 19, 1901; A.R. Cratty, "Pittsburg Points," *Sporting Life*, January 19, 1901.
47. "Kerr Hopeful," *Sporting Life*, January 19, 1901; "Dreyfuss' Deed," *Sporting Life*, January 19, 1901; A.R. Cratty, "Pittsburg Points," *Sporting Life*, January 19, 1901; Richter, "Doughty Dreyfuss."
48. Richter.
49. "Facts About the Deal," *The Sporting News*, March 2, 1901.
50. Francis C. Richter, "Dreyfuss Wins Out," *Sporting Life*, February 23, 1901.

# How Many Hits Did Ty Cobb Make in His Major League Career? What Is His Lifetime Batting Average?

## Herm Krabbenhoft

Among baseball's most iconic career numbers are 714 and 4,191, the first Babe Ruth's *official* career home runs total and the second Ty Cobb's *official* career hits total. But if you look at many baseball statistics sources today, including websites and encyclopedias, you will find Cobb's number has been altered. This paper seeks to use all available evidence to determine the most accurate total for Cobb's lifetime hits, at-bats, and batting average.

According to the most-recently published baseball encyclopedias and 2019 baseball websites, Ty Cobb's lifetime hit total is *unofficially* 4,189—two fewer hits than the 4,191 obtained from his originally-generated *official* Day-By-Day (DBD) records.[1] In addition, Cobb's career at-bats total has been changed from the *official* 11,429 to the *unofficial* 11,434—five more than before.[2] This was the state of affairs in fall 2018, prior to the completion of my research to ascertain accurate runs-scored numbers and runs-batted-in numbers for the players on the 1908 Detroit Tigers. These *unofficial* changes in Cobb's hits and at-bats also precipitated a lowering of his career batting average—from a rounded-up *official* .367 (.36670) to an *unofficial* as-is .366 (.36636).[3]

As summarized in Appendix 1 (available online at SABR.org), these changes to Cobb's hits and at-bats are attributable to the corrections of errors in Cobb's official DBD records for three seasons:

- 1906 (the games on April 22 and April 23)

- 1910 (the second game of the doubleheader on July 24)

- 1912 (the first game of the doubleheader on July 12)

There have been numerous other reports of discrepancies. Two other games from 1910 (May 26 and August 10) had been reported previously as containing at-bat errors—by Paul MacFarlane in the 1981 *Daguerrotypes* record book published by *The Sporting News*.

However, the requisite supporting documentation for these alleged at-bat errors was not provided and were completely ignored by *Total Baseball*, *The ESPN Baseball Encyclopedia*, Baseball-Reference.com, Baseball Almanac, and Retrosheet. The Retrosheet "Discrepancy File" listed five other games which, according to the Retrosheet box scores, contained discrepancies with the originally-generated DBD records for Cobb's at-bats: 1905 (September 13), 1911 (May 20), 1913 (August 9), 1916 (June 6), and 1919 (the first game of the double header on July 4). Again, the requisite supporting documentation (i.e., batter-by-batter play-by-play details) for these alleged at-bat errors was not provided. And, while doing my research on the 1908 season, I discovered yet another at-bat error in the official DBD records for the Genius in Spikes—in the Boston-Detroit game on May 15.[5] I made it my goal to search out and compile all the requisite documentation to corroborate or to refute each of the above-mentioned alleged discrepancies in Cobb's at-bats.

### RESEARCH PROCEDURE

For the May 15, 1908, game between the Tigers and Red Sox in Boston, I obtained ten game accounts, six from Boston and four from Detroit. In Boston I used the *Globe* (BG), *Herald* (BH), *Post* (BP), *Daily Advertiser* (BDA), *Journal* (BJ), and *Traveler* (BT). From Detroit the accounts came from the *Free Press* (DFP), *Journal* (DJ), *News* (DN), and *Times* (DT). From these accounts I was able to construct an unambiguous record of Cobb's at-bats and hits in the game.

I provided this documentation to Retrosheet's Tom Ruane and Dave Smith for their review, upon which we achieved 100% agreement and the at-bats and hits for Cobb were incorporated in the Retrosheet Box Score File (and Cobb's derived Player Daily File).[6] John Thorn and Pete Palmer also concurred with my conclusions for Cobb's at-bats and hits.[7] I also ascertained the complete details for each of the plate appearances Ty Cobb had in the 1910 games on May 26 and August 10 and in the five above-mentioned games

*Ty Cobb and Joe Jackson*

from Retrosheet's Discrepancy File. (See Appendices 2 and 3) I also provided this information to Ruane, Smith, Palmer, and Thorn, who concurred with each of my conclusions for Cobb's at-bats and hits in these seven games.[8]

## RESULTS

Two independent batter-by-batter play-by-play descriptions of the May 15, 1908, game were provided in the BP and BJ game accounts (See Appendix 4). While similar, these "scorecard" summaries are not identical. Based on these two scorecards, here's what Cobb did in each of his four plate appearances:

1. Second Inning—Cobb flied out to the right fielder (Cravath).

2. Fourth Inning—Cobb doubled. He was subsequently retired on a play from the left fielder (Thoney) to the second baseman (McConnell). Boss Schmidt flied out to Thoney who then threw to McConnell, catching Cobb off second.

3. 7th Inning—According to the BP scorecard, Cobb was safe on an error by the pitcher (Young). Cobb advanced to second and to third

on a base hit by the first baseman (Rossman). Cobb advanced to home on a fielder's choice and scored. According to the BJ scorecard, Cobb singled and advanced to third on a base hit by the first baseman (Rossman) and then scored when Schmidt hit into a 4–3 groundout.

4. 8th Inning—With Schaefer on third base with one out, Cobb was retired on a flyout to left. Schaefer advanced from third to home and scored on Cobb's flyout [which, according to the official 1908 scoring rules, was a sacrifice hit (fly)]. The BP scorecard recorded the event "sh F7" while the BJ scorecard recorded the play "F7."

Thus, for the entire game, according to the BP scorecard summary, Cobb achieved one hit (a double) in three at-bats and one sacrifice hit (fly). However, according to the BJ scorecard, Cobb collected two hits (one double and one single) in four at-bats (and no sacrifice hits). According to the *official* DBD records, Cobb had two (2) hits in four (4) at-bats and no sacrifice hits (i.e., the May 15 cell in the "SH" column was left blank).

The 1908 season was the first season in which run-scoring flyouts were officially scored as sacrifice hits (flies) and, therefore, a player was not charged with an at bat when he batted in a run on a flyout. (See Appendix 5 for the relevant official scoring rules before 1908 and from 1908 forward.) Therefore, the BJ scorecard summary is not accurate since Cobb's eighth-inning performance should have been recorded as "sh F7" as it was in the BP scorecard summary. Thus, the official DBD record, which shows Cobb with four (4) at-bats, is also not accurate. That the official DBD record and the BJ account are identical suggests that the official scorer was the BJ journalist. (See Appendix 6 for definitive information on this.) With regard to Cobb's seventh inning performance—safe on a fielding error by the pitcher according to the BP scorecard or safe on a base hit according to the BJ scorecard, the official DBD records show Cobb with two (2) hits and Young with no errors. Additional discussion of Cobb's seventh-inning performance is provided in Appendix 6.

To further investigate the eighth-inning at-bat discrepancy between the official DBD records and the "scorecard" summaries given in the BP and BJ game accounts, I examined the game accounts presented in several other newspapers. Here are the text descriptions for the run scored by Detroit in the eighth inning given in the various daily newspapers published in Detroit and Boston:

**DFP**—"Detroit fetched another run in the eighth, on a hit by Schaefer, [first baseman] Unglaub's poor throw off Crawford, and Cobb's out to [left fielder] Thoney."

**DJ**—"Schaefer hit safely. He went from first to third on Unglaub's poor throw to first on Crawford's grounder. Schaefer scored on Cobb's fly to Thoney, but the Boston scorers failed to give Cobb a sacrifice which he was entitled to."

**DN**—There was no mention of the eighth-inning run.

**DT**—"The Tigers got another [run] in the eighth just to give Killian an easy margin." No further details were provided in the DT game account.

**BG**—"The Tigers scored their sixth run in the eighth on Schaefer's single, a putout [i.e., Crawford's sacrifice and subsequent out for interference], and Rossman's single." [NOTE: The BG description is not in alignment with the BP and BJ scorecard summaries and omits what Cobb did—Cobb was the player who batted immediately before Rossman]

**BH**—"In the eighth a single by Schaefer, a sacrifice hit by Crawford, and a long sacrifice fly by Cobb added another run."

**BP** text description—"In the eighth Schaefer's hit, Crawford's sacrifice and Unglaub's error, followed by Rossman's third hit, made the score 6 to 4." [NOTE: The BP text description is not in alignment with the BP scorecard summary and does not include what Cobb did (following Crawford's at bat and preceding Rossman's at bat).]

**BDA**—There was no mention of the eighth-inning run.

**BJ** text description—"In the eighth the Tigers made another run on Schaefer's hit, Crawford's sacrifice and Unglaub's accompanying error, and Cobb's fly out." [NOTE: The BJ text description is in perfect synch with the BJ scorecard summary.]

**BT**—"Detroit added another run in the eighth on Schaefer's single and Unglaub's error on Crawford's bunt, and Cobb's fly to Thoney."

The DFP, DJ, BH, BJ, and BT text descriptions and the BP and BJ "scorecard" summaries are in complete alignment with each other and state that Cobb batted in Schaefer with a flyout—which according to the official scoring rules for 1908 means that Cobb should have been credited with a sacrifice hit (fly) and should not have been charged with an at bat. The BG and BP text descriptions, however, state that Schaefer scored on a single by Rossman (but make no mention of what Cobb did in his plate appearance immediately before Rossman singled).

Examination of the box scores reveals numerous inconsistencies between a given box score and the accompanying text. And comparison of one box score with another reveals that there are several inconsistencies, especially with respect to players being credited with sacrifice hits. Appendix 6 provides transcripts of the various box scores along with a synopsis of the sacrifice-hit numbers for all players and the base-hit numbers for Cobb.

## DISCUSSION

How does one deal with the conflicting information? From my perspective, the most important information is that presented in the batter-by-batter play-by-play scorecard summaries provided in the BP and BJ game accounts. As documented in these scorecard summaries for the eighth inning, Schaefer got a base hit, advanced to second on a sacrifice hit by Crawford, took third on an error by the first baseman (which also allowed Crawford to reach first base, but who was then called out for interference by umpire O'Loughlin), and scored on a sacrifice hit (fly) by Cobb, who was retired on a flyout to the left fielder. That Schaefer scored on Cobb's flyout to left is also stated in the BH, BJ, BT, DFP, and DJ text descriptions. Indeed, as indicated in the Results section, the BH and DJ text descriptions specifically mention that Cobb hit a sacrifice (fly). The BH writer (no by-line given) stated, "*and a long sacrifice fly by Cobb.*" The DJ author (no by-line given) wrote "*…but the Boston scorers failed to give Cobb a sacrifice which he was entitled to.*" Thus, I contend that Schaefer did score in the eighth inning as a consequence of Cobb's plate appearance, which was a sacrifice fly to the left fielder. With regard to the statements given in the BG and BP text descriptions that Schaefer scored on a single by Rossman, I contend that they are erroneous—chiefly because they are not supported by the batter-by-batter play-by-play summaries in the BP and BJ "scorecards" and they do not mention what Cobb did, Cobb having batted immediately before Rossman singled.

My conclusion is that the preponderance of the evidence is that in the game on May 15, 1908, Germany Schaefer scored from third base in the eighth inning on a one-out sacrifice flyout hit by Ty Cobb. Cobb should not have been charged with an at bat in his eighth-inning plate appearance, Therefore, Cobb actually achieved two (2) hits in three (3) at-bats, not two (2) hits in four (4) at-bats as given in his official DBD records.

The appropriate changes have since been made in Retrosheet, which now shows Cobb with three (3) at-bats and one sacrifice hit. Pete Palmer has also made the appropriate corrections in his database of baseball statistics. These changes are visible on Retrosheet.org and Baseball-Reference.com.[9]

Turning now to consideration of the documentation collected in Appendices 1–3, Table 1 (below) summarizes the corrections of the errors in at-bats and hits in Cobb's originally-generated official DBD records for the twelve games with errors in hits and/or at-bats investigated for this article.

Among the changes made at Retrosheet and Baseball-Reference, one exception that has not been made visible to the public yet is the 1905 correction which I completed in December 2018, after Retrosheet's Fall 2018 Update and after Palmer's Fall 2018 Update.[10] Table 1 shows that the corrections of the errors in Cobb's hits and at-bats result in small changes in his relevant full-season batting averages. For his career, Cobb amassed 4,189 hits in 11,439 at-bats (not 4,191 hits in 11,429 at-bats), which affords him an *unofficial* .366 batting average (.36620), not a rounded-up .367 (.36670) as obtained from his *official* DBD records.

Two important questions emerge from the correction of these errors in the official DBD records for Cobb's at-bats and hits:

1. Is the number of errors, consisting of twelve games with fourteen errors (three errors in the number of hits and eleven errors in the number of at-bats), extraordinary?

2. Are these corrected numbers the final-absolute values for Cobb's at-bats, hits, and batting average, particularly for his career?

The answer to the first question is "No." Several years ago, Steve Hirdt, executive vice-president of the Elias Sports Bureau (the official statistician for Major League Baseball) stated, "Around the time that Rickey Henderson was challenging Ty Cobb's all-time runs-scored record, there was some focus on someone's claim that, by God, a mistake had been found in Cobb's game-by-game statistics and that Cobb should be credited with one more run than Elias showed [i.e., 2246 vs. 2245]. I say it's amusing, because we knew not only of that particular error, but more than a dozen [errors] dealing with Cobb's run-scored total."[11] The fourteen instances of errors in Cobb's hits and at-bats identified in this paper are in line with the "more than a dozen" errors for his runs-scored.

The answer to the second question is "Hopefully." Thanks to the dedicated efforts of the Retrosheet volunteers, Retrosheet has generated balanced box scores for every game that Cobb played in his major league career. As presented in Appendix 3, my research has conclusively resolved each of the five games which had at-bat discrepancies between the

**Table 1. Corrections of Errors in At-Bats and Hits in Ty Cobb's Official DBD Records**

| Year | Game | Official H/AB | Actual H/AB | Official H/AB | Official AVG | Actual H/AB | Actual AVG |
|------|------|------|------|------|------|------|------|
| 1905 | 9–13 | 1/3 | 1/4 | 36/150 | .24000 –> .240 | 36/151 | .23841 –> .238 |
| 1906 | 4–22 | –/– | 0/3 | | | | |
| | 4–23 | –/– | 1/5 | 112/350 | .32000 –> .320 | 113/358 | .31564 –> .316 |
| 1908 | 5–15 | 2/4 | 2/3 | 188/581 | .32358 –> .324 | 188/580 | .32414 –> .324 |
| 1910 | 5–26 | 2/4 | 2/5 | | | | |
| | 8–10 | 1/3 | 1/4 | 196/509 | .38507 –> .385 | 194/508 | .38189 –> .382 |
| | 9–24 (2) | 2/3 | –/– | | | | |
| 1911 | 5–20 | 3/4 | 3/5 | 248/591 | .41962 –> .420 | 248/592 | .41892 –> .419 |
| 1912 | 7–12 (1) | 1/2 | 0/2 | 227/553 | .41049 –> .410 | 226/553 | .40868 –> .409 |
| 1913 | 8–09 | 1/2 | 1/3 | 167/428 | .39019 –> .390 | 167/429 | .38928 –> .389 |
| 1916 | 6–06 | 1/2 | 1/3 | 201/542 | .37085 –> .371 | 201/543 | .37017 –> .370 |
| 1919 | 7–04 (1) | 0/0 | 0/1 | 191/497 | .38431 –> .384 | 191/498 | .38353 –> .384 |
| Career | | | | 4,191/11,429 | .36670 –> .367 | 4,189/11,439 | .36620 –> .366 |

Retrosheet box scores and the official DBD records. Likewise, as presented in Appendices 1 and 2, each of the other six previously-identified games with errors in Cobb's official DBD records for at-bats and/or hits has been conclusively resolved. And, as described in this article, the correction of Cobb's 1908 at-bat error has been accepted by Retrosheet and Pete Palmer. So, I am optimistic that all of the errors in Cobb's official at-bats and hits (and derived batting averages) have been discovered and corrected. However, it is possible that future research could turn up additional errors in Cobb's at-bats and/or hits—like the missed 1908 non-at-bat sacrifice fly described in this article. Nonetheless, it can be stated right now that—based on the research described in this article (including Appendices 1, 2, and 3)—the at-bats and hits (and derived batting averages) for Ty Cobb are the most complete and most accurate they have ever been.

## CONCLUDING REMARKS

The 2018 edition of *The Elias Book of Baseball Records* shows Ty Cobb having the record for the highest lifetime batting average in the major leagues with a .367 mark.[12] Similarly, Elias shows Cobb having the record for the most hits, lifetime, in the American League with 4,191 hits.[13] However, it no longer shows the number of at-bats Cobb accumulated in his 24-year career (1905–28). According to the 1982 edition of *The (Elias) Book of Baseball Records*, Cobb was the AL record holder in career at-bats with 11,429—the number obtained from the official DBD records.[14] Since Elias still uses 4,191 for Cobb's lifetime hits and .367 for his lifetime batting average, Elias apparently also uses 11,429 for Cobb's lifetime at-bats. With 4,191 hits, the number of at-bats needed to yield a .367 batting average is between 11,405 (which gives a batting average of .36747) and 11,435 (which gives a batting average of .36650).

Since Elias has declined to incorporate corrections to the previously-documented errors in Cobb's official DBD records for 1906, 1910, and 1912, it seems unlikely that they will incorporate the correction of the at-bat error discovered in Cobb's official DBD record for the 1908 season (or the other at-bat errors shown in the Appendices). Although Elias has not corrected the at-bats and hits errors in Cobb's 1906, 1910, and 1912 seasons, they did correct Cobb's runs-scored errors for the years 1909 and 1911—seasons in which Cobb topped the AL in runs scored.[15]

Elias's strict adherence to the previously derived statistics may stem from a directive issued by MLB

*Cobb demonstrates the split grip he used to get all 4,189 of his hits.*

NATIONAL BASEBALL HALL OF FAME AND LIBRARY, COOPERSTOWN, NY

Commissioner Bowie Kuhn in 1981 which stated, "The passage of 70 years, in our judgment, also constitutes a certain statute of limitation as to recognizing any changes in the records with confidence of the accuracy of such changes."[16] Kuhn's declaration has caused an intriguing dilemma, as Kirk Kenney points out in his 2015 article, "Did Rose Really Set Hits Record Against Padres?" SABR, *Total Baseball*, Baseball-Reference.com, Baseball Almanac, and Retrosheet list 4,189 hits for Cobb, while MLB and the Elias Sports Bureau have 4,191 hits. Kenney summarizes this dilemma thus: "*Total Baseball* is MLB's official encyclopedia and historical record. Elias is MLB's official statistician. And they don't agree. What the heck?"[17] Kenney concluded his article with a quotation by MLB's Official Historian, John Thorn, which makes a fitting conclusion for this article, as well: "A statute of limitations on the truth? When you discover truth, you have to report it." ∎

**NOTE**: All appendices can be accessed at https://sabr.org/node/54547.

## Dedication

Herm Krabbenhoft gratefully dedicates this article to his good friend Gary Stone. Because of Gary's very generous help in making photocopies of game accounts from microfilmed newspapers numerous times at several libraries in upstate New York over the past thirty-some years, my baseball research has been greatly facilitated. We've also enjoyed many baseball games and times together. Thanks so much, Gary, and all the best to you and Barbara!

## Acknowledgments

I gratefully thank Pete Palmer and John Thorn for their inputs and guidance on the discovery of errors in Ty Cobb's official DBD records for at-bats and hits for the 1906, 1910, and 1912 seasons. I gratefully thank Dixie Tourangeau, Gary Gillette, and Jerry Nechal for providing photocopies and scans of articles from various Boston and Detroit newspapers. I also wish to thank Steve Elsberry for providing me with Ty Cobb's hits for the 1912 season as given in the second and third editions of *Total Baseball*. And I thank Retrosheet's Tom Ruane and Dave Smith and Pete Palmer and John Thorn for reviewing the evidence I collected on the May 15, 1908, game and the games in Appendices 2 and 3.

## Notes

1. John Thorn, Phil Birnbaum, Bill Deane, *Total Baseball* (New York: Sport Media Publishing, 2004); Gary Gillette, Pete Palmer, *The ESPN Baseball Encyclopedia* (New York: Sterling Publishing, 2008); Baseball-Reference.com—accessed on October 10, 2018; Baseball Almanac—accessed on October 10, 2018; Retrosheet—accessed on October 10, 2018.

2. Ibid.

3. Herm Krabbenhoft, "Accurate Runs-Scored Records for Players of the Deadball Era: The Players on the 1908 Detroit Tigers," *The Inside Game*, Volume XVIII, Number 5 (November 2018) 10; Herm Krabbenhoft, "Accurate RBI Records for Players of the Deadball Era: Part 16—The Players on the 1908 Detroit Tigers," *The Inside Game*, Volume XIX, Number 1 (February 2019) 9.

4. Paul Mac Farlane, "Lajoie Beats Out Cobb," *The Sporting News*, (April 18, 1981) 3; Paul Mac Farlane, *Daguerreotypes of Great Stars of Baseball* (St. Louis: C.C. Johnson Spink, 1981) 56.

5. Krabbenhoft, "Accurate Runs."

6. Tom Ruane and Dave Smith, email correspondence with Herm Krabbenhoft, September 3, 8, and 9, and October 12–15, 2018. I submitted supporting documentation for RBI statistics for 66 games for which Retrosheet had no RBI numbers and 18 games for which my evidence disagreed with the RBI statistics shown in the Retrosheet box scores—including the May 15, 1908, game for which I wrote, "Also consider crediting Cobb with a sacrifice fly and one less at bat." On September 8, Ruane replied, "That was it. In all the other cases [i.e., with the exception of the second game of the July 7 double header (for which

I had made a transcription error)] I concur with your conclusions." The corrected box score for the May 15, 1908, game for Boston-vs.-Detroit on Retrosheet (Figure 12 in Appendix 6) was accessed October 1, 2018.

7. Pete Palmer, email correspondence with Herm Krabbenhoft, October 10, 11, 13–16, 2018— On October 10, Palmer wrote to Krabbenhoft, "You have done very detailed analyses of these games. I would certainly be willing to make any changes that you have verified, as I have done with the runs and RBI research you have done on the Tigers and Lou Gehrig." On October 11, Palmer wrote to John Thorn and Krabbenhoft (and four others), "My position is for the most part to accept the original records as close approximations. However, if someone like Herm does the necessary research or prove a particular cause, I am happy to include the change."

8. Email correspondence, as previously cited.

9. Baseball-Reference.com—accessed on February 1, 2019; Retrosheet— accessed on February 1, 2019.

10. Tom Ruane and Dave Smith, email correspondence with Herm Krabbenhoft, December 2–9, 2018 and February 6–9, 2019. Ruane and Smith agreed 100 percent with my deduced PBP description of the September 13, 1905, game and have incorporated the information in the Retrosheet box score and derived player daily file, which is expected to be included in Retrosheet's Spring 2019 release of updated information; Pete Palmer and John Thorn, email correspondence with Herm Krabbenhoft, February 9, 2019. Palmer agreed 100 percent with my deduced PBP description of the September 13, 1905, game and will incorporate the information in his database of baseball statistics in the fall of 2019.

11. Steve Hirdt, *The SABR Bulletin*, (July–August, 2006) 6.

12. Seymour Siwoff, *The Elias Book of Baseball Records*, (New York: Seymour Siwoff, 2018) 7.

13. Ibid, 13.

14. Seymour Siwoff, *The Book of Baseball Records*, (New York: 14 Seymour Siwoff, 1982) 12.

15. Herm Krabbenhoft, "Accurate Runs-Scored Numbers for Players of the Deadball Era: The Players on the 1909 Detroit Tigers," *The Inside Game*, Volume XVIII, Number 3 (June 2018) 4; Herm Krabbenhoft, "Accurate Runs-Scored Numbers for Players of the Deadball Era: The Players on the 1911 Detroit Tigers," *The Inside Game*, Volume XVII, Number 4 (September 2017) 4.

16. Mac Farlane, "Lajoie Beats Out Cobb."

17. Kirk Kenney, "Did Rose Really Set Hits Record Against Padres?" *The San Diego Union-Tribune*, September 11, 2015, https://www.sandiegouniontribune.com/sports/padres/sdut-pete-rose-breaks-ty-cobb-hit-record-4192-2015sep11-story.html—accessed October 6, 2018.

# New Books from SABR

Part of the mission of the Society for American Baseball Research has always been to disseminate member research. In addition to the *Baseball Research Journal*, SABR publishes books that include player biographies, historical game recaps, and statistical analysis. All SABR books are available in print and ebook formats. SABR members can access the entire SABR Digital Library for free and purchase print copies at significant member discounts of 40 to 50% off cover price.

### JEFF BAGWELL IN CONNECTICUT:
*A Consistent Lad in the Land of Steady Habits*
This volume of articles, interviews, and essays by members of the Connecticut chapter of SABR chronicles the life and career of Connecticut's favorite baseball son, Hall-of-Famer Jeff Bagwell, with special attention on his high school and college years.
**Edited by Karl Cicitto, Bill Nowlin, & Len Levin**
**$19.95 paperback (ISBN 978-1-943816-97-2)**
**$9.99 ebook (ISBN 978-1-943816-96-5)**
**7"x10", 246 pages, 45 photos**

### 1995 CLEVELAND INDIANS:
*The Sleeping Giant Awakens*
After almost 40 years of sub-.500 baseball, the Sleeping Giant woke in 1995, the first season the Indians spent in their new home of Jacob's Field. The biographies of all the players, coaches, and broadcasters from that year are here, sprinkled with personal perspectives, as well as game stories from key matchups during the 1995 season, information about Jacob's Field, and other essays.
**Edited by Joseph Wancho**
**$19.95 paperback (ISBN 978-1-943816-95-8)**
**$9.99 ebook (ISBN 978-1-943816-94-1)**
**8.5"X11", 410 pages, 76 photos**

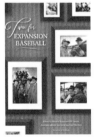

### TIME FOR EXPANSION BASEBALL
The LA Angels and "new" Washington Senators ushered in MLB's 1960 expansion, followed in 1961 by the Houston Colt .45s and New York Mets. By 1998, 10 additional teams had launched: the Kansas City Royals, Seattle Pilots, Toronto Blue Jays, and Tampa Bay Devil Rays in the AL, and the Montreal Expos, San Diego Padres, Colorado Rockies, Florida Marlins, and Arizona Diamondbacks in the NL. *Time for Expansion Baseball* tells each team's origin and includes biographies of key players.
**Edited by Maxwell Kates and Bill Nowlin**
**$24.95 paperback (ISBN 978-1-933599-89-7)**
**$9.99 ebook (ISBN 978-1-933599-88-0)**
**8.5"X11", 430 pages, 150 photos**

### Base Ball's 19th Century "Winter" Meetings 1857-1900
A look at the business meetings of base ball's earliest days (not all of which were in the winter). As John Thorn writes in his Foreword, "This monumental volume traces the development of the game from its birth as an organized institution to its very near suicide at the dawn of the next century."
**Edited by Jeremy K. Hodges and Bill Nowlin**
**$29.95 paperback (ISBN 978-1-943816-91-0)**
**$9.99 ebook (ISBN 978-1-943816-90-3)**
**8.5"x11", 390 pages, 50 photos**

### MET-ROSPECTIVES:
*A Collection of the Greatest Games in New York Mets History*
This book's 57 game stories—coinciding with the number of Mets years through 2018—are strictly for the eternal optimist. They include the team's very first victory in April 1962 at Forbes Field, Tom Seaver's "Imperfect Game" in July '69, the unforgettable Game Sixes in October '86, the "Grand Slam Single" in the 1999 NLCS, and concludes with the extra-innings heroics in September 2016 at Citi Field that helped ensure a wild-card berth.
**edited by Brian Wright and Bill Nowlin**
**$14.95 paperback (ISBN 978-1-943816-87-3)**
**$9.99 ebook (ISBN 978-1-943816-86-6)**
**8.5"X11", 148 pages, 44 photos**

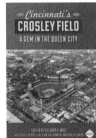

### CINCINNATI'S CROSLEY FIELD:
*A Gem in the Queen City*
This book evokes memories of Crosley Field through detailed summaries of more than 85 historic and monumental games played there, and 10 insightful feature essays about the history of the ballpark. Former Reds players Johnny Edwards and Art Shamsky share their memories of the park in introductions.
**Edited by Gregory H. Wolf**
**$19.95 paperback (ISBN 978-1-943816-75-0)**
**$9.99 ebook (ISBN 978-1-943816-74-3)**
**8.5"X11", 320 pages, 43 photos**

### MOMENTS OF JOY AND HEARTBREAK:
*66 Significant Episodes in the History of the Pittsburgh Pirates*
In this book we relive no-hitters, World Series-winning homers, and the last tripleheader ever played in major-league baseball. Famous Pirates like Honus Wagner and Roberto Clemente—and infamous ones like Dock Ellis—make their appearances, as well as recent stars like Andrew McCutcheon.
**Edited by Jorge Iber and Bill Nowlin**
**$19.95 paperback (ISBN 978-1-943816-73-6)**
**$9.99 ebook (ISBN 978-1-943816-72-9)**
**8.5"X11", 208 pages, 36 photos**

### FROM SPRING TRAINING TO SCREEN TEST:
*Baseball Players Turned Actors*
SABR's book of baseball's "matinee stars," a selection of those who crossed the lines between professional sports and popular entertainment. Included are the famous (Gene Autry, Joe DiMaggio, Jim Thorpe, Bernie Williams) and the forgotten (Al Gettel, Lou Stringer, Wally Hebert, Wally Hood), essays on baseball in TV shows and Coca-Cola commercials, and Jim Bouton's casting as "Jim Barton" in the *Ball Four* TV series.
**Edited by Rob Edelman and Bill Nowlin**
**$19.95 paperback (ISBN 978-1-943816-71-2)**
**$9.99 ebook (ISBN 978-1-943816-70-5)**
**8.5"X11", 410 pages, 89 photos**

*To learn more about how to receive these publications for free or at member discount as a member of SABR, visit the website: sabr.org/join*

# Hits in Consecutive ABs

*Investigating the Nineteenth Century*

## Brian Marshall

While playing for the Cleveland Indians over the course of four consecutive games in July 1920, Tris Speaker got hits in eleven consecutive at bats, setting both the American League and major league record. Although Speaker is now tied for third on that list, this article's subject is what happened regarding the hits in consecutive at bats record before Speaker's feat, not after. According to *Total Baseball*, the previous record of ten was shared by two players, Ed Delahanty and Jake Gettman, who both accomplished the feat in 1897 in the National League. The NL portion of "Most Consecutive Hits" table in *Total Baseball* also includes Joe Kelley with nine.[1] But there is one additional nineteenth century player, Jake Stenzel, who must be included in this discussion, and my research has uncovered a discrepancy in the number of hits comprising the actual record.[2] This article will detail the hits in consecutive ABs streaks related to each of the NL leaders, including Stenzel, as well as provide the details related to the hits discrepancy for Delahanty and Kelley.

### JAKE STENZEL

In 1893, Jake Stenzel, then of the Pittsburgh Pirates, registered a streak of eleven hits in consecutive ABs, a performance which was detailed by Al Kermisch in the *Baseball Research Journal* in 1991.[3] As stated by Kermisch, the Stenzel streak began on July 15, in a game against the Washington Senators, with three hits. Although he had five hits that day, the first five-hit performance of his career, it was the final three of those hits that began Stenzel's streak.[4] On July 17 against the Cleveland Spiders, Stenzel went four-for-four, with two walks, to bring the total to seven hits in seven consecutive at bats. The Kermisch article incorrectly dates the next game on July 19—it was July 18—but nevertheless the streak was continued with four singles in six ABs.

I researched six relevant newspaper articles covering the game but unfortunately they only provide the details of when the first three hits occurred (singles in the first, second and fourth innings) as well as a ninth-inning strikeout.[5] It isn't clear in which at bat the fourth hit occurred. The Kermisch article didn't include references, but it seems fair to presume that Kermisch based his conclusion that "Stenzel singled in his first 4 times at bat to make it 11 hits in a row" on sound evidence. Eleven hits in eleven consecutive times at bat is significant of course, because it increases by one the

*Jake Stenzel*

NL record over that listed in *Total Baseball* and means that Speaker's performance only tied the MLB record rather than set it.

But that's not all. My research shows that Ed Delahanty also had eleven hits in consecutive ABs, rather than the 10 listed *in Total Baseball*.

### ED DELAHANTY

The Delahanty streak is demonstrably 11 hits in 11 at bats. It began with the doubleheader games on July 13, 1897, with Delahanty playing for Philadelphia against the Louisville Colonels. In the first game he went four-for-four and in the second game five-for-five, making nine hits on the day. The streak continued the next day, also against Louisville, when Delahanty managed to get two more hits in his first two times at bat—in the first and fourth innings. That would make eleven hits in eleven consecutive ABs to equal the MLB record set by Stenzel in 1893.

Let us examine the evidence. The home and away newspapers covering the first game of the July 13 doubleheader differ markedly in their batting statistics for Delahanty. The Louisville newspapers listed Delahanty with only three hits in three at bats.[6] The Philadelphia newspapers listed him with four hits in four at bats.[7] The box score in *Sporting Life* along with the ICI game-by-game data sheets for Delahanty in 1897 each also indicated four hits in four at bats.[8] After the Delahanty

Joe Kelley's consecutive hits feat went underreported at the time, and subsequently underreported in the record books.

hit spree, the *Cleveland Plain Dealer* newspaper commented:

> Delahanty [sic], the Phillies' heavy hitting outfielder, must be afraid that Burkett may become the three-time champion batter. When he saw that the Cleveland hitter was crawling up, the Quaker champion took out a fresh supply of bats, and the way he has been hitting the ball is wonderful. Out of fifteen times at bat in the last three games, he has made fourteen hits [sic]. That is a record for the season.[9]

Crediting Delahanty with only three hits in three at bats appears to be unique to the Louisville newspapers. The discrepancy apparently stems from whether or not Delahanty reached on an error in the seventh when his ball got past Clark at second base for Louisville. If the play was interpreted by the Louisville press as an error, that should have been reflected accordingly in the box score of the Louisville papers. Strangely, they neglected to do so. It is clear from the newspaper articles that Delahanty made a hit every time he came to bat and *The Louisville Courier-Journal* specifically alluded to Clark failing to corral balls off the bats of Delahanty and Lajoie.[10] This could mean Clark had a shot at fielding the Delahanty hit in the seventh but wasn't up to the task. If that was the case, then by rule Delahanty should be credited with a hit rather than Clark being charged with an error on the

play.[11] (There was also another discrepancy regarding the reporting of the first game on July 13, 1897, which is not relevant to this article.[12])

## JOE KELLEY

Delahanty isn't the only one whose achievements seem to be under-recorded. There is a discrepancy in the number of hits during consecutive ABs for Joe Kelley of the Baltimore Orioles during the 1894 season. As mentioned, *Total Baseball* lists Kelley with nine hits in consecutive ABs. My research shows the streak was actually ten.

The Kelley streak began with the game on September 1, 1894, with a hit in his final at bat, and finished with the doubleheader games on September 3, 1894, against the Cleveland Spiders. That day he went four for four in the first game and five for five in the second game, to add nine hits to the one that ended the previous game, totaling ten.

As with Delahanty, I examined multiple newspaper accounts of Kelley's performance. In the September 1 game Kelley managed two hits—a double and a single—in three ABs and also reached on a base on balls. The September 1 game was played in Baltimore, the Orioles won, 5–2 and it wasn't necessary for them to bat in the ninth inning.[13] *The Cleveland Leader* reports that Kelley managed a double in the first and a single in the seventh, which implies that Kelley's two other plate appearances were likely in the third and fifth innings.[14] One of them was a walk and the other had to be the second hit. (Kelley also came within one batter of batting in the eighth inning but Kid Gleason appears to have been the final out.) The ICI game-by-game data sheets also indicate that Kelley had a BB to go along with a double and a single.[15] At the very least, his final at bat on September 1 was unquestionably a hit.

Then we come to the doubleheader of September 3 in which Kelley went nine-for-nine across the two games. In fact, his performance in the second game is noteworthy because four of his five hits were doubles, which tied the NL (and MLB) record for most doubles in a game by an individual. Not only that, it was done in a six-inning game against none other than Cy Young. Baltimore had 22 hits, 12 of them doubles, off Young in that game, which may have been the most hits that Young gave up in six innings in his career. One reason for the preponderance of doubles may have been a ground rule that limited extra-base hits to two, and Kelley lost a home run due to this.[16] Umpire Tim Keefe called the game on account of darkness after six full innings had been played.

THE RUCKER ARCHIVE

*Jake Gettman*

### JAKE GETTMAN

The last consecutive ABs with a hit performance that needs to be included in this discussion is that of Jake Gettman, who played with the Senators in 1897 and at the time of his acquisition by Washington was known as the "Keeler of the Texas League."[17] Gettman registered a mark of ten hits in ten consecutive ABs that began on September 10, 1897, with a four-for-four performance against the Cleveland Spiders, continued with a five-for-five performance on September 11 in the first game of a doubleheader against the Cincinnati Reds, and concluded with a single in his first AB in the second game. As I have just demonstrated, Gettman's streak equaled the third best record of the nineteenth century—Kelley's 10 in 1894—and was third to Jake Stenzel's 11 in 1893 and Delahanty's 11 of a few months earlier in July 1897. In their coverage of Gettman's feat, the *Washington Post* described him "…making ten successive hits out of ten turns at the bat, which will stand as a batting achievement for the season."[18] The *Post* were apparently unaware that Delahanty had recorded eleven hits in eleven consecutive ABs earlier in the 1897 season. *Sporting Life* published a short article that read:

> Washington, D.C., Sept. 12.—President Nick Young announced yesterday afternoon that Gettman's feat of making 10 safe hits out of 10 consecutive times at the bat established a record in the National League. In Friday's game against Cleveland Gettman made four hits, with a total of eight bases—two singles, a double and home run—and Saturday the first six times he faced the Cincinnati pitchers he drove out four singles, a three bagger and a home run, a total of 11 bases, and a grand total consecutively of 19 bases. This record is liable to stand unmarked for a long time.[19]

Young may have been caught up in the fact that Gettman played for Washington, but apparently he, like the *Washington Post*, was not aware of the Delahanty performance, not to mention the previous performances of both Stenzel and Kelley.

### CONCLUSION

This article has identified five errors in the record of hits in consecutive at bats as published in the sixth edition of *Total Baseball*. The sources of these errors vary, but it would appear that, based on erroneous contemporary statements by both the National League president and published newspaper reports, there was general unawareness of the individuals who recorded streaks of hits in consecutive at bats, at least through the time when the 1927 issue of *Balldom* was published.[20] The following nineteenth-century changes should be made to create an accurate list of record holders:

1. Jake Stenzel holds the NL record at 11 hits in 11 consecutive ABs and should be added to the list.

2. Ed Delahanty also had 11 hits in 11 consecutive ABs, not 10.

3. Joe Kelley had 10 hits in 10 consecutive ABs, not 9.

4. The NL record should stand as 11 hits in 11 consecutive ABs; shared by 2 players.

5. Tris Speaker tied, rather than set, the MLB record at 11 hits in 11 consecutive ABs. ∎

### Notes

1. Pietrusza, Editors with Matthew Silverman and Sean Lahman. *Total Baseball: The Official Encyclopedia of Major League Baseball*, Sixth Edition. New York, NY: Total Sports, 1999, 236–37.

2. The SABR record book lists Tom Parrott, Nap Lajoie, and Ed Konetchy with 10 as well as Stenzel. SABR, *The SABR Baseball List & Record Book* (New York: Simon & Schuster, 2007), 146.

3. Al Kermisch. "Stenzel May Own NL Consecutive Hit Mark." *Baseball Research Journal* 20 (1991): 32.

4. Stenzel's first career five-hit performance went as follows: First inning single, second inning home run, fourth inning reached on an error, fifth inning bases-clearing triple, sixth inning single, eighth inning single.

5. "THE FATAL SIXTH: Pittsburgh Men Were Winners Up to That Inning," *Pittsburgh Chronicle-Telegraph*, July 19, 1893, 2.; "CLEVELAND'S CLINCHING: They Handily Take the Second Game From Pittsburgh," *Pittsburgh Press*, July 19, 1893, 5; "THIS IS SAD INDEED: Our Own Spanked and Sat Upon By Those Cleveland Yawps—Stenzel Figures Largely in the Game," *Pittsburgh Commercial Gazette*, July 19, 1893, 6; "EASY, VERY EASY: Gumbert Was Very Wild and Gifts Were Plenty—Stenzel's Dirty Work," *Cleveland Plain Dealer*, Wednesday, July 19, 1893, 5; "ONLY NINE NOW: Cleveland Won From Pittsburgh Just the Same as Usual," *The Cleveland Leader*, Wednesday, July 19, 1893; "NATIONAL LEAGUE: The Record: Games Played Tuesday July 18," *Sporting Life*, Volume 21, Number 17, July 22, 1893, 4.

6. "DROPPED TWO: Crippled Infield Responsible for Double Defeat: Pitchers Poorly Supported," *Louisville Courier-Journal*, Wednesday Morning, July 14, 1897; "HARD GAMES TO LOSE: Colonels Should Have Won Both From the Phillies," *Louisville Times*, Wednesday, July 14, 1897.

7. "OUR PHILLIES THROW THE COLONELS TWICE: Both Were Mighty Interesting Games and We Won Solely on Our Merits," *Philadelphia Inquirer*,

Wednesday Morning, July 14, 1897, 4; "THE PHILLIES SCORE TWO VICTORIES OVER LOUISVILLE: Manager Stallings Reads the Riot Act to His Men with Good Results," *Philadelphia Public Ledger*, Wednesday, July 14, 1897, 14; "PHILLIES WIN TWO GAMES: Double Victory at Louisville by Good Ball Playing: Delahanty Makes Nine Hits," *Philadelphia Record*, Wednesday Morning, July 14, 1897.

8. "THE LEAGUE RACE: Games Played Tuesday July 13," *Sporting Life*, Volume 29, Number 17, July 17, 1897, 3; For those who aren't familiar with ICI, David Neft was the man behind ICI and it was the ICI research and subsequent resultant data that formed the basis for the Macmillan Baseball Encyclopedia of 1969.

9. "Baseball Notes," *Cleveland Plain Dealer*, Thursday, July 15, 1897, 3.

10. "DROPPED TWO," *Louisville Courier-Journal*.

11. Baseball rules, as published in the 1897 *Reach Base Ball Guide* which governed the 1897 playing season. Rule 71: Scoring, Section 3 (under Batting) reads, "In the third column should be placed the first base hits made by each Player. A base hit should be scored in the following cases: (1) When a hit ball is hit so sharply to an Infielder that he cannot handle it in time to put out the Batsman. In case of doubt over this class of hits, score a base hit, and exempt the Fielder from the charge of an error. (2) When a hit ball is hit so slowly toward a Fielder that he cannot handle it in time to put out the Batsman." Then in Section 7 (under Errors) it reads, "In scoring errors of batted balls see Section 3 of this Rule."

12. There is an inconsistency regarding the written game article(s) in the newspaper(s) and the scoring by inning indicated below the box score having to do with the specific inning Philadelphia scored their final two runs; were the runs scored in the seventh or the eighth inning?

13. "AGAIN THE ORIOLES WON: The Clevelands Lost the Second as They Did the First," *Baltimore American*, Sunday, September 2, 1894, 5; "ANOTHER FOR BALTIMORE: Cleveland Defeated in an Interesting and Exciting Contest," *Baltimore Sun*, Monday Morning, September 3, 1894, 6; "A HARD FIGHT: Cleveland Made a Worthy Struggle for Yesterday's Game," *Cleveland Plain Dealer*, Sunday, September 2, 1894, 3.

14. "A TRIBE OF JONAHS: That's What the Cleveland Ball Club Is," *Cleveland Leader*, Sunday, September 2, 1894.

15. 1894 ICI Data Sheets for Joe Kelley.

16. Regarding the doubleheader games on September 3, 1894, at Baltimore, between Baltimore and Cleveland, there was a ground rule that limited the hits to two bases. In fact, in the first game, Kelley apparently lost a HR due to the two base ground rule. The record books incorrectly indicate the record for most triples in a game by a single team as nine, by the Baltimore Orioles, in the first game of the doubleheader on September 3, 1894, which, of course, was impossible given the ground rule that was in effect. A possible source for the error may have been *Sporting Life* since in their coverage for the first game the hits were identified as "Three-base hits" below the box score, no "Two-base hits" were listed, while for the second game *Sporting Life* correctly indicated the hits as Two-base hits, again due to the ground rule. According to the author's research the NL record for most triples in a game by a single team during the nineteenth century appears to be seven, accomplished by the Athletics on June 14, 1876, against the Cincinnatis, while in the AA it also appears to be seven, again accomplished by the Athletics on August 27, 1884, against the Brooklyns.

17. "Washington Gets 'The Keeler of Texas,'" *Baltimore Sun*, Wednesday Morning, August 11, 1897, 6.

18. "HONORS WERE DIVIDED: Game Each for the Senators and Cincinnatis," *Washington Post*, Sunday, September 12, 1897, 8.

19. "A BATTING RECORD: Credited to Young Gettman, of the Washington Club," *Sporting Life*, Volume 29, Number 26, September 18, 1897, 1.

20. George L. Moreland. *Balldom: The Britannica of Baseball, Fascinating Facts For Fans,* Fourth Edition. (Youngstown, OH: Balldom Company, Incorporated, 1927.)

Table 1. Hits in Consecutive ABs by an Individual, Nineteenth Century

| # AB | Player/Team | Date | Opponent | AB | Hits | BA | 1B | 2B | 3B | HR | TB | SLG | EBH | Innings |
|---|---|---|---|---|---|---|---|---|---|---|---|---|---|---|
| 11 | Jake Stenzel, Pittsburgh Pirates | | | | | | | | | | | | | |
| | Streak Game 1 | July 15, 1893 | Washington Senators | 6 | 5 | 0.833 | 3 | 0 | 1 | 1 | 10 | 1.667 | 2 | 9 |
| | | last 3 ABs of Gm 1 | Fifth Inning | | | | | | 1 | | | | | |
| | | | Sixth Inning | | | | 1 | | | | | | | |
| | | | Eighth Inning | | | | 1 | | | | | | | |
| | | | Streak Game Totals | 3 | 3 | | | | | | | | | |
| | Streak Game 2 | July 17, 1893 | Cleveland Spiders | 4 | 4 | 1.000 | 2 | 2 | 0 | 0 | 6 | 1.500 | 2 | 9 |
| | Streak Game 3 | July 18, 1893 | Cleveland Spiders | 6 | 4 | 0.667 | 4 | 0 | 0 | 0 | 4 | 0.667 | 0 | 9 |
| | | first 4 ABs of Gm 3 | First Inning | | | | 1 | | | | | | | |
| | | | Second Inning | | | | 1 | | | | | | | |
| | | | Fourth Inning | | | | 1 | | | | | | | |
| | | | Unknown Inning | | | | 1 | | | | | | | |
| | | | Streak Game Totals | 4 | 4 | | | | | | | | | |
| | | | Overall Streak Totals | 11 | 11 | 1.000 | 8 | 2 | 1 | 0 | 15 | 1.364 | 3 | |
| | | | | | | | | | | | | | | |
| | Ed Delahanty, Philadelphia Phillies | | | | | | | | | | | | | |
| | Streak Game 1 | July 13, 1897 (1) | Louisville Colonels | 4 | 4 | 1.000 | 4 | 0 | 0 | 0 | 4 | 1.000 | 0 | 9 |
| | Streak Game 2 | July 13, 1897 (2) | Louisville Colonels | 5 | 5 | 1.000 | 4 | 0 | 1 | 0 | 7 | 1.400 | 1 | 9 |
| | Streak Game 3 | July 14, 1897 | Louisville Colonels | 5 | 4 | 0.800 | 2 | 1 | 0 | 1 | 8 | 1.600 | 2 | 9 |
| | | first 2 ABs of Gm 3 | First Inning | | | | | | | 1 | | | | |
| | | | Fourth Inning | | | | 1 | | | | | | | |
| | | | Streak Game Totals | 2 | 2 | | | | | | | | | |
| | | | Overall Streak Totals | 11 | 11 | 1.000 | 9 | 1 | 1 | 0 | 14 | 1.273 | 2 | |
| | | | | | | | | | | | | | | |
| 10 | Joe Kelley, Baltimore Orioles | | | | | | | | | | | | | |
| | Streak Game 1 | September 1, 1894 | Cleveland Spiders | 3 | 2 | 0.667 | 1 | 1 | 0 | 0 | 3 | 1.000 | 1 | 9 |
| | | last AB of Gm 1 | Seventh Inning | | | | 1 | | | | | | | |
| | | | Streak Game Totals | 1 | 1 | | | | | | | | | |
| | Streak Game 2 | September 3, 1894 (1) | Cleveland Spiders | 4 | 4 | 1.000 | 3 | 1 | 0 | 0 | 5 | 1.250 | 1 | 9 |
| | Streak Game 3 | September 3, 1894 (2) | Cleveland Spiders | 5 | 5 | 1.000 | 1 | 4 | 0 | 0 | 9 | 1.800 | 4 | 6 |
| | | | Overall Streak Totals | 10 | 10 | 1.000 | 5 | 5 | 0 | 0 | 15 | 1.500 | 5 | |
| | | | | | | | | | | | | | | |
| | Jake Gettman, Washington Senators | | | | | | | | | | | | | |
| | Streak Game 1 | September 10, 1897 | Cleveland Spiders | 4 | 4 | 1.000 | 2 | 1 | 0 | 1 | 8 | 2.000 | 2 | 9 |
| | Streak Game 2 | September 11, 1897 (1) | Cincinnati Reds | 5 | 5 | 1.000 | 3 | 0 | 1 | 1 | 10 | 2.000 | 2 | 9 |
| | Streak Game 3 | September 11, 1897 (2) | Cincinnati Reds | 3 | 1 | 0.333 | 1 | 0 | 0 | 0 | 1 | 0.333 | 0 | 7 |
| | | first AB of Gm 3 | Second Inning | | | | 1 | | | | | | | |
| | | | Streak Game Totals | 1 | 1 | | | | | | | | | |
| | | | Overall Streak Totals | 10 | 10 | 1.000 | 6 | 1 | 1 | 2 | 19 | 1.900 | 4 | |

The Henry Chadwick Award was established by SABR to honor baseball's great researchers—historians, statisticians, analysts, and archivists—for their invaluable contributions to making baseball the game that links America's present with its past.

Apart from honoring individuals for the length and breadth of their contribution to the study and enjoyment of baseball, the Chadwick Award will educate the baseball community about sometimes little known but vastly important contributions from the game's past and thus encourage the next generation of researchers.

The contributions of nominees must have had public impact. This may be demonstrated by publication of research in any of a variety of formats: books, magazine articles, websites, etc. The compilation of a significant database or archive that has facilitated the published research of others will also be considered in the realm of public impact.

## Allan Roth

### by Andy McCue

LIBRARY OF CONGRESS

Allan Roth pushed the analysis of baseball statistics to a new level. He promoted himself into a job earlier analysts only aspired to. Roth "was the only zealot lucky enough to work for a major league team and to get to test his theories first hand," wrote Alan Schwarz.

Abraham Roth was born in Montreal on May 10, 1917, the son of Nathan and Rose (Silverheart). Nathan worked as a tailor and the family moved around Ontario province before returning to Montreal during Abraham's high school years, when he attended Strathcona Academy, playing all the major sports. He also spent many free hours from age 13 to 16 compiling statistics for the International League and his hometown Montreal Royals. He passed the entrance examination for McGill University, where older brother Max was already studying. Family circumstances, however, prevented paying for a second college student, so Abraham took a job. He worked as a salesman, first of magazines and later of men's ties, suspenders, belts, and mufflers. In 1940, he married Esther Machlovitch and changed his name to Allan before going into the Canadian army.

Roth started his quest for a major league career by writing Brooklyn Dodgers president Larry MacPhail in December 1940. MacPhail was, at best, non-committal. After his 1944 discharge for medical reasons, Roth's attention returned to the Dodgers, but this time focused on Branch Rickey, MacPhail's successor and an executive Roth considered the most innovative man in sports.

Roth's four-page letter contained proposals to track a wide range of statistics. Some of these were standard, but others, such as where the ball was hit and the count it was hit on, hadn't been compiled regularly. Roth also proposed to break the statistics down into various categories that would reveal tendencies which the front office and the manager could use to win ball games.

Breakdowns that are mundane to us now—performance against left-handers and right-handers, in day games versus night games, in the various ballparks, in situations with runners in scoring position—were rarely compiled or used, and never part of the public discussion in Roth's time. The letter was intriguing enough to get a meeting with a still-skeptical Rickey. The conversation turned positive, Roth said, when Rickey asked him about runs batted in. Roth said he didn't think much of runs batted in unless they were correlated with the chances to drive them in, then differentiated again by which base they'd been driven in from.

With postwar restrictions on visas for foreigners, it took until 1947 for Rickey to get Roth on the Brooklyn payroll. And, then, he kept him under wraps. Roth's work went only to Rickey. In his first season, for example, Roth used one of his innovations—spray charts marking the location of all a player's batted balls—to show that an increasing number of Dixie Walker's hits were going to the opposite field, a sign his bat speed was fading. Rickey, following his own dictum that it was better to trade a player a year too early, sent Walker to the Pirates. "The People's Cherce" batted .316 in 1948, but was down to .282 the next year, his last in the majors.

Unlike contemporary statistical analysts, Roth generally ignored higher mathematics. "The figures concerned in baseball statistical work don't call for integral calculus or even advanced algebra," he said. He summed up his philosophy: "Baseball is a game of percentages—I try to find the actual percentage, which is constantly shifting, and apply it to the situation where it will do the most good."

Rickey's departure from the Dodgers after the 1950 season meant changes for Roth. The new president, Walter O'Malley, was dedicated to the business side of the organization. The new manager, Charlie Dressen, managed by the seat of his pants. Roth was moved into the radio booth to feed timely material to the Dodgers announcers and quickly struck up a strong friendship with Vin Scully. "If you had some question that came to you in the middle of a game, he would reach down into the bag, and next thing you knew you'd have your answer. It was marvelous," said Scully.

In 1954, Roth's work hit the big time—with a heavy coating of Branch Rickey. *Life* ran an article titled "Goodby (sic) to Some Old Baseball Ideas." The article said it had been written by Branch Rickey, whose picture graced the first page. Roth's back is visible in the background of that photo, and he is pictured on the article's third page. Clearly, the multipart equation in the background was the work of Roth. Rickey called the equation "the most disconcerting and at the same time the most constructive thing to come into baseball in my memory." Thirty years later, John Thorn and Pete Palmer wrote in their seminal book, *The Hidden Game of Baseball*, that "Rickey and Roth's fundamental contribution to the advancement of baseball statistics comes from their conceptual revisionism, their willingness to strip the game down to its basic unit, the run, and reconstruct its statistics accordingly."

In many ways "The Equation" was years ahead of its time. The equation, which contained eight different terms, was vastly complicated for contemporary baseball organizations. In his history of baseball analytics, *The Numbers Game*, Alan Schwarz summarizes the impact of Roth's equation: "No evidence exists that anyone took it seriously."

Roth returned to the role he had played under Rickey. But now his analysis was not going just to Rickey, but to the manager and directly to individual players. On Friday, September 18, 1959, the Dodgers arrived in San Francisco for a key series against the Giants. They needed a sweep to have any realistic hope of making the World Series. Friday night's game was rained out and manager Walt Alston announced that Don Drysdale, who'd been scheduled to start Friday, would pitch the Saturday afternoon game.

Roger Craig would start the evening game. Roth went to Alston and pointed out that Drysdale's night-game record was substantially better than his daytime performance while Craig showed little difference. Alston switched the pitchers, Los Angeles won both games, and Sunday as well. The Dodgers finished the season in a tie with the Braves, won the playoffs and the World Series for an improbable championship.

After the move to Los Angeles, Roth started to attend spring training in Vero Beach. He and a coach would meet with each player to go over his performance of the previous year, both positives and negatives, and suggesting changes that could improve the player's statistics. Sandy Koufax would credit such sessions in the early 1960s with helping him learn to emphasize first-pitch strikes and taking something off the ball.

In 1964, Roth left the Dodgers and expanded his freelance work. Within weeks, he was contributing regularly to *The Sporting News*. He revived a monthly column he'd written for *Sport* magazine from 1952 until 1960. He continued to edit the annual *Who's Who in Baseball*, which he'd done since the 1954 issue. He contributed statistical data for *Koufax*, by Sandy Koufax and Ed Linn, and the publisher felt it important enough to be included in advertising for the book. He collaborated with Harold Rosenthal on the spring training magazines from MACO publishing.

In 1966, NBC came calling with its new contract for the Game of the Week, the All-Star Game, and the World Series. *The Sporting News* column disappeared and for the next decade, Roth would sit between Curt Gowdy and Tony Kubek, feeding them the kind of statistical nuggets he'd supplied to Scully for years. A few years later, he moved to ABC to provide the same service.

While spending his time producing statistical nuggets for the broadcasters, Roth continued his exploration of ways teams could use statistics to improve performance. He consulted for 20 major league teams and identified Joe Morgan as the league's most valuable player long before voters did. Harking back to his early talks with Branch Rickey, Roth focused on Morgan's on-base percentage, power, and stolen base success.

Ill health forced Roth to retire in the late 1980s and he died of a heart attack in Brotman Medical Center in Culver City on March 3, 1992. "He was the guy who began it all," said Bill James. "He took statisticians into a brave new world." ∎

# Leonard Koppett

## by Dan Levitt

NATIONAL BASEBALL HALL OF FAME LIBRARY, COOPERSTOWN, NY

Leonard Koppett (1923–2003) was a long-time sportswriter known for his intellectual rigor and evidence-based analysis. Koppett wrote for many of the leading New York newspapers before relocating to the Bay Area and writing for several West Coast dailies. He also wrote a column for *The Sporting News* for many years. His articles and columns demonstrated an understanding of historical context, a statistical savvy ahead of his time, and a keen recognition of the relationship among events. He authored 17 books on sports, including three highly influential baseball books: *The Thinking Fan's Guide to Baseball* (1967), *The Man in the Dugout* (1993), and *Koppett's Concise History of Major League Baseball* (1998). He received the J.G. Taylor Spink Award from the National Baseball Hall of Fame and Museum in 1992, and the Curt Gowdy Media Award from the Naismith Memorial Basketball Hall of Fame in 1994, and he remains the only writer to win both prestigious awards.

Koppett was born in Moscow after his parents moved there from the Crimea. His parents both had the opportunity to receive a higher education because restrictions on Jews had been rolled back somewhat after the social unrest of 1905. In the late 1920s his father came to the United States with the foreign trade office, and the family followed shortly thereafter. When Stalin came to power in 1929, his parents realized they might be in danger and stayed in the US. In New York the family moved among the boroughs—he first realized he wanted to be a sportswriter when he was nine years old and lived a block away from Yankee Stadium—and by Koppett's high school years they lived in the Sea Gate area of Brooklyn.

After high school Koppett enrolled at and graduated from Columbia, though his college years were interrupted by WWII and just under three years in the army. While at Columbia he worked for the school paper and became a stringer—Columbia football was big at the time—for a couple of the daily papers. Koppett started his formal sportswriting employment with the *New York Herald Tribune* in 1948. He later regarded the *Herald Tribune* of that era as the best overall newspaper of his career. In 1954 he moved to the *New York Post* because he was too often being confined to a desk job. He soon became acquainted with the "chipmunks,"

a loose-knit group of younger, irreverent sportswriters. Koppett described himself as too "orthodox" to follow their nontraditional approach.

Sportswriting for most dailies paid poorly in the early 1960s, and Koppett decided to leave the *Post* in 1962 to find a higher paying job in public relations or a similar business line. Fortunately for baseball enthusiasts, a spot opened up at the higher-paying *New York Times*, and Koppett jumped at the opportunity. In 1973 Koppett moved to Palo Alto, California, as the West Coast sports correspondent for the *Times*. He left in 1978 when the travel was finally becoming a burden, and he wanted to spend more time with his family and growing children. A couple years later he joined the *Peninsula Times Tribune* as columnist, also spending a few years as the overall editor for the paper.

As a young high-schooler, I learned how to explore questions and craft arguments by reading Koppett's columns in *The Sporting News*. He had a seemingly straightforward but thought-provoking way of defining the underlying assumptions and approaches to questions he wanted to answer. One, in particular, struck me: an article in 1976 on how to determine if a player was overpaid. To systematically analyze the problem, Koppett devised a framework, reasoning "that there are only three possible approaches to an objective definition of 'overpaid.'"

- One is a "share" concept: how much money is generated by this employes [sic] activity and what share of that income should go to him?

- A second is a "comparability" concept: what do other employes, in other fields or other places, get paid for comparable effort or comparable status or comparable special qualities?

- The third is "productivity": what are the services provided by the employe "worth" to the business?

This systematic approach, often bolstered by a rare contextual understanding of statistics (for the time), offered Koppett's readers a dimension they didn't often get from other sources.

When *The Thinking Fan's Guide to Baseball* came out in 1967, it provided the first comprehensive look at all the aspects of baseball, from a manager's tactical decisions on the field, to the business of baseball, to the intricacies of hitting and pitching. And it offered it all up with an intelligent dose of historical and statistical context. More recently, *Koppett's Concise History of Major League Baseball* weaved between the game on and off the field, while delivering a deeper understanding of the connections among the various elements of both.

Koppett was a great sportswriter who brought a historical and contextual appreciation to his work. Through his many columns, long-form articles, and books, Koppett's comprehensive and reasoned explorations and explanations enriched generations of baseball followers. ■

## Rob Neyer

### by Mark Armour

COURTESY OF ROB NEYER

Rob Neyer (1966–) received his big break in 1989 when Bill James hired him as his research assistant. Rob has never been hesitant to tell this story, of a young, unsettled guy working as a roofer in Lawrence, Kansas—armed with a love of baseball and the written word, and a willingness to work hard—being granted the opportunity to work with the most famous baseball researcher in the world. And this is all true, as far as it goes.

Also true: Rob seized this opportunity and forged his own career path, a path he essentially invented. When he began writing for ESPN.com in 1996, he became the first widely read, analytically savvy writer on the Internet. In this role, he not only influenced a steadily growing pool of like-minded readers, he influenced future writers, who could now envision such a path for themselves. "[Rob] paved the way for the next generation of writers to make their living on the Internet, instead of going through the motions at the local paper," says Jonah Keri of *The Athletic*. "It's not a stretch to say I owe a gigantic chunk of my existence as a sportswriter to Rob's work back in the 90s at ESPN."

Years earlier, Rob's childhood was spent moving around the Midwest before settling in Kansas City in 1976 just as the Royals were becoming a great team. He followed all the major sports as a kid, and was not immune to the popularity and success of the local nine, who became his entrée into the great game. He played a lot of baseball, but his love of the game would far eclipse his playing career.

After a few years at the University of Kansas and some time on local roofs, Rob landed his dream job. He spent four years with James, working extensively on all three editions of Bill's annual *Baseball Book* (1990–92)

and the first edition of his *Player Ratings Book* (1993). He spent three more years working on various publications for STATS, Inc. before arriving at ESPN in 1996.

During his 15 years at ESPN, writing five columns a week for a while and eventually evolving into what we now call a "blogger," Rob increasingly acted as the public voice (on radio, on television, at conference panels) for a new way of thinking about the game. Michael Lewis's 2003 book *Moneyball* further legitimized Rob and his readers. "If Bill's *Abstracts* are recognized as the birth of contemporary sabermetrics," says Cory Schwartz of MLB Advanced Media, "it was Rob's column that lifted those ideas out of the margins of fandom and made them familiar and accessible to a national audience. That spirit inspires not only much of what happens where I work, but dozens of baseball websites and blogs, and probably all 30 MLB front offices."

Rob's influence extended beyond simply writing well. He also used his platform to tout talented baseball writers who were struggling to find an audience. Craig Calcaterra, then an Ohio attorney, began blogging about baseball daily in 2007. Rob linked to one of Craig's pieces, then another, and soon Craig found a readership. He soon left the law for a brand-new career as lead baseball writer for NBCSports.com. "Rob didn't have to do it," Craig says. "But he did because he's a selfless and decent man. Rob has done more to advance baseball thought and discourse over the past couple of decades than anyone, yet he has never hesitated to elevate the work of others before promoting himself. Anyone who does what I do now is in his debt."

While doing all of this, Rob also found time to write seven books, including *Baseball Dynasties* (with Eddie Epstein, 2000), *Rob Neyer's Big Book of Baseball Lineups* (2003), and *The Neyer/James Guide to Pitchers* (with Bill James, 2004), which was awarded the *Sporting News*-SABR Baseball Research Award in 2005.

Rob left ESPN in 2011 to become the National Baseball Editor for *SB Nation*, and three years later joined FoxSports.com. Rob has been mainly freelancing for the past few years. After a decade hiatus from writing books, his 2018 effort, *Power Ball—Anatomy of a Modern Baseball Game*, won the Casey Award as the best baseball book of the year.

Rob married Angela in 2014, and their daughter Olive came aboard in 2015. In 2019, Rob will serve his second year as the Commissioner of the West Coast League, a collegiate wooden bat league in the Pacific Northwest. He is also tapped to host SABR's brand-new baseball podcast, the start of what will likely be yet another successful chapter in the baseball life of Rob Neyer. ■

# Contributors

**MARK ARMOUR** Mark Armour is the founder of the Baseball Biography Project, and currently serves as Co-chair of the Baseball Cards Committee.

**BOB BAILEY** has been a SABR member since 1982. He has contributed over twenty articles to the *Baseball Research Journal*, *The National Pastime*, and other SABR publications. He is currently the Vice Chairman of the Nineteenth Century Committee and editor of the Committee's newsletter, *Nineteenth Century Notes*. He lives in Gainesville, Florida.

**GABRIEL B. COSTA** is a Catholic priest and mathematics professor who is currently on an extended Academic Leave from Seton Hall University. He is a member of SABR and has published in the *BRJ* in the past. You can contact him at gabriel.costa@westpoint.edu.

**CHUCK HILDEBRANDT** has served as chair of the Baseball and the Media Committee since its inception in 2013. Chuck is a two-time Doug Pappas Award winner for his oral presentations "'Little League Home Runs' in MLB History" (2015) and "Does Changing Leagues Affect Player Performance, and How?" (2017), and authored the cover story for the Spring 2015 *Baseball Research Journal*, "The Retroactive All-Star Game Project." Chuck lives with his lovely wife Terrie in Chicago, where he also plays in an adult hardball league. Chuck has also been a Chicago Cubs season ticket holder since 1999, although he is a proud native of Detroit. So, while Chuck's checkbook may belong to the Cubs, his heart still belongs to the Tigers.

**DOUGLAS JORDAN** is a professor at Sonoma State University in Northern California where he teaches corporate finance and investments. He has been a SABR member since 2012. He runs marathons when he's not watching or writing about baseball. Email him at douglas.jordan@sonoma.edu.

**HERM KRABBENHOFT**, a SABR member since 1981, is a retired research chemist. His baseball research has included ultimate grand slam homers, leadoff batters, five-tool players, President George H.W. Bush's collegiate baseball career at Yale, quasi-cycles, the uniform numbers of Detroit Tigers players, consecutive games on-base-safely streaks, and the RBI records achieved by Babe Ruth, Lou Gehrig, and Hank Greenberg.

**BILL LAMB** is the editor of *The Inside Game*, the quarterly newsletter of SABR's Deadball Era Committee, and the author of *Black Sox in the Courtroom: The Grand Jury, Criminal Trial and Civil Litigation* (McFarland, 2013). Prior to his retirement, he spent more than 30 years as a state/county prosecutor in New Jersey.

**DAN LEVITT** is the author of several baseball books and numerous essays. He is a longtime SABR member and a recipient of the Davids Award and the Chadwick Award. His books have won the Larry Ritter Book Award, the *Sporting News*-SABR Baseball Research Award, and have twice been finalists for the Seymour Medal.

**DAVID MACIAS** is a Faculty Member at Sonoma State University in Northern California where he teaches Accounting and Income Tax. David has also been a manager in a Research Organization and a SABR member since 2018. The article "Team Batting Average: A comprehensive Analysis" is his first contribution to the *BRJ*. He plays golf when he's not watching baseball. Contact David at maciadav@sonoma.edu.

**BRIAN MARSHALL** is an Electrical Engineering Technologist living in Barrie, Ontario, Canada, specializing in the application of power electronics as it relates to machine automation. Brian is a long time researcher in various fields including power electronic engineering, entomology, NFL, Canadian Football and MLB. Brian has written many articles, winning awards for two of them, and two books in his 63 years. Brian has been a SABR member for over four years and is a long time member of the PFRA. Growing up, Brian played many sports, including football, rugby, hockey, and baseball, along with participating in power lifting and arm wrestling events, and aspired to be a professional football player, but when that didn't materialize, he focused on Rugby Union and played off and on for 17 seasons in the "front row."

**ANNE C. MARX SCHEUERELL** is an Associate Professor of Sport Management in the Francis J. Noonan School of Business at Loras College in Dubuque, Iowa. Her research is in sport analytics and sport as a platform for socio-cultural change. She earned her master's degree from Arizona State University and her doctorate degree from the University of Arkansas.

**DAVID B. MARX** is a Professor Emeritus of Statistics at the University of Nebraska in Lincoln, Nebraska. He works in the area of spatial statistics as well as in sports statistics. His Ph.D. is from the University of Kentucky and he was previously employed at the University of Arizona and University of Arkansas.

**ANDY McCUE**, a former SABR president, is the author of *Mover and Shaker: Walter O'Malley, the Dodgers, and Baseball's Western Expansion*, winner of the 2015 Seymour Medal. He heads SABR's Baseball Index project (www.baseballindex.com).

**A.J. RICHARD** is a graduate student and graduate assistant at the University of Northern Iowa studying Leisure/Youth/Human Services and Women and Gender Studies. In 2015, A.J. "discovered" girls and women in baseball when a friend told her about Jackie Mitchell striking out Babe Ruth. That year she started "Women Belong in Baseball" on Facebook and Twitter to increase awareness of girls and women in baseball and the barriers they face. A.J. has been a member of SABR since 2016. A.J. can be emailed at womenbelonginbaseball@gmail.com.

**JOAN WENDL THOMAS**, a freelance writer, also writes under the name Joan M. Thomas. A long time SABR member, she is a regular contributor to the Biography project, and has written several book reviews for the Deadball Era Committee. Her published books on baseball include *St. Louis' Big League Ballparks*, *Baseball's First Lady*, and *Baseball In Northwest Iowa*. A former resident of St. Louis, she now lives in her home town of Le Mars, Iowa. She can be reached by email at JTh8751400@aol.com.

**DUSTY TURNER** is a Major in the United States Army who is currently an Assistant Professor at the United States Military Academy at West Point and teaches Sabermetrics. He has previously served as an Army Engineer and Operations Research Systems Analyst. Contact Dusty at dusty.s.turner@gmail.com or via twitter @dtdusty

**NAVNEET S. VISHWANATHAN** is a recent graduate of Georgetown University where he studied International Economics. A former Baseball Operations Intern for the San Diego Padres, Vishwanathan currently works for a major consulting firm in Washington, D.C. He is passionate about labor economics and trade and is keen on pursuing a career in the baseball industry. Vishwanathan presented his research on arbitration at SABR 48 in Pittsburgh in June 2018. He can be contacted at navneetv54@gmail.com.

**ROBERT D. WARRINGTON** is a native Philadelphian who writes about the city's baseball past.

# Society for American Baseball Research

Cronkite School at ASU
555 N. Central Ave. #416, Phoenix, AZ 85004
602.496.1460 (phone)
SABR.org

## Become a SABR member today!

If you're interested in baseball — writing about it, reading about it, talking about it — there's a place for you in the Society for American Baseball Research. Our members include everyone from academics to professional sportswriters to amateur historians and statisticians to students and casual fans who enjoy reading about baseball and occasionally gathering with other members to talk baseball. What unites all SABR members is an interest in the game and joy in learning more about it.

SABR membership is open to any baseball fan; we offer 1-year and 3-year memberships. Here's a list of some of the key benefits you'll receive as a SABR member:

* Receive two editions (spring and fall) of the *Baseball Research Journal*, our flagship publication
* Receive expanded e-book edition of *The National Pastime*, our annual convention journal
* 8-10 new e-books published by the SABR Digital Library, all FREE to members
* "This Week in SABR" e-newsletter, sent to members every Friday
* Join dozens of research committees, from Statistical Analysis to Women in Baseball.
* Join one of 70+ regional chapters in the U.S., Canada, Latin America, and abroad
* Participate in online discussion groups
* Ask and answer baseball research questions on the SABR-L e-mail listserv
* Complete archives of *The Sporting News* dating back to 1886 and other research resources
* Promote your research in "This Week in SABR"
* Diamond Dollars Case Competition
* Yoseloff Scholarships

* Discounts on SABR national conferences, including the SABR National Convention, the SABR Analytics Conference, Jerry Malloy Negro League Conference, Frederick Ivor-Campbell 19th Century Conference, and the Arizona Fall League Experience
* Publish your research in peer-reviewed SABR journals
* Collaborate with SABR researchers and experts
* Contribute to Baseball Biography Project or the SABR Games Project
* List your new book in the SABR Bookshelf
* Lead a SABR research committee or chapter
* Networking opportunities at SABR Analytics Conference
* Meet baseball authors and historians at SABR events and chapter meetings
* 50% discounts on paperback versions of SABR e-books
* Discounts with other partners in the baseball community
* SABR research awards

We hope you'll join the most passionate international community of baseball fans at SABR! Check us out online at SABR.org/join.

--- ✂ ------------------------------------------------------

## SABR MEMBERSHIP FORM

|  | Annual | 3-year | Senior | 3-yr Sr. | Under 30 |
|---|---|---|---|---|---|
| **Standard:** | ❑ $65 | ❑ $175 | ❑ $45 | ❑ $129 | ❑ $45 |
| *(International members wishing to be mailed the Baseball Research Journal* | | | | | |
| *should add $10/yr for Canada/Mexico or $19/yr for overseas locations.)* | | | | | |
| Canada/Mexico: | ❑ $75 | ❑ $205 | ❑ $55 | ❑ $159 | ❑ $55 |
| Overseas: | ❑ $84 | ❑ $232 | ❑ $64 | ❑ $186 | ❑ $55 |
| Senior = 65 or older before Dec. 31 of the current year | | | | | |

### Participate in Our Donor Program!

Support the preservation of baseball research. Designate your gift toward:
❑General Fund    ❑Endowment Fund    ❑Research Resources    ❑_____
❑ I want to maximize the impact of my gift; do not send any donor premiums
❑ I would like this gift to remain anonymous.

Note: Any donation not designated will be placed in the General Fund.
SABR is a 501 (c) (3) not-for-profit organization & donations are tax-deductible to the extent allowed by law.

Name _____

E-mail* _____

Address _____

City _____ ST_____ ZIP_____

Phone _____ Birthday _____

**\* Your e-mail address on file ensures you will receive the most recent SABR news.**

**Dues**              $_____

**Donation**          $_____

**Amount Enclosed**   $_____

Do you work for a matching grant corporation? Call (602) 496-1460 for details.

*If you wish to pay by credit card, please contact the SABR office at (602) 496-1460 or sign up securely online at SABR.org/join. We accept Visa, Mastercard & Discover.*

Do you wish to receive the *Baseball Research Journal* electronically? ❑ Yes    ❑ No
Our e-books are available in PDF, Kindle, or EPUB (iBooks, iPad, Nook) formats.

**Mail to: SABR, Cronkite School at ASU, 555 N. Central Ave. #416, Phoenix, AZ 85004**

# SABR Books on Great Teams and Great Games

The Society for American Baseball Research, the top baseball research organization in the world, disseminates some of the best in baseball history, analysis, and biography through our publishing programs. The SABR Digital Library focuses on a tandem program of paperback and ebook publication, making these materials widely available for both on digital devices and as traditional printed books.

*THE 1986 BOSTON RED SOX:*
*THERE WAS MORE THAN GAME SIX*
One of a two-book series on the rivals that met in the 1986 World Series, the Boston Red Sox and the New York Mets, including biographies of every player, coach, broadcaster, and other important figures in the top organizations in baseball that year.
**Edited by Leslie Heaphy and Bill Nowlin**
**$19.95 paperback (ISBN 978-1-943816-19-4)**
**$9.99 ebook (ISBN 978-1-943816-18-7)**
**8.5"X11", 420 pages, over 200 photos**

*THE 1986 NEW YORK METS:*
*THERE WAS MORE THAN GAME SIX*
The other book in the "rivalry" set from the 1986 World Series. This book re-tells the story of that year's classic World Series and this is the story of each of the players, coaches, managers, and broadcasters, their lives in baseball and the way the 1986 season fit into their lives.
**Edited by Leslie Heaphy and Bill Nowlin**
**$19.95 paperback (ISBN 978-1-943816-13-2)**
**$9.99 ebook (ISBN 978-1-943816-12-5)**
**8.5"X11", 392 pages, over 100 photos**

*SCANDAL ON THE SOUTH SIDE:*
*THE 1919 CHICAGO WHITE SOX*
The Black Sox Scandal isn't the only story worth telling about the 1919 Chicago White Sox. The team roster included three future Hall of Famers, a 20-year-old spitballer who would win 300 games in the minors, and even a batboy who later became a celebrity with the "Murderers' Row" New York Yankees. All of their stories are included in Scandal on the South Side with a timeline of the 1919 season.
**Edited by Jacob Pomrenke**
**$19.95 paperback (ISBN 978-1-933599-95-3)**
**$9.99 ebook (ISBN 978-1-933599-94-6)**
**8.5"x11", 324 pages, 55 historic photos**

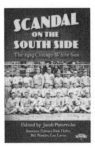 

*WINNING ON THE NORTH SIDE*
*THE 1929 CHICAGO CUBS*
Celebrate the 1929 Chicago Cubs, one of the most exciting teams in baseball history. Future Hall of Famers Hack Wilson, '29 NL MVP Rogers Hornsby, and Kiki Cuyler, along with Riggs Stephenson formed one of the most potent quartets in baseball history. The magical season came to an ignominious end in the World Series and helped craft the future "lovable loser" image of the team.
**Edited by Gregory H. Wolf**
**$19.95 paperback (ISBN 978-1-933599-89-2)**
**$9.99 ebook (ISBN 978-1-933599-88-5)**
**8.5"x11", 314 pages, 59 photos**

*DETROIT THE UNCONQUERABLE:*
*THE 1935 WORLD CHAMPION TIGERS*
Biographies of every player, coach, and broadcaster involved with the 1935 World Champion Detroit Tigers baseball team, written by members of the Society for American Baseball Research. Also includes a season in review and other articles about the 1935 team. Hank Greenberg, Mickey Cochrane, Charlie Gehringer, Schoolboy Rowe, and more.
**Edited by Scott Ferkovich**
**$19.95 paperback (ISBN 9978-1-933599-78-6)**
**$9.99 ebook (ISBN 978-1-933599-79-3)**
**8.5"X11", 230 pages, 52 photos**

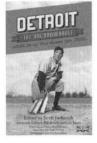 

*TIGERS BY THE TALE:*
*GREAT GAMES AT MICHIGAN AND TRUMBULL*
For over 100 years, Michigan and Trumbull was the scene of some of the most exciting baseball ever. This book portrays 50 classic games at the corner, spanning the earliest days of Bennett Park until Tiger Stadium's final closing act. From Ty Cobb to Mickey Cochrane, Hank Greenberg to Al Kaline, and Willie Horton to Alan Trammell.
**Edited by Scott Ferkovich**
**$12.95 paperback (ISBN 978-1-943816-21-7)**
**$6.99 ebook (ISBN 978-1-943816-20-0)**
**8.5"x11", 160 pages, 22 photos**

*MAJOR LEAGUE BASEBALL A MILE HIGH:*
*THE FIRST QUARTER CENTURY OF THE COLORADO ROCKIES*
*A look at the first 25 years (1993–2017) of the MLB team in Denver, the Colorado Rockies. Including essays on the birth of the Rockies, biographies of 24 of the most important players, managers, and club executives, and "ballpark bios" of the two fields on the Rockies have called home: Mile High Stadium and Coors Field. In addition, 18 memorable and historic games are recapped.*
**Edited by Bill Nowlin and Paul T. Parker**
**$19.95 paperback (ISBN 978-1-943816-77-4)**
**$9.99 ebook (ISBN 978-1-943816-76-7)**
**8.5"X11", 272 pages, 32 photos**

*THE TEAM THAT COULDN'T HIT:*
*THE 1972 TEXAS RANGERS*
Articles in this book cover the effort to bring a team to North Texas and the story of Tom Vandergriff, the man now known as "the father of the Rangers." Biographies of every man to play—or coach—for the 1972 team are presented, including Frank Howard, Larry Bittner, Horacio Pina and Tom Grieve, and broadcasters Don Drysdale and Bill Mercer. Owner Bob Short and Arlington Stadium itself are given full write-ups as well.
**Edited by Steve West and Bill Nowlin**
**$29.95 paperback (ISBN 978-1-943816-93-4)**
**$9.99 ebook (ISBN 978-1-943816-92-7)**
**8.5"X11", 414 pages, 60 photos**

*SABR Members can purchase each book at a significant discount (often 50% off) and receive the ebook edtions free as a member benefit. Each book is available in a trade paperback edition as well as ebooks suitable for reading on a home computer or Nook, Kindle, or iPad/tablet.*

*To learn more about becoming a member of SABR, visit the website: sabr.org/join*